Pragmatemes in Audiovisual Translation in English, French, and Polish

ŁÓDŹ STUDIES IN LANGUAGE

Edited by Barbara Lewandowska-Tomaszczyk and Łukasz Bogucki

Volume 78

Judyta Mężyk

Pragmatemes in Audiovisual Translation in English, French, and Polish

PETER LANG
Berlin · Bruxelles · Chennai · Lausanne · New York · Oxford

Bibliographic Information published by the Deutsche Nationalbibliothek
The Deutsche Nationalbibliothek lists this publication in the Deutsche Nationalbibliografie; detailed bibliographic data is available online at http://dnb.d-nb.de.

Library of Congress Cataloging-in-Publication Data
A CIP catalog record for this book has been applied for at the Library of Congress.

Publication co-financed by the University of Silesia in Katowice

UNIVERSITY OF SILESIA
IN KATOWICE

This publication is a revised version of the PhD thesis entitled *Pragmatemes in Audiovisual Translation in English-French-Polish Language Pairs* written under supervision of prof. Lucie Gournay and prof. Andrzej Łyda as a joint thesis at the University of Silesia in Katowice, Poland, and the Paris-East Créteil University in Paris, France, defended on the 15th of May 2024 in Sosnowiec, Poland.

ISSN 1437-5281
ISBN 978-3-631-93180-6 (Print)
ISBN 978-3-631-93181-3 (E-PDF)
ISBN 978-3-631-94009-9 (E-PUB)
DOI 10.3726/b23023

Published by Peter Lang GmbH, Berlin (Germany)
info@peterlang.com

This publication has been peer reviewed.
www.peterlang.com

Contents

Acknowledgments

Without counsel plans fail, but with many advisers they succeed.

Proverbs 15:22, The English Standard Version

First, I would like to express my gratitude to my PhD supervisors, Prof. Lucie Gournay from the Université Paris-Est Créteil and Prof. Andrzej Łyda from the University of Silesia in Katowice. Thank you for agreeing to supervise this joint thesis, sharing your knowledge with me, guiding me through this research, suggesting revisions, and offering your support throughout the entire process. Thank you for helping me become the researcher I am today.

I would also like to extend my gratitude to other people who had a direct impact on me and my research. I would like to especially thank my tutor, Prof. Łukasz Bogucki from the University of Łódź, for his invaluable insights into audiovisual translation, our many enriching conversations on the topic, and his patience in listening to all my ideas throughout the process. Prof. Bogucki was also a member of my Polish evaluating committee, and with that, my sincere thanks go also to the other members of my Polish and French evaluating committees, who helped me by asking profound questions and offering valuable advice: Prof. Magdalena Bartłomiejczyk and Prof. Ewa Gumul from the University of Silesia, Prof. Dominique Ducard from the Université Paris-Est Créteil, and Dr. Hab. Raluca Nita from the Université de Poitiers. I am also grateful to Dr. David Schauffler for proofreading this thesis, and to the reviewers of my PhD thesis, who suggested valuable adjustments for this publication: Prof. Mikołaj Deckert from the University of Łódź, Prof. Łukasz Grabowski from the University of Opole, and Prof. Graham Ranger from the Université d'Avignon. This publication would not have been possible also without the people from the Peter Lang Group, to whom I am immensily grateful. Additionally, I thank all the researchers who generously shared their knowledge and experience with me during the span of this doctoral project. There are too many of you to name here individually, but I hope you all recognize the impact you had on me in conducting this research.

This research could not have been conducted without the financial support from various institutions. Above all, I thank the University of Silesia for their constant support, both throughout my time in the Doctoral School leading up to my PhD defense, and during my following work at the Institute of Linguistics. Here, I would like to especially thank Prof. Adam Wojtaszek, the Director of The Institute of Linguistics, for supporting this publication. Then, I would like to express my gratitude to the institutions that provided me with funds that made this research possible: the Polish government for the monthly scholarship provided to every PhD student and the French embassy in Poland and Campus France for the French government scholarship that facilitated my travels to Paris and stays at the Université Paris-Est Créteil. Furthermore, I would like to acknowledge other institutions that financed my participation in conferences and summer schools, namely the IMAGER laboratory at the Université Paris-Est Créteil and the Polish National Agency for Academic Exchange, and the President of my city, Świętochłowice, Daniel Beger, for granting me a scholarship that covered various smaller expenses. Lastly, my gratitude extends to l'École Universitaire de Recherche du Grand Paris "Francophonies et Plurilinguismes: Politique des langues" from the Université Paris-Est Créteil for providing a scholarship that assisted in covering any additional expenses.

On a more personal note, I express my deepest gratitude to my husband, Bruno, for his unwavering patience during my writing process, for taking care of our puppy, our apartment, and me when I was restlessly immersed in research. I thank all my friends and mentors who never asked me how my thesis was going, who never abandoned me despite all the meetings I missed due to my unusual profession, and who always succeeded in convincing me not to quit when I felt like doing so. I thank my family, especially my mom and dad, for sharing in my joys and always cheering me on. I extend my thanks to all my collegues, whose research journeys and words of encouragement, especially during our meetings at various conferences, IDEAL research group sessions, and Koło Naukowe Doktorantów Językoznawstwa gatherings, have been a great source of inspiration. I must also express my appreciation to my students from the University of Silesia, the Tischner European University in Cracow, and various dance schools, for their compassionate understanding, especially during moments when my mind felt more chaotic than usual.

Last but certainly not least, I thank God. I thank God for being my greatest support, my most enthusiastic cheerleader, my best adviser. Thank you Jesus for leading me to this point and being with me every step of the way.

List of figures

List of tables

General Introduction

A substantial portion of our daily language use includes formulaic units such as idioms, metaphors, collocations, and other similar constructs. We are often unaware of the widespread nature of these units and their crucial role in everyday communication; at least until we start learning a new language, when it becomes evident that these units present challenges due to the fact that they are rather to be treated as single units than be subject to the analysis by the means of grammar. According to Wood (2015), formulaic units (formulaic sequences or formulas) are language units of multiple words that are characterized by a single function or meaning and are mentally stored and retrieved as if they were single words. Some scholars, such as Fillmore (1979), argue that the proficient use of formulaic sequences significantly contributes to language fluency, with formulaic language not only facilitating the achievement of communication goals (Kecskés 2003), but also helping to do so without imposing a processing overload (Wray 2002).

Studies on formulaic language are not a novelty, as the formal approach to this subject was already tackled by early grammarians (e.g., Jesperson 1924). Yet, since the 1970s, research on formulaic language has experienced exponential growth with the development of technology (Wood 2015). The issue has been studied from various perspectives, including sociolinguistic (e.g., Mazur 1990), ethnolinguistic (e.g., Bartmiński 2007), psycholinguistic (e.g., Wray 2002), and pedagogical (Durrant and Mathews-Aydınlı 2011), among others. It is also with the rise of corpus linguistics that formulaicity has proved to be prevalent in language data (Wray 2002). However, despite numerous studies focusing on units such as collocations (e.g., Sinclair 1991, Mel'čuk 1998) and idioms (e.g, Skandera 2004, Genzel 1991, Wood 1986), relatively little attention has been directed toward other units vital to our everyday communication, among which undoubtedly are pragmatemes, i.e, fixed utterances used in typical, repeatable, and specific situations of communication.

While the term *pragmateme* was first introduced in 1995 within the typology of phrasemes proposed by Mel'čuk, the phenomenon had been acknowledged long before that, for instance, by Coulmas (1979) in his study on routine formulas, i.e., expressions linked to repetitive social situations. Pragmatemes are units that often escape notice but are pervasive in our everyday lives, with examples found among commonplace interactions (e.g., *How are you?*), celebrations (e.g., *Merry Christmas!*), official communication (e.g., *All rise!*), and written instructions (e.g., *Best before*). Given the examples, it is evident that a lack of understanding of pragmatemes may cause serious communicational problems. In literature, phenomena resembling pragmatemes not only appear under different names, such as *pragmatic phraseologisms* (Dziadkiewicz 2007), *stereotyped language acts* (Kauffer 2019), *situation-bound utterances* (Kecskés 2000), among others, but are also accompanied by varying definitions. Fortunately, despite the terminological chaos, researchers have pursued investigations into pragmatemes from diverse perspectives, such as psycholinguistic (e.g., Myles, Hooper, and Mitchell 1998), literary (e.g., Barnas 2017), and, probably most extensively, lexicographic (e.g., Blanco and Mejri 2018, Kauffer 2011, Krzyżanowska, Grossmann, and Kwapisz-Osadnik 2021). Furthermore, some research has been conducted from the translational perspective (e.g., Sułkowska 2023, Martín 2018), although without delving into the examination of these units within actual texts and their translations.

Consequently, the primary objective of this thesis is to conduct an in-depth examination of pragmatemes from a comparative and translational standpoint. The study delves into pragmatemes across three languages: English, French, and Polish– a set that, thus far, has not been collectively explored in terms of pragmatemes. Furthermore, one of the key research questions posed in this project aims to lay out a universal definition of pragmateme, as it is argued that the definitions existing in the literature are applicable only to the given languages of particular studies (e.g., the unit *Joyeux anniversaire* [Eng. *Happy birthday*], a pragmateme prototypical in Blanco and Mejri's [2018] definition, loses its prototypicality in its Polish equivalent, *Sto lat* [Eng. *A hundred years*], due to its lack of compositional nature). Thanks to the literature review conducted on the topic across different languages, the theoretical part aims to bridge the apparent language gap between the research conducted in different languages and propose a pragmateme definition applicable universally across languages. This study also seeks to identify linguistic universals of pragmatemes, i.e., examine whether any linguistic properties, such as the presence of question forms, ellipsis, and others, characterize pragmatemes as a linguistic phenomenon, which may help identifying them within texts. Last but not least, the study attempts to examine pragmatemes from a translational perspective. In order to stress the importance of context in certain pragmatemes, a complex translation type was chosen for the analysis, and that is audiovisual translation, specifically, subtitling. This approach aims to elucidate how context influences the translation of pragmatemes within audiovisual content.

To answer these research questions, first, corpora were collected. As this study aims to focus on everyday conversational language, subtitles and captions from TV series portraying ordinary life were collected with the use of Language Reactor, a Google Chrome extension for Netflix. The English corpus comprised 770,836 tokens, the French 664,508 tokens, and the Polish 138,516 tokens. At the same time, pragmatemes in the languages of the study, i.e., English, French, and Polish, were identified in secondary sources. However, at this stage, not within the corpora. According to both Wood (2015) and Bardovi-Harlig (2012), starting the research with preidentified formulas is a more common practice than searching for them on the frequency basis, given the specific nature of these units. Therefore, 45 reliable sources, including language dictionaries and phrasebooks, among others, were used. In total, 1205 English pragmatemes (some used in speech, others in writing), 1167 French pragmatemes, and 1503 Polish pragmatemes were identified across the sources used. Additionally, these sources helped to identify pragmatemic patterns (e.g., *See you* + TIME). With the prepared list of preidentified pragmatemes and the corpora in place, the units were searched for within the corpora using corpus linguistic software, Unitex. This search resulted in finding 290 pragmatemes in English, 186 in French, and 106 in Polish. These units were then subjected to linguistic analysis considering factors such as complexity, frequency, imperativeness, variantivity, presence of question forms, presence of verbless forms, deixis, ellipsis, speech acts, and pragmateme type. Furthermore, one type of pragmatemes underwent translational analysis. French and Polish translations of English charged pragmatemes, i.e., units which are ambiguous without any context and can be compositional or idiomatic, were investigated in terms of the used translation techniques. Due to their ambiguous nature, charged pragmatemes were chosen for this analysis as possibly the most intriguing and challenging in translation, considering the constraints of the dissertation's time and space. The translational analysis, conducted accordingly to technique typologies already outlined by various researchers (namely Molina and Hurtado Albir 2002, Hejwowski 2015, and Díaz-Cintas and Remael 2007), revealed a gap regarding the approach toward context in audiovisual translation. Consequently, a new set of techniques was proposed as a result of the analysis. Finally, the two analyses – linguistic and translational – were aligned by comparing the linguistic properties of source language pragmatemes with their target language equivalents. The comparison helped to find a link between the findings of both analyses.

The current research project builds upon the theoretical groundwork laid by previous researchers who have investigated the nature of pragmatemes. It is hoped that this study, by presenting a comprehensive research methodology and theoretical foundations, may inspire similar investigations focusing on the practical use of pragmatemes across various texts, which would give deeper insights into the typology and characteristics of these units across different registers and languages. Additionally, it is hoped that the set of translation techniques proposed in this project helps to underscore the significance of context in audiovisual translation, not solely concerning pragmatemes but also extending to other linguistic units.

At this juncture, it seems appropriate to offer some predicted answers to the research questions posed in this project. First, the study is expected to offer a universal definition of a pragmateme that can be embraced by different linguists regardless of their language background. Yet, given the diverse language families represented in the analysis (English, a West Germanic language; French, a Romance language; and Polish, a Slavic language), the likelihood of discovering universal linguistic characteristics of pragmatemes is not high. Although there may be some similarities, given the fact that these languages share an Indo-European origin, these similarities are not expected to be significant enough to be considered universal. Nevertheless, the linguistic analysis is expected to challenge certain traits of pragmatemes that some researchers consider defining, such as compositionality and polylexicality (e.g., Blanco and Mejri 2018). Then, from the translational perspective, it is anticipated that charged pragmatemes, due to their ambiguous nature and high context-sensitivity, may pose challenges to translators. Facing these challenges may require the use of a number of different techniques crucial for maintaining the intended meaning of these pragmatemes within the context, while also adapting to the constraints imposed by subtitling.

The thesis is organized into five chapters. Following the present introduction, Chapters 1 delves into the theoretical background essential for understanding the concept of pragmatemes and situates these units within the landscape of formulaic language. Chapter 2 explores the complexity of audiovisual translation and its various modes, especially subtitling. Chapter 3 is dedicated to outlining the methods employed in this study. It offers a description of the tools used, such as Language Reactor and Unitex, highlighting their roles in the research process. Chapters 4 and 5 are devoted to the analysis of the collected data. The contrastive linguistic analysis is presented in Chapter 4, which scrutinizes the identified pragmatemes across the languages under study, while Chapter 5 centers on the translation analysis, specifically examining the techniques used in the translation of charged pragmatemes. Finally, the conclusions drawn from the research findings are put forward in the last section, along with addressing the study limitations and proposing potential avenues for future research.

CHAPTER 1

Pragmatemes and Formulaic Language

Pragmatemes are language units which are all around in our everyday lives. These are units such as *For sale* written on a sign by the house that one can buy, *Cash or credit?* asked by a cashier in a shop during the transaction, *You are under arrest* stated by a police officer while making an arrest, etc. These examples reveal that pragmatemes are used in specific pragmatic situations. Nevertheless, there is a question of interpretation in what *specific situations* really means and what the place of pragmatemes in a language is. That is why the linguistic phenomenon of what is called here a *pragmateme* has been discussed from many different points of view in the literature. Rey, in the preface to Blanco and Mejri's *Les Pragmatèmes* (2018: 9), recognizes that various researchers give similar theories different names, and Barnas (2017: 5) lists over ten different terms researchers use in relation to the phenomenon of pragmatic expressions (e.g., *communicational phraseologisms* by Burger [1973], *pragmatic phraseologisms* by Dziadkiewicz [2007], *stereotyped language acts* by Kauffer [2019] and *situational phrases* by Anscombre [2011], among others). Acknowledging the complex nature of the issue, Fléchon, Frassi, and Polguère (2012) even ask in the title of their article, *do pragmatemes have an undefinable charm?*[1]. To approach this question, this chapter discusses different concepts behind various definitions of a pragmateme (and other similar terms) proposed by different authors over the years, the role of pragmatemes in the formulaicity of language, and how these units can be approached in translation.

1.1 What is a pragmateme?

It is argued that the phenomenon of pragmatemes is a complex one, and this can be supported by the number of different approaches that this section

[1] Original title: *Les pragmatèmes, ont-ils un charme indéfinissable ?*. If not stated otherwise, all translations in this thesis are made by myself.

presents. The aim of this section is not only to enumerate research already done on the topic but also to compare it critically, and, in the end, propose a new, comprehensive approach to pragmatemes that will also encompass the strong points of existing definitions in a consistent way.

1.1.1 Pragmatemes in Mel'čuk's division of phrasemes

The present review of different approaches to pragmatemes starts with the one proposed by Mel'čuk (1995), as he is considered to be the first linguist to name a particular type of language units *pragmatemes*[2]. In the 1995 article "Phrasemes in language and phraseology in linguistics", a definition of a phraseme is put forward, along with its subtypes, one of which is the pragmateme. Mel'čuk developed the topic in many of his later works, for instance, in the 2012 article "Phraseology in the language, in the dictionary, and in the computer", where a more complex division is suggested, with phrasemes being divided into two main groups: lexical (non-compositional, i.e., idioms, and compositional, i.e., collocations) and semantic-lexical ones, i.e., clichés.

According to Mel'čuk (2012), a pragmateme is a subtype of a cliché. The most general term in Mel'čuk's approach is a phraseme (or *phraseological expression*), which is a non-free phrase, meaning that "at least one of its lexical components L_i is selected by the speaker in a linguistically constrained way – that is, as a function of the lexical identity of other component(s)" (ibid: 219). Then, regarding a semantic-lexical phraseme (or *cliché*), both the components of its lexical expression and the components of its meaning "are selected by the Speaker in a constrained way", for instance, *Happy birthday* or *Will you marry me?* (ibid: 220). Mel'čuk considers these units to be the most common type of phrasemes, which partially explains why they are also the most difficult to study and the least researched so far (Mel'čuk goes so far as to say that they are "seriously understudied", ibid). This group is divided into two: pragmatically non-constrained clichés (i.e., compositional proverbs and sayings, e.g., *A watched pot never boils*, and compositional complex proper names, e.g., *City*

[2] In fact, Charles Bally is believed to have been the first one to present the foundation of what we call today a pragmateme, with a description of fixed, situationally constrained units in his 1909 book *Traité de stylistique française*. Mel'čuk refers to this work as one of the primary inspirations for his phraseme theory (Mel'čuk 2012).

of Light) and pragmatically constrained clichés. It is necessary to note that pragmatic constraints can apply to all types of phrasemes but clichés constitute the majority of them, and that is why Mel'čuk (ibid) proposes a separate name for this group: pragmatemes. They are units that, apart from lexical and semantic-lexical constraints, are also affected by situational (pragmatic) constraints, which means that it is not the situation described by the cliché that limits the choice of means of language, but the situation of their use which demands the choice of a particular cliché. As an example, Mel'čuk (ibid) presents the warning written on food containers: *Best before...* in English, *Najlepiej spożyć przed...* in Polish, or *À consommer avant...* in French.

Bogacki (2012), who uses Mel'čuk's definition of a pragmateme, highlights the triple character of this unit, i.e., the meaning-form-situation character. The meaning and form represent the characteristics of a language sign, while the situation corresponds to the pragmatic side of a pragmateme.

Fléchon, Frassi, and Polguère (2012: 83) elaborate on Mel'čuk's original approach (1995) and call what he defines as a pragmateme, "pragmatème au sens étroit" [pragmateme in the narrow sense], noting that in his original terminology, a pragmateme can only be an independent phrase (not a single word or expression inserted into a sentence). Therefore, to fill the apparent gap, Fléchon, Frassi, and Polguère (2012: 83) propose a new term, namely "pragmatème au sens large" [pragmateme in the broad sense], which contains both Mel'čuk's idea (*pragmatemes cliché*), pragmatemes which are lexemes (*lexemic pragmatemes*)[3] and pragmatemes which are not compositional, i.e., their meaning does not include the meaning of their lexical components (*idiomatic pragmatemes*). In this approach, pragmatically constrained lexemes such as *Hello?* as a response made after picking up the phone, and idiomatic expressions such as *Chaud devant!* (a French expression meaning "mind your back!" used particularly by waiters trying to pass through a crowd) can also be considered pragmatemes (ibid).

3 It has to be pointed out that the article by Fléchon, Frassi, and Polguère was published in 2012, and as Bogacki (2012) notes, by that time Mel'čuk had already published his article "Tout ce que nous voulions savoir sur les phrasèmes, mais..." (2011) in which he acknowledged that there exist pragmatemes which are not phrasemes due to their monolexical character.

1.1.2 Blanco and Mejri's research on pragmatemes

In 2018, Blanco and Mejri published *Les Pragmatèmes*, a comprehensive study on pragmatemes from theoretical and practical (lexicographical among others) points of view. The approach is based on the one proposed by Mel'čuk (1995), with the sole focus on the phenomenon of a pragmateme and its specification.

In this approach[4], for a linguistic unit to be called a pragmateme, it has to be:

1) autonomous, i.e., it can be never considered a part of a phrase. This trait of a pragmateme highlights its predicative nature (that is why Mejri [2018] suggests that pragmatemes can be also called *fixed predicates*). However, it has to be noted that a pragmateme can be a homonym of a lexical unit or of a separate phraseme and the two should not be confused. For instance, the French pragmateme *En panne* written on an elevator that is broken and the phraseme *être en panne* that can be integrated as a verbal expression to any phrase (Blanco and Mejri 2018: 27);
2) constrained in its signified, i.e., there is a preexisting semantic form (or a number of forms) that should be used by the speaker to express what they want to say. What is more, in the majority of cases, this semantic form also demands the use of particular lexical units (ibid: 27). Therefore, in a situation such as delivering a package, the couriers say *Sign here, please* as they are not linguistically free to choose to say for example *Write your name on this document;*
3) polylexical; however, according to Blanco and Mejri (ibid: 31) around five to sever percent of pragmatemes are monolexical (for example, *Congratulations!* expressing praise after an achievement). Furthermore, they observe that most monolexical pragmatemes are interjections of illocutionary value (e.g., *Attention!*) or expressive value (e.g., *God!*). It should be stressed nonetheless that onomatopoeic interjections of

[4] While Blanco and Mejri's (2018) approach appears to be applicable to all languages, it has to be noted that they focus on French pragmatemes. However, in the discussion of examples in this subsection, English equivalents are given where possible.

different noises, such as *Bang!*, "ne sont pas des pragmatèmes puisqu'elles ne sont pas sémantiquement restreintes par la situation de communication" [are not pragmatemes because they are not semantically constrained by the situation of communication[5]] (ibid: 31);

4) semantically compositional, i.e., the meaning of a pragmateme can be understood through the meaning of every component of it. Sometimes the meaning has to be actualized with spatio-temporal coordinates or other extralinguistic factors, for instance *No smoking* is a ban effective only in a place where there is such a sign (ibid: 31). Nevertheless, this rule is not obligatory as there are pragmatemes which are not semantically compositional; *Bless you* uttered after someone has sneezed cannot be interpreted by a simple interpretation of its semantic components (ibid: 26). Units which are usually not compositional are in the majority elliptic or hyperbolic utterances, as well as monolexical pragmatemes (ibid: 33-34);
5) ritualized[6], i.e., pragmatemes are created in a diachronic process that can be either quick (if the unit is widely spread from an authorized source) or slow (which often results in many variants of one unit). Furthermore, Blanco and Mejri (ibid) mention a number of rules codifying the ritual use of pragmatemes, such as precise anchorage of the utterance (space, time, etc.), whether the unit exists in spoken or written language, lexical form and the consequences of not using the appropriate unit in a given situation[7], among others (ibid: 35).

Therefore, in Blanco and Mejri's approach, the definition of a *prototypical pragmateme* is as suggested: "un énoncé autonome polylexical, sémantiquement compositionnel, qui est restreint dans son signifié par la situation de

5 All translations are my own unless otherwise noted.

6 The authors acknowledge the fact that certain linguists (e.g., Coulmas 1981) call fixed units of a ritual nature used for performative function in given situations (e.g., in religious rituals) *routine formulas*; nevertheless, in Blanco and Mejri's approach, the term *routine formula* is not used as it seems to be one of different realizations of a pragmateme (Blanco and Mejri 2018: 34-35).

7 The fact of possible consequences existing in the case of not using the appropriate pragmateme (using a wrong one or not using any) in a given situation is what distinguishes pragmatemes from proverbs (Blanco and Mejri 2018: 36).

communication dans laquelle il est produit" [an autonomous, polylexical, semantically compositional utterance that is constrained in its signified by the situation of communication[8] in which it is produced] (ibid: 25). While it is undeniable that Blanco and Mejri's work (ibid) is one of the most extensive so far, it does not seem to be without shortcomings. The concept of a prototypical pragmateme excludes way too many examples (including a number of examples that appear in the index list the researchers present at the end of their study) to say that one can focus on the prototypical units in their research. Therefore, it should be asked if imposing such narrow criteria is the right way to approach pragmatemes. With this in mind, the next subsection presents a different point of view on pragmatemes, one that has been proposed by Kauffer (2011).

1.1.3 Kauffer's stereotyped language acts

Kauffer (2011) proposes the coining of a new term, *stereotyped language act* (in short ALS, abbreviation of the French name *acte de langage stéréotypé*). Kauffer's work is focused on presenting ALS's connection with context (2018) and how to approach them in bilingual dictionaries (2011).

According to Kauffer (2011: 155), ALS "are phraseological expressions which are characterised by their enunciative status, their idiomaticity and their pragmatic function. They are language acts which express a threat, a refusal, an approbation, etc.", for example *Big deal!*. Kauffer states that ALS are a type of pragmatic phraseologisms, i.e., units which do not only have a referential function but have to be considered on a pragmatic level (2019: 150), next to pragmatemes[9] and conversational formulas[10].

---

8 In Blanco and Mejri's approach the specification of the situation of communication is very important as this is the trait that distinguishes pragmatemes from clichés (contrary to Mel'čuk's [1995] approach, where pragmatemes were a subtype of clichés) (Blanco and Mejri 2018: 52).

9 Kauffer uses the term *pragmateme* as defined by Blanco and Mejri's theory, but he also notes the existence of a similar term, *routine formula*, used mainly by German researchers. Nevertheless, he acknowledges that *routine formula* is a broader term and the research on these units is focused on their ritualization and function in communication (Kauffer 2019: 152).

10 Conversational formulas are expressions (however, some of them are single lexemes) which, in general, are: (1) not directly connected to a given situation, (2) somewhat fixed on morpho-syntactic level, (3) of weak semantical idiomaticity, (4) of functions

There are three defining conditions of ALS. First, they are autonomous and polylexical utterances. Second, their meaning is not semantically compositional. The semantic idiomaticity trait of ALS can be divided into three categories: (1) ALS which have both literal and phraseological meaning and are of weak semantic idiomaticity, (2) ALS which have both literal and phraseological meaning and are of strong semantic idiomaticity, and (3) ALS which have only the phraseological meaning (Kauffer 2018). Third, their phraseological meaning is always pragmatic, as ALS "are defined by the precise function of communication" (Kauffer 2019: 155), and the level of their idiomaticity often depends on context. Furthermore, the pragmatic function means that ALS are a reaction to what has been said or done, which according to Kauffer (2011: 156) is primarily observable in dialogues. It is thanks to their pragmatic function that these units can be broadly defined as speech acts in terms of Austin and Searle's approach as they may be used for expressing approval, confirmation, surprise, etc., so their nature may be performative and affective (Kauffer 2018: 52).

The characteristic traits of ALS may resemble the defining traits of the aforementioned pragmatemes. However, Kauffer (2018: 50) distinguishes one from the other, stressing that while pragmatemes are pragmatically constrained, i.e., they can be used in only one specific situation of communication (except being used differently than their primary meaning, e.g., as irony), ALS have *contextual plasticity* (*plasticité contextuelle*, ibid: 52), i.e., they can be used in different situations and often convey a different meaning, according to the context of a given situation (e.g., *You must be joking!* is a response that can be made to a number of utterances that can cause surprise, disapproval, etc.)[11], "[i]l n'y a donc pas de routinisation de l'ALS dans une situation donnée" [so there is no routinization of ALS in a given situation] (ibid: 53). Kauffer (ibid) also notes that there are three major issues in the description of pragmatemes:

concentrated on the discourse level (e.g., organization of a conversation), and (5) sometimes autonomous, but most often a part of a phrase, for instance *in my opinion, in short* (Kauffer 2018: 151).

[11] Nevertheless, it seems that some of the pragmatemes given as examples by Blanco and Mejri (2018) can be applied in various situations and convey different meanings, e.g., the interjection *Tu parles!* can express disbelief (*You must be joking!*) or agreement (*And how!*).

(1) the fact that their polylexicality is not a restrictive trait as there seems to be a large number of pragmatemes which are single lexemes[12], (2) the fact that the connection to a given situation of communication is a defining criterion of a pragmateme, while it is very complicated to precisely describe such a situation and sometimes units which are said to be pragmatemes can apply to more than one situation, and (3) there seems to be no agreement among researchers whether pragmatemes are autonomous utterances (e.g., Blanco and Mejri's approach) or not (e.g., Mel'čuk's theory). Finally, Kauffer in his theory (2019: 165) acknowledges that polylexical pragmatemes can be considered sub-types of ALS and that ALS and pragmatemes complement each other in the field of phraseology.

Furthermore, Kauffer in his works acknowledges that properly categorizing and defining different phraseologisms can be problematic, which is evidenced by the fact that a lot of different typologies and definitions have already been drawn up by various researchers around the world. He notes that pragmatic phraseologisms are especially diverse in terms of the terminology associated with them (2018: 150). For example, in his 2011 article, Kauffer compares the notion of ALS to similar units in three typologies: (1) as units belonging to two categories according to Burger's (1982) typology: communicative phraseologisms (because of their pragmatic function) and phraseologisms which are autonomous utterances, (2) as routine formulas (which focus on ritualization of expressions but do not stress their autonomous character), according to Coulmas's (1981) typology, and (3) as routine formulas in the approach of Lüger (1999), who highlights the non-compositional meaning of the unit but who also states that it does not have to be an autonomous utterance (i.e., it can allow slots, e.g., *in my opinion*).

Kauffer (2018, 2019) also stresses that, when categorizing a unit as a type of phraseologism, the context is often a factor that should be taken into account. In terms of ALS, he presents a list of contextual factors that can influence the meaning of these units: anaphoric relations to the preceding context, deictic relations, elimination of ALS's contextual ambiguity by specifying their meaning, enrichment of the meaning (by using two ALS of a similar

12 However, Kauffer (2019: 163) states that there are also ALS which are monolexical (e.g., *basta*). Therefore, it seems that in his terminology, it is not a restrictive trait either.

meaning together or by adding affective elements) and (de)phraseologization (meaning that thanks to the context one is able to determine whether a unit is an ALS or not) (Kauffer 2018: 53-56). The strong connection to the context of pragmatic phraseologisms (pragmatemes, conversational formulas and ALS), and therefore their direct relation to their usage is the important factor that, according to Kauffer (2018: 57), should place these units at the center of research on phraseology, and that is one of the reasons why they are also placed at the center of this thesis.

1.1.4 Kecskés's situation-bound utterances (SBUs)

Another term depicting a concept very similar to the concept of a pragmateme is a situation-bound utterance[13] (SBU) as in Kecskés (2000, 2003, 2010, 2014, 2017). According to Kecskés (2000: 606), SBUs are "highly conventionalized, prefabricated pragmatic units whose occurrence is tied to standardized communicative situations." Therefore, they are units which are often obligatory and predictable in social situations, hence their name. Contrary to Blanco and Mejri (2018), Kecskés (2000: 607) argues that the meaning of SBUs is not compositional, but functional. In other words, their pragmatic function is not encoded in the linguistic form but in the situation in which they are used, thanks to which they can be distinguished from "their freely generated counterparts" (e.g., *I'll talk to you later* may be used as an SBU and thus is a way to say goodbye or as a compositional structure and then literally means to talk to somebody on a different occasion). However, by studying their etymology, it is clear that SBUs are phrases that used to be freely generated but have become delexicalized (completely or at least partially) by being frequently used in conventionalized situations to convey the pragmatic motivation of a speaker (ibid). Therefore, through repetition, they became frozen in the language and "are a part of collectively shared social background knowledge" (Kecskés 2017: 202) that one can gain through participation in

[13] Kecskés (2010) acknowledges the existence of a variety of other terms describing a similar linguistic phenomenon; however, he argues for the term *situation-bound utterances* being the most suitable one as it directly refers to their main feature, i.e., "their strong tie, their boundedness to a particular situation" (Kecskés 2010: 3) and is not as broad as terms such as *routine formula* and not as specific as terms such as *institutionalized expression*.

social practices. Thanks to the knowledge of SBUs one can feel that one is a part of the group in which those SBUs are used and they provide assurance of not being misunderstood. What is more, SBUs are selective in that they constitute a preferred way of conveying a certain meaning in a given situation (even though there exist many different ways, among them various freely generated and idiomatic phrases, to express the same meaning) and completive, i.e., they always evoke a particular situation, unlike freely generated utterances (Kecskés 2010).

In terms of their part in formulaicity of language, SBUs are conversational routines (CRs), like speech formulas and discourse markers (Kecskés 2010). Consequently, all SBUs are CRs but not all CRs are SBUs. While it is not always possible easily to distinguish which CRs are SBUs and which are not, one of the main factors to take into account is that the most salient meaning of SBUs is situational and other CRs are simply functional. Furthermore, other CRs usually have discourse functions rather than purely situational functions. SBUs are also different from idioms in "origin, purpose and use" (Kecskés 2010: 4). The main differences are that semantic idioms are usually used unpredictably (while the use of SBUs can be predicted) and they are usually the result of a creative act (while SBUs are characterised by frequent repetition); furthermore, SBUs may have a transparent freely generated counterpart while semantic idioms are not transparent at all. For instance, conversational routines such as *to tell you the truth* can be used in different social contexts, while SBUs are only linked to a particular pragmatic context, e.g., *Welcome aboard* which is uttered to someone boarding a ship or a plane or starting a new job (Bardovi-Harlig 2012: 209).

Kecskés (2000) in his approach distinguishes two key features of SBUs, the first one being that their meaning applies within a relevant frame, i.e., they are "more or less fixed and predictable" (ibid: 610) and therefore have a communicative function. To understand them, Kiefer (1995) calls for the use of frame semantics, as a frame is where the script of every situation takes place. For example, the frame of the SBU *You are welcome* would be "reacting to thanks" (Genzel 1991: 54). Thanks to this frame the pragmatic property of an SBU is created and the SBU come to mean the same thing for all speakers of a given community. Still in regard to the first key feature of SBUs, that is, the applicability of their meaning within a particular frame, Mey's (2001) pragmatic act theory is relevant. Mey (ibid) argues against classic speech act theory and stresses that speech acts have to be situated to be effective. In Mey's (ibid) approach, the aim is to characterize what he calls a *pragmeme*, i.e., "a general situational prototype" (Kecskés 2010: 2), which is realized through an SBU (an *individual pragmatic act* or a *pract*[14] in Mey's [2001] terminology), which is both situation-derived and situation-constrained. For instance, a pragmeme for the SBU *How can I help you?* would be [offering one's help][15]. Therefore in Mey's theory context (both linguistic and extralinguistic) is essential for understanding pragmatic acts, because "no conversational contribution at all can be understood properly unless it is situated within the environment in which it was meant to be understood" (Mey 2001: 217).

Nevertheless, Kecskés (2000: 610) notes that "predictability and boundedness to a specific sub-event are, of course, a matter of degree rather than absolutes"[16], which is important in examining specific SBUs.

The second key feature of SBUs is that they behave like words (ibid). This is true for all linguistic units of formulaic language, whose meaning cannot be derived from its semantics. However, Kecskés (ibid) argues that SBUs are not simply lexical units, because due to their referring to a given frame they are rather pragmatic units. To put it another way, "words are rarely tied to particular situations only" while SBUs "are usually tied to one or more particular situations" (Kecskés 2010: 5). Therefore, in examining SBUs it has to be remembered that not only do they behave like words, but they are inseparable from their situational meanings and pragmatic functions[17].

---

14 However, it seems that not all practs are SBUs. As an example, Kecskés (2010: 6) presents the pragmeme [greeting a new employee] which can be realized by various practs such as *Welcome aboard* or *Hope you will like it here*, though only the former seems to be an SBU due to its unanalyzable structure which is tied to the situation of the pragmeme.

15 Mey (2001) proposes that pragmemes be introduced in square brackets.

16 The more an SBU is repeated, the more its meaning is encoded in the structure and hence a particular pragmatic function of the unit is getting conventionalized, i.e., its meaning will be the same for most native speakers (Kecskés 2010).

17 That is why Kecskés (2010) argues that when describing SBUs, register-oriented and/or situation-bound frequency and not general frequency (which is used for words) should be taken into account.

1.1.5 Other researchers on the topic

This section started with the description of Mel'čuk's (1995) ideas, as he is thought to have been the first one to use the term *pragmateme*. Three similar concepts were then presented: Blanco and Mejri's (2018) pragmatemes, Kauffer's (2011, 2018, 2019) ALS, and Kecskés's (2000, 2003, 2010, 2014, 2017) SBUs. These concepts have been discussed in separate subsections because their expositions by the researchers are comprehensive and cover different aspects (conceptual, lexicographic and didactic, among others). However, there is a plethora of other research in which similar concepts are noted, but since they do not seem to be as extensive as those already discussed, a selection of them will be discussed together in this subsection.

In Polish phraseology, the term *phraseme* (Polish: *frazem*), proposed by Chlebda[18] (1993), is the most similar to the notion of a pragmateme as viewed by Blanco and Mejri (2018). Chlebda describes phrasematics, or *phraseology of the addresser* (*frazeologia nadawcy*, 1993: 335) as a research field in the center of which there is a person addressing somebody in a given situation and with a particular goal. The unit researched by phrasematics is called a phraseme, which is defined as follows: "względnie stała forma językowa, która w danej sytuacji stała się – niezależnie od swych cech strukturalnych i semantycznych – przyjętym (nierzadko jedynym) sposobem wyrażania danego potencjału treściowego" [a relatively fixed language form which became (regardless of its structural and sematic characteristics) the accepted (and often the only) way of expressing a given message] (ibid: 336). Furthermore, and similarly to Kauffer (2018), Chlebda stresses the importance of context as it makes phrasemes relative units of meaning depending on how, by whom and to whom they are used in a conversation. A phraseme is therefore a very broad notion with only one feature[19] that has to be present, i.e., its reproducibility

---

[18] In Polish literature, the term *frazem* [*phraseme*] also appears in reference to the original Mel'čuk's (1995) definition, i.e., as repeatable multiword expressions which are frequent in given types of texts. Such a definition is adopted, for example, in Arabski, Łyda, and Warchał's (2009) dictionary of English academic phrasemes (*Słownik angielskich frazemów akademickich*).

[19] Nevertheless, Benenowska (2001: 209), while discussing Chlebda's approach, presents a more detailed description of a phraseme and states that it "ma kilka cech, np. występowanie w bezpośredniej komunikacji razem z intonacją, kontekstowa zależność,

in a given situation and to express a given message; Chlebda himself highlights the fact that this definition results in a radical increase in the number of language units to be counted as such, e.g., while describing and classifying phrasemes in a dictionary.

Gębka-Wolak and Moroz (2014) propose the addition of a new type of semantic phraseme to Mel'čuk's typology, the *non-free syntactic group*. These are units characterized by their non-compositional meaning (semantic and syntactic irregularity, i.e., the whole has different semantic and syntactic traits than do its components), which can be understood thanks to "swoistą konfigurację komponentów segmentalnych i suprasegmentalnych" [a specific configuration of components-segments and components-suprasegments] (ibid: 54). Furthermore, as they claim, these units can also transmit a *pragmatic parameter* (*parameter pragmatyczny*, ibid: 53). As an example Gębka-Wolak and Moroz give the exclamation *What a girl!* where the word *girl* can be replaced by another noun. Nevertheless, researchers examining non-free syntactic groups can be faced with a number of difficulties, such as having to determine whether these units should be considered lexical units or syntactic constructions. As the authors note, non-free syntactic groups are "not complete enough" for lexical units because at least one of their elements is a lexical variable and can be freely substituted, but the syntactic mechanism behind their components is too individual for syntactic constructions (ibid: 58-59). Therefore, while it can be argued that Gębka-Wolak and Moroz's observations are noteworthy, the factor of what they call a pragmatic parameter seems too vague for these units to be considered pragmatemes (if that was the case, one would have to think, for example, that all verbless exclamatory sentences are pragmatemes).

Another approach is proposed by Barnas (2017), who, having presented a large number of different researchers' views on pragmatemes, proposes her

brak możliwości sprowadzenia do mowy zależnej, odtwórczy charakter (ponieważ jako całość jest reprodukowana z pamięci dyspozycyjnej użytkownika)" [has several features, for example, being present in direct communication along with intonation, context-dependence, lack of possibility of being transformed into indirect speech, reproducibility (because it is reproduced as a whole from the user's memory)].

own definition of the language unit that she too calls a *pragmateme*, which is an expression:

- composed of at least one lexeme;
- obligatory fixed;
- the use of which is associated with a given situation;
- which functions "indépendamment dans une situation de communication, quel que soient le canal, l'émetteur, le récepteur du message, le code ou le contexte" [independently in the situation of communication, regardless of the canal, transmitter, receiver of the message, code or context] (ibid: 21);
- which is predictable (ibid: 22).

Furthermore, according to Barnas (2017: 22), "chaque pragmatème est un acte de parole" [every pragmateme is a speech act] and therefore elements such as insults, curses, exclamations, affective phrases, etc. which are "délimitées de deux côtés par des signes de ponctuation ou fonctionnant indépendamment" [delimited by punctuation marks or which function independently] (ibid) should be considered pragmatemes. Barnas in her study focuses on non-compositional pragmatemes, which she calls *the most interesting* (*les plus intéressants*, ibid: 44). She also gives her opinion that the criteria of polylexicality and semantic compositionality, which are often proposed in regard to the research on pragmatemes, should be rejected because they do not concern all pragmatemes (ibid: 22). Barnas's approach may not seem novel in regards to the concepts already discussed, as all of these traits have been already proposed in one way of another, but what is different in this approach is how all-inclusive it is, while still referring to situation-bounded units. At first, her definition of a pragmateme may even seem too general, since there are no factors that would strictly limit the scope of the study, as also does, for instance, Blanco and Mejri's (2018) argument about semantic compositionality. However, thanks to a general definition, there is no need to explain the exceptions to the rule, as is the case, e.g., for Blanco and Mejri (ibid). The study can be limited to the preferential choice of the researcher, such as the choice of non-compositional polylexical units in Barnas's own study (2017), but the primary definition of a pragmateme remains all-encompassing.

Other researchers, for example, Dziadkiewicz (2007), make use of other approaches in their research, for instance, the approach suggested by the German school represented by Burger (1973, 1982), who presents the concept under the term *pragmatic phraseologisms* (PrPs)[20] which are "un large groupe de formulations conventionnelles réalisant des actes de langage déterminés qui ne peuvent être décrits que dans un cadre pragmatique, c'est-à-dire faisant référence à la situation de leur énonciation" [a large group of conventional formulas that perform specific speech acts and which can only be described from a pragmatic perspective, i.e., by referencing the situation of the utterance] (as discussed in Dziadkiewicz 2007: 1). As an example of a PrP, Burger (discussed in Dziadkiewicz 2007) gives both closed fixed expressions such as *Guten Tag* (*Good morning*) and open lexicogrammatical constructions, e.g., *Würden Sie mir bitte den Zucker herüberreichen?* (*Would you pass me the sugar, please?*). Dziadkiewicz (2007: 4) also acknowledges the fact that PrPs can be single lexemes functioning as phrases, expressions functioning as phrases, polylexical formulas, or lexicosyntactic constructions.

A few further names of similar linguistic phenomena can be listed. For example, Bardovi-Harlig (2012: 208) suggests the term *pragmatic routines*, using characteristics outlined by Myles, Hooper, and Mitchell (1998: 325) to describe situationally dependent units that are two morphemes or more of length, phonologically coherent (meaning they are articulated without hesitance), and used repeatedly without changes in form by a whole community. Myles et al. (1998: 325) in their examination also mention three psycholinguistic criteria for what Bardovi-Harlig calls pragmatic routines: they are not related to the productive patterns of speech, are more complex compared to the speaker's other linguistic output, and may be inappropriate or idiosyncratic (semantically, syntactically, or pragmatically). Marque-Pucheu (2007) suggests the term *énoncé lié* [*connected utterance*] for a language unit which is recurrent, connected to a very specific situation of communication in which it is automatically produced, and rarely semantically compositional, e.g., *You must be joking!* (the definition and the provided example show therefore that this

[20] However, it has to be noted that Burger published another paper in 2003 in which he presents the concept of communicative phraseologisms, as discussed before by Kauffer (2011).

concept can be compared to Kauffer's aforementioned concept of ALS and Kecskes's SBUs; however, both of these theories seem much more detailed).

Lastly, Longhi and Sarfati (2012) give yet another definition of what they call a pragmateme: "Le pragmatème c'est l'unité minimale de sens et d'interaction. Il permet une réorganisation de la répartition des unités du lexique (en partie du discours), selon la perspective pragmatique" [A pragmateme is a minimal unit of meaning and interaction. It makes the reorganization of the repartition of lexical units (which are a part of the discourse) possible from the pragmatics perspective] (ibid: 125). Longhi and Sarfati are among researchers who note the importance of interaction in the pragmateme definition, which could put some examples among adjacency pairs (e.g., *Good morning, class. – Good morning, teacher*). Furthermore, Sarfati (1997) gives a more detailed description of a pragmateme in which he highlights the importance of examining the words (1) thanks to which speech acts are accomplished (e.g., *promise*), (2) that describe speech acts (e.g., *convince*), and (3) that transmit the pragmatic traits (e.g., grammatical words) in the research on pragmatemes.

1.1.6 Different typologies of pragmatemes

The subsections presented above suggest that theories on pragmatemes vary, at least slightly, from researcher to researcher. Most of them have not only proposed their own definition of the concept but have also suggested how it can be classified on a number of criteria, which will be further discussed in this subsection.

Firstly, Fléchon, Frassi and Polguère (2012) while examining Mel'čuk's approach suggest the use of a pragmateme of broader definition and distinguish three types: pragmateme cliché, lexemic pragmateme and idiomatic pragmateme (see p. 28).

Then, while Rey briefly mentions three types of pragmatemes (spoken-written, only spoken, only written) in the preface to Blanco and Mejri's *Les Pragmatèmes* (2018: 12), these authors themselves highlight the importance of the situation of communication which demands the use of a certain pragmateme as that which constitutes the main characterization of the notion. That is why they classify pragmatemes on the basis of the given situation of communication (2018: 36-50), according to:

- spatial coordinates: for a number of pragmatemes to be interpretable, a spatial coordinate needs to be present (for example, *Best before*[21] cannot be interpreted if not written on a food or cosmetics product);
- temporal coordinates: e.g., popular pragmatemes such as *Good morning* and *Good afternoon* can be only uttered at a particular time of the day;
- situational coordinates: some pragmatemes can be uttered only in a given situation; Blanco and Mejri further distinguish five subtypes of this type of pragmateme:
  - accidental situations – such as a car accident;
  - organized events – such as a marriage ceremony;
  - periodic events – such as Christmas;
  - situations-actions – such as an attack;
  - situations-states – such as a disease.

  Furthermore, the researchers stress that the last two subtypes have to be "considérés du point de vue événementiel" [considered from a situational point of view] (ibid: 41). For this category, examples of pragmatemes are *Bless you* uttered after someone sneezes and *My condolences*.
- action coordinates: according to Blanco and Mejri (ibid: 43), "[i]l y a un grand nombre de pragmatèmes liés par une situation de communication qui doit comprendre une action donnée" [there are many pragmatemes connected to a given situation of communication which must contain a given action], and by "action" they understand every utterance in which the verb can be replaced by *do* (e.g., instead of saying *I called Mary* one can say *I did that*). In this category there are pragmatemes that demonstrate for instance presentations or formal announcements (e.g., *I have the pleasure to inform you that* + phrase), but there are also pragmatemes that are performative acts such as *I pronounce you husband and wife*[22].

---

21 As in the subsection devoted to Blanco and Mejri's (2018) approach (see p. 30), in this subsection, the examples are either given by myself or are English equivalents of the French pragmatemes originally discussed by Blanco and Mejri (ibid).

22 Nevertheless, "[t]ous les pragmatèmes (sauf quelques interjections) ont une valeur illocutive, mais seulement un petit nombre a une valeur performative" [all pragmatemes (except a few interjections) are illocutionary acts, but only a small number of them are performative] (Blanco and Mejri 2018: 44).

- state coordinates: visible through all stative verbs. States can be divided into transitional (e.g., *be tired*) and situational (e.g., *be late*). Pragmatemes such as *Open/Closed* and *Wet paint*[23] belong to this category.
- entity coordinates: pragmatemes belonging to this category describe the characteristics of objects, humans, animals or plants – "entities" having dimensions and physical traits such as width, length, weight, color (ibid: 46) – for instance: *Push to open*, *Best before*[24] and *Serve chilled*. Also, pragmatemes describing location (e.g., *Elevator*) or the object's composition (e.g., *100% cotton*) also belong to this category. Blanco and Mejri (ibid: 49-50) add that these pragmatemes do not describe the situation of communication in terms of the form of an object but the signified they represent, e.g., the sign *Fragile* written on a box does not simply describe the characteristics of the object inside but also implies that the package should be handled with care.

Interestingly, in 2013, a few years before publishing *Les Pragmatèmes* with Mejri, Blanco published an article in which he proposed classifying pragmatemes according to a number of different, more formal traits:

- whether the unit belongs to the spoken or written language;
- whether it is a part of regional or official language;
- whether its register is formal or informal;
- whether it comes from a foreign language;
- the time when it was in use (whether it is currently in use, if it is a neologism or an anachronism);
- the domain in which it is used (technical, scientific, artistic language, etc.);
- what kind of connotations are associated with it (if it is pejorative or whether it is a euphemism);
- the frequency of use;
- linguistic correctness (Blanco 2013: 18-20).

---

23 It can be noted that the pragmatemes mentioned here can be also considered to be part of the spatial coordinates type. Therefore, it seems that some pragmatemes may belong to two or more of the categories suggested by Blanco and Mejri (2018) as it can be difficult to specify which of a pragmateme's coordinates are the most important.

24 From this particular example it can be concluded that in Blanco and Mejri's classification, one pragmateme may belong to more than one type; *Best before* belongs both to the group with spatial coordinates and that with entity coordinates.

Some of the characteristics presented above are also mentioned by Chlebda (1993), who states that phrasemes can be classified depending first on when they were in use. From the lexicographical point of view, determining this factor is impossible due to the fact that new phrasemes are constantly being created. Phrasemes can also be classified according to the area of their reproducibility (whether they function as such in the language of a whole nation, region, particular environment, a family, etc.). Nevertheless, Chlebda (1993: 337-339) focuses on the classification of phrasemes according to their function. He elaborates on Halliday's systemic functional linguistics, presenting phrasemes of:

- ideational function, i.e., connecting the speaker to the outside world and how they view it (Chlebda 1993: 337); in this group there are phrasemes naming various objects and phenomena (e.g., *plant butter*[25]), names of certain beliefs and convictions (e.g., *Tarot will tell you the truth*), laws and quasi-laws (e.g., $E = mc^2$), and descriptions of psychological and emotional states (e.g., *I'm on cloud nine*);
- interpersonal function, i.e., connecting people to one another (Chlebda 1993: 338); in this group there are phrasemes which are warnings (e.g., *Beware of the dog*), bans (e.g., *No smoking*), notice (e.g., *No complaints will be considered after that time*), encouragements (e.g., *Yes we can!*), and wishes (e.g., *Merry Christmas!*), etc.;
- textual function: in this group there are phrasemes that describe the text in a text (Chlebda 1993: 338), i.e., they present its parameters, structure, etc., so they can be called *metaphrasemes*, e.g., *so called*, *as stated before*[26], etc.

Further elaborating on Chlebda's approach to phrasemes, Benenowska (2001: 209-210) adds that these units can be classified by taking many different factors into account, for instance "w odniesieniu do stopnia konwencjonalizacji (…), funkcji (prymarną i sekundarną), specyfikacji użycia (stwierdzenie, zaprzeczenie, (…) itd.), struktury składniowej, (…), etc." [the degree

[25] The examples presented here are English equivalents of Chlebda's Polish examples.

[26] In this sense, pragmatemes of textual function greatly resemble lexical bundles (see more: p. 64)

of conventionalization, function (primary and secondary), use (statement, negation, etc.), syntactic structure, etc.] In her study, she classifies phrasemes of oral language on the basis of film dialogues with reference to Awdiejew's (1998) typology of functions: modal, emotive, behavioral and persuasive functions on the interactional level and function of text organization and content organization on the discourse level.

The next typology to be mentioned is the classification of discourse particles and routine formulas according to their discourse functions that was made by Stede and Schmitz (1997). Discourse particles are "words that are not uttered because of their propositional content, but because of some pragmatic function for the ongoing discourse." For example, *right* initiates "some kind of break in the conversation" (Stede and Schmitz 1997: 3), while routine formulas are "expressions whose occurrence is closely tied to types of recurrent social situations" (Coulmas 1979: 239) with the following characteristics: "the form as a recurrent sequence, its occurrence in specific social contexts, and the idea of the social contract which extends to members of a particular speech community"[27] (Bardovi-Harlig 2012: 207). These concepts are similar to some of the definitions of a pragmateme presented before and that is why this classification is taken into account in this part of the thesis. According to Stede and Schmitz (1997: 5), these units can represent four different discourse functions: structuring (further divided into push, pop, uptake, check, and repair), coherence-marking, attitudinal (positive, negative, indifferent, given, and surprise), and smoothening (with a sub-type called *filler*).

Structuring functions help to make the discourse understandable, with the push and pop functions marking "the beginning of a sub-topic or digression, and the return to the previous topic, respectively" (Stede and Schmitz 1997: 6), e.g., *by the way*; the uptake function signalizing turn-taking or turn-holding in a conversation, e.g., *okay, now*; the check function seeking feedback, e.g., *isn't it?*; and the repair function helping with problems that occur in expressing a given content, e.g., *I mean, sorry*.

[27] Stede and Schmitz (1997) also stress the non-compositional (idiomatic) meaning of routine formulas; this feature, however, does not seem to appear in all research on this type of units.

The coherence-marking function "can be employed to facilitate the embedding of the utterance within the context, and to check the common basis of the participants" (ibid: 7).

The attitudinal functions help to convey a given (positive, negative, indifferent) attitude towards a specific content, to express surprise at something another person has said (surprise function) or to reveal a presupposition towards the speaker's own utterance (given function).

Thanks to the smoothening function the discourse is made appropriate and polite, and the filler sub-type specifically helps the speaker organize their utterance and "plan the output" (ibid).

The last typology to be mentioned in the present subsection is the one made by Kecskés (2000). His classification of SBUs borrows from the approach presented by Cruse (1992) who discussed the relationship between words and their concepts. In short, Cruse claimed that various lexical routes can lead to a single concept and therefore distinguished two types of linguistic units: plain, which have semantic properties decoding a particular meaning of the word, and charged, which cannot be semantically decomposed in order to understand the meaning and have additional modulatory effects. For instance, the concept [DIE] can be presented with the plain word *die* or with the charged term *snuff it* (Kecskés 2000: 611). Kecskés (ibid) adapted Cruse's theory and distinguished three types of SBUs:

- Plain SBUs are units such as *It is good to see you*, whose meaning is compositional and which can be semantically decoded. Therefore, their communicative meaning usually is the same as their semantic meaning;
- Charged SBUs are units that can be ambiguous without any context. They can be either compositional or functional depending on the situation they are used in; therefore their meaning is *charged* by the situation. For example, *get out of here* can be used as "go away" or "don't fool me" (ibid: 614);
- Loaded SBUs are units used to convey rituals such as greeting someone and apologizing which have been so frequently used that they are completely delexicalized, i.e., they have lost their compositionl meaning and cannot be decoded semantically. Their pragmatic function is the primary one and the original etymology may be difficult to trace. The situations they are usually used in are thought of even without context (e.g., *Welcome*

aboard); therefore they are *loaded* with a new function which is "no longer depended only on the situation" (ibid: 614) as their meaning is already encoded in the expression itself[28].

In this and previous subsections, a part of the existing literature on different concepts similar to that of a pragmateme was reviewed, thanks to which it is now possible to discuss the approach which will be the basis for the analytical part of this thesis research.

1.1.7 Approach towards pragmatemes in this thesis

As has been shown in the previous subsections, there is a variety of terms concerning language units that can be called pragmatemes. The reason for this may be that these units can be particularly difficult to define precisely, but also, as Kecskés (2000: 607) suggests, that they are used in various fields of both theoretical and applied linguistics, sometimes by linguists who are not interested in searching outside their own research fields. Having discussed the approaches to the topic made by different researchers, it would also seem sensible to add that this variety of terms and definitions may also result from a lack of communication between researchers from different countries. This dissertation, by presenting approaches published in English, French, and Polish, aims to overcome this lack of communication, to show the similarities between comparable research that is often conducted simultaneously, but in different languages, and to suggest a possible term and definition that could be used internationally.

Many theories on the topic of pragmatemes, phrasemes, routine formulas, pragmatic idioms and situation-bound utterances have been presented in this thesis in the previous subsections. Therefore, it is now possible to suggest a main definition that would connect the above-mentioned approaches. In this dissertation, the use of the term *pragmateme* is argued for, since it is connected to the well-known phraseme theory by Mel'čuk (2012), and also depicts the relation with pragmatics, and seems fairly easy to understand, as

---

[28] This classification may be compared with Kauffer's (2019) classification of ALS depending on the level of their idiomaticity; however, Kecskés's (2000) typology seems more detailed.

it is neither lengthy nor an abbreviation. Following in Barnas's (2017) and Kecskés's (2000) footsteps, an inclusive definition is proposed: pragmatemes are language units that are fixed, i.e., used without changes in their form, in a language and predictably used in situations of communication which are typical, repeatable, and specific. Furthermore, pragmatemes themselves trigger a mental representation of the specific communication situation. This definition encompasses units that are either mono- or polylexical, semantically compositional or not, and allowing for slots[29] or not. The reason to make the proposed definition rather broad is simple: it is intended to be used internationally and this is only possible with and all-encompassing approach such as the one proposed here. The fact that the proposed definition may be used across different languages may be its biggest advantage in comparison to the other approaches presented in this section. If the definition of a pragmateme excluded monolexical units, some pragmatemes could be considered as such in one language but not another (e.g., the monolexical French *Bonjour* and its Polish polylexical equivalent *Dzień dobry*). Similarly, if the definition excluded idiomatic units, equivalents of some pragmatemes in other languages could not be considered pragmatemes (e.g., the compositional English *Happy birthday* and its Polish idiomatic equivalent *Sto lat*, which literally means *A hundred years*). Furthermore, one of the important characteristics of a pragmateme in this definition is the predictability of the utterance in a given situation. For example, on entering a dance class in France, women may expect the dance teacher to greet them with *Bonjour, ça va les filles?* (lit. *Hello, how are you, girls?*) instead of directly starting the class; the same however does not apply in a similar setting in Poland, where *How are you?* (*Jak się masz?*) is usually not used as a greeting but rather an actual question inviting a factual response. Another example is that when one receives a package, one may expect the courier to say *Sign here, please* and probably not *For the reception of this package, I need your signature on this document.*

[29] Pragmatemes with slots typically incorporate a vocative element, such as *Good morning [NAME]*. Slots can also be seen in pragmatemic patterns (see p. 138), for instance, *See you [TEMPORAL EXPRESSION]*. In this regard, the central aspect of the pragmateme remains fixed, as does the categorical nature of the slot.

Addressing the elephant in the room, i.e., what can be understood by the *specific situation of communication*, it is up to the researcher to decide upon every individual case, which can be considered a weak point of the proposed approach. For instance, for some researchers, units such as *You must be joking* can be considered pragmatemes because their use can be clearly described (e.g., "showing surprise at what the interlocutor has just said"). However, in this thesis, such a unit is not considered a pragmateme because *You must be joking*, even though it always conveys the same message, can be an answer to a countless number of different statements. Similarly, *Thank you* is regarded here as too wide in its usage to be a pragmateme, as one can give thanks for a countless number of things. Yet *Thank you for coming* is considered here a pragmateme since its usage is limited to a situation that can be easily specified. *I love you*, although it can be predictable and is definitely a fixed and repeatable unit, is not specifically related to any given situation of communication (it can be uttered in many different moments of one's life) and therefore cannot be considered a pragmateme; however, *Love you*, used as a part of saying goodbye, is a pragmateme in that sense. Therefore, it is argued that pragmatemes are separate from utterances which can have a pragmatemic usage. In the first case, the utterance evokes the situation of communication in which it is usually used even in an abstract context, without the actual situation happening. For instance, if one thinks about the utterance *Check*, it immediately evokes three situations: checking if elements on a list are completed, asking for a check (in that case, usually with a *please*), and in the game of chess when the king is threatened. That is why *Check* is a pragmateme. However, one of its French equivalents, referring to checking a list, *C'est bon* (lit. *It's good*), does not evoke the same situation if it stands on its own, for example in a dictionary; on the contrary, *C'est bon* on its own may mean a number of things (e.g., *I'm fine*, *Check*, *It's good*, etc.) That is why it only has a pragmatemic usage in a particular context.

In terms of typology, Kecskés's (2000) division into plain, charged, and loaded units is applied, with a slight change to the charged category. Charged pragmatemes are those which are ambiguous and need context to be properly understood. They can be either compositional in one setting, and idiomatic in another, or (and this is what differs from Kecskés's original definition) compositional or idiomatic in two (or more) different settings. Furthermore, the compositional/idiomatic factor may not be even applicable, as is the case in one-word pragmatemes. In that case, the label *compositional* could be assigned to monolexical pragmatemes whose meaning is similar to the most common one noted in a dictionary, while the label *idiomatic* could refer to its meaning outside of the ordinary one. For instance, the English pragmateme *Clear* is different from the adjective use presented in most dictionaries, as it may be used by police officers to indicate that there is nobody in a room or by anyone in a conversation to indicate that a message has been understood. Therefore, context is needed to understand with which of these meanings the pragmateme is used, and that is why *Clear* is a charged pragmateme. This trait is often visible in translation, because such a pragmateme often has two different equivalents depending on its situational meaning: the first meaning would be translated into the Polish *Czysto* while the latter would be *Zrozumiano* (lit. *Understood*) or *Jasne* (similarly in French: the first meaning would be represented with *Il n'y a personne* [lit. *There's nobody*], while the latter with *C'est noté* [lit. *It's noted*]).

Furthermore, it is argued here that pragmatemes can be investigated not only from the point of view of their type, but also from that of their linguistic features. For instance, in this thesis research, pragmatemes will be examined according to how many words they contain, and whether they are imperatives, questions, elliptic utterances, and verbless units. The presence of deictic markers and variations to one pragmateme will be also investigated. Finally, it is argued that for all pragmatemes, one (or more) particular speech act that they perform can be assigned.

As has been shown many times throughout this section, pragmatemes are a complex topic to research. Now, having set the ground from the micro-scale, i.e., starting from the single unit that is a pragmateme, it is possible to present a larger topic, similarly, not easily definable, i.e., formulaic language, of which pragmatemes are a part.

1.2 Research on Formulaic Language: different perspectives

The present section will focus on different theoretical perspectives regarding formulaic language, to which pragmatemes belong. This section is an overview of an immense phenomenon which is impossible to fully grasp.

As Chlebda (2003: 17) puts it, presenting the paradigms of formulaic language is a "karkołomne zadanie" [back-breaking task] since not only there is a huge number of works published on the topic but also a "chaos terminologiczny" [terminological chaos], and both factors make it difficult to gather and coherently present the ideas on the topic, especially in works whose literature review includes research in more than one language, such as this one. This section seeks to set out pragmatemes on the confluent landscape of formulaic language.

Grabowski (2018: 67) distinguishes three characteristics of a language: (1) "szablonowość" [richness in regular patterns], meaning that the user's choice of the means of expression is limited, (2) "formuliczność" [formulaicity], which is the repeatable use of formulas (both single and multi-word) that have specific pragmatic functions or perform speech acts, and (3) "standaryzacja" [standardization] which means that languages aim for the precision of speech, which leads to the use of formulas and regular patterns. Formulas (formulaic sequences or formulaic units) are "a linguistic solution to non-linguistic problems" (Kecskés 2003: 79), with these problems being two human needs: (1) the need to achieve certain social communicational goals, and (2) the need to both produce and understand language without a processing overload[30] (Wray 2002). Formulaic sequences are generally understood as multi-word expressions that are lexicalized, i.e., stored in memory as if they were single lexemes, processed without reference to their composition (Wood 2012). Formulaicity is a long-recognized phenomenon, with Jespersen (1924/1976: 85) observing that "a language would be a difficult thing to handle if its speakers had the burden imposed on them of remembering every little item separately." His definition of a formula entails not only whole sentences and group of words, but also single words (which is the case for some pragmatemes, see p. 34) and even parts of a word, with the most important factor being that "it must always be something which to the actual speech instinct is a unit which cannot be further analyzed or decomposed in the way a free combination

[30] These needs are in line with Sperber and Wilson's (1995: 260) principle of relevance, according to which "human cognition tends to be geared to the maximization of relevance."

can" (Jespersen 1924/1976: 88). Nowadays, one of the most commonly used definitions of formulaic sequences is provided by Wray and Perkins (2000: 1):

> a sequence, continuous or discontinuous, of words or other meaning elements, which is, or appears to be, prefabricated: that is, stored and retrieved whole from memory at the time of use, rather than being subject to generation or analysis by the language grammar.

According to Wray (2002: 9), this definition was created to be as inclusive as possible in order to be applicable to any type of linguistic unit that has been described as formulaic in any type of research so far. In accordance with this definition, pragmatemes, being repeatable language units, can also be considered a type of formulaic sequences (although some of them are single lexemes) and are therefore a part of formulaic language, the amount of research on which has been growing since the 1970s (Wood 2015: 4). To begin with, it is essential to define formulaic language along with other terms vital for the understanding of the topic.

Firstly, the notion of *formulaic language* is often not coterminous with the notion of *phraseology*. The first term can be used to describe the collective of formulaic sequences, most often understood as multi-word units of a single meaning or function that are "prefabricated or stored and retrieved mentally as if a single word" (Wood 2015: 3)[31], whereas the latter refers rather to the study of formulaic language (Wood 2015: 2). However, since the division between phraseology and formulaic language appears to be fluid, in this dissertation, they are considered to be interchangeable.

One approach to the research on formulaic language is the linguistic (or formal) approach in which formulaicity is perceived as grammatical and lexical language patterns, and formulaic sequences are studied as fixed[32]

---

[31] Nonetheless, this is a very general definition and many more can be found by various researchers. For example, Schmitt and Carter (2004: 2) note that "[i]n fact, formulaic sequences seem to exist in so many forms that it is presently difficult to develop a comprehensive definition of the phenomenon."

[32] Fixedness of formulaic sequences is a characteristic that has its limitations, since often the context plays a vital role (e.g., when a person transforms a formulaic sequence to make a joke or to create art, which is the case for instance in the Polish Proverbs

lexical connections in terms of phraseology (Grabowski 2018: 69-70). The general focus is on the non-compositionality[33] of the units and the degree of their predictability in the phrase (Durrant and Mathews-Aydınlı 2011: 59). Examples of the linguistic approach to formulaic language can be already found in the works of early grammarians (e.g., Jesperson's 1924 research on free and fixed expressions) and the Eastern European school of phraseology (e.g., Vinogradov 1947).

Secondly, in the sociolinguistic approach, the research focuses on situational and cultural conditions of formulaicity, based on the fact that the use of formulas depends on the type of text and situational context or speech act (Grabowski 2018: 71); therefore, some formulaic sequences are more frequent than others if used in situations that are more common than others. An example of this approach to pragmatemes would be the study of pragmemes (see p. 37). For the sociolinguistic approach, the definition by Mazur (1990: 72-73) can be presented, according to which formulaicity is "wybór wzorca tekstowego charaktestystycznego dla danej czynności, wybór wariantu realizacyjnego wzorca w konkretnej sytuacji, w związku z określonymi intencjami nadawcy, wybór konwencjonalnych znaków językowych orz tradycyjnej formy tekstu przy wprowadzeniu elementów indywidualnych" [the choice of a textual pattern characteristic to a particular activity, the choice of a variable of the pattern in a given situation, according to the intention of the sender of the message, and the choice of conventionalized language signs and traditional text form along with individual elements] (cited in Grabowski 2018: 71).

Word-Play project by Agata Dondzik, source: https://www.behance.net/gallery/6712111/Illustrated-Proverbs-Word-Play, accessed on June 27, 2022), and, as Wray (2002: 34) notes, "only a small subset of formulaic sequences are entirely fixed", while others permit insertions.

33 While non-compositionality is a trait often associated with formulaic sequences, Wray (2012: 239) notes that although there are formulaic sequences which are completely impenetrable (e.g., *hocus pocus*), there are also those which are entirely transparent (e.g., many frequent pragmatemes such as *have a nice day*), and those that are in between these two categories (e.g., *all of a sudden*, *spill the beans*). Furthermore, Taylor (2002: 550) argues that the distinction into two groups: compositional and non-compositional is not right to begin with, as expressions (most of them according to Taylor, and all of them according to Wray [2012: 249]) are non-compositional to a certain degree when interpreted in their context.

Formulaic language is also an important factor in research on oral tradition, both in terms of literature (e.g., Parry's 1928, 1930, and 1932 works on formulaic language in Homer's poetry) and folkloric studies (e.g., Malinowski in his 1935 study on the Trobriand Islanders notes their use of formulaic sequences in magical rituals). Similarly, in his ethnolinguistic approach, Bartmiński (2007) compares formulas to stereotypes and stresses the importance of their social and cultural dependence.

In the psycholinguistic approach, the focus of the research is on the way language data is stored and processed in the mental lexicon (Grabowski 2018: 69). Wray (2002: 9) perceives formulaic sequences not as units created by means of grammar but as wholes that are prefabricated and retrieved from memory as a preferable lexical choice in the communication process. Therefore, the more a unit is used, the more likely it will be stored in memory as a whole and used again in similar contexts[34]. In cognitive linguistics, the process of strengthening linguistic elements in memory through repetition is referred to as cognitive routinization or automatization (Diessel 2019). This ability to use automatized sequences stored in memory in a spontaneous speech is thought to be an important factor in language fluency (Wood 2015: 7). Wray (2002: 97) also notes a few key functions of formulaic language, some helping the speaker's production, and others facilitating the hearer's comprehension. These are, in part:

- controlling the flow of information of communication;
- saving time in mental processing, therefore allowing the speaker to put the focus on other elements of communication;
- organizing the discourse.

The pedagogical point of view offers an approach similar to the psycholinguistic one, with Palmer (1933: 4) describing what he calls a *collocation* as

[34] However, not all researchers agree that if a unit is used with high frequency, it means that it must be automatically stored in the mental lexicon as a whole, especially by a collective of all users of a language (see for example Ellis 2012 or Myles and Cordier 2016).

a sequence of words that "must or should be learnt, or is best, or most conveniently learnt as an integral whole or independent entity" which resembles the later psycholinguistic studies on formulaic sequences (e.g., Wray 2002). Durrant and Mathews-Aydınlı (2011: 60) elaborate on Palmer's definition, adding that formulas are not only sequences of words but also "other linguistic entities", e.g., parts of speech or grammar patterns, and the reason why they are best learned as wholes is 1) because they cannot be produced or understood without specific knowledge, and 2) because this will facilitate language fluency due to their high frequency.

In terms of the role of the speaker, two approaches to formulaic language can be distinguished: the speaker-external and speaker-internal approach (Grabowski 2018: 72). In the first, the focus is on the communicational context of the text, taking into account factors such as formal criteria, frequency, and pragmatic functions, whereas the second stresses the importance of the internal (mental) lexicon in which the units are stored. For the purposes of this thesis, the first approach will be applied (see methods presented in Chapter 3, p. 123).

Lastly, the corpus linguistic approach stresses the importance of the frequency of use of formulaic sequences and the degree of their fixedness (Grabowski 2018: 69). In this approach, formulas are defined as "strings of linguistic items (including words, parts of speech, and semantic fields) which have a statistical tendency to co-occur in corpora" (Durrant and Mathews-Aydınlı 2011: 59). According to Wray (2002: 13), it is thanks to corpus linguistics that formulaicity was revealed to be pervasive in terms of language data, as it has shown that "words belong with other words not as an afterthought but at the most fundamental level."

As this section has briefly presented, the research on formulaic language is multidimensional and extensive. The approaches presented above often overlap, and, as noted by Durrant and Mathews-Ayıdnlı (2011: 59), "common to all is the idea that formulas are linguistic strings which, though they have the potential to be analyzed into multiple components, are – for one reason or another – better left unanalyzed." To discuss the complexity of the matter, Wray (2012) proposed a diagram to present the links in the discussion space of current research on the topic of formulaic language:

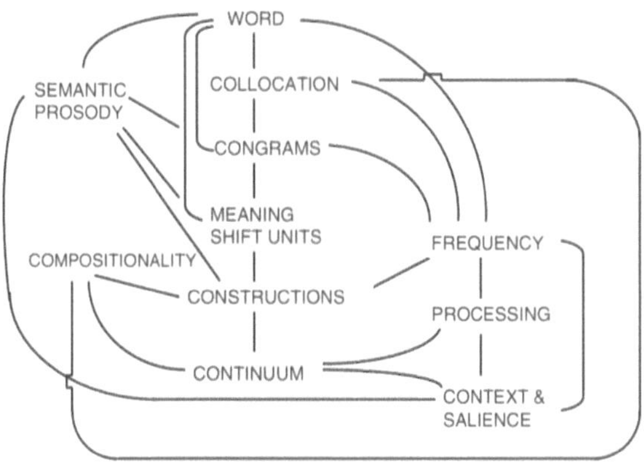

Figure 1. "The complex discussion space of current research into formulaic language" (reprinted from Wray 2012: 238)[37]

Wray comments on the diagram she presents as being "alarmingly complicated" (2012: 238), and adds that in spite of the fact that some areas of research are clearly linked (e.g., frequency and context/salience), one has to be careful determining the relationship between other features (e.g., collocation and context/salience). She sums up the complexity of the topic by comparing the research on formulaic language to an elephant being differently described by blind men (2012: 239):

> We may imagine that in due course our work will join up and we will grasp the nature of the whole beast. But the point of the metaphor is that the blind men don't know if they are in fact describing aspects of the same thing, because they can't see the elephant. And we, for the moment at least, cannot necessarily assume that there is a single phenomenon at the heart of our different activities, or if there is, that there are not also a few small rodents skulking about in the room too, confusing the description of the elephant and, perhaps, also influencing how it behaves. We can describe what we find, and call it formulaic language. But the elephant in the room is that we do not know if there is just one elephant in the room.[35]

[35] It seems that the blind men lack distance vision in the field and so are concerned only with a single part of the elephant. Perhaps, to fully grasp the whole beast, more works assembling its parts are needed.

Furthermore, as Wood (2015: 160) notes, a large number of questions remain. For example, in terms of psycholinguistic research on formulaic language, there is still the question of why certain units are processed holistically, as wholes, while others are not. It seems that neurological research may be used as an aid, as it has already helped to indicate that holistic processing of formulaic units is held in the right hemisphere (Wood 2015: 162). Answering this question may also be helpful to determine in what way adult learners acquire formulaic sequences. However, the lack of a unifying theory of language formulaicity is the most prominent research issue (Wood 2015: 167). For instance, in terms of identification of formulaic units, despite the many methods in use, such as using frequency, expert or native speaker judgment, or checklists of formulaicity characteristics (methods discussed in more detail later in this thesis, see p. 70), "they still lack precision and we are left dependent on listener judgment rather than a firm set of standards" (Wood 2010: 179), and therefore, "in many cases absolute certainty in identification is likely difficult to achieve" (Wood 2015: 160), with Forsyth and Grabowski (2015: 3) adding that formulaic language is such a complex phenomenon that a single method cannot be expected to cover its all aspects. Similarly, there is not one unified classification of formulaic sequences and the already existing definitions may overlap or be considered imprecise. Furthermore, even the current state of knowledge about what exactly constitutes a formulaic sequence is fluid[36] (Wood 2010: 178). That is why there is still a lot to be done, and there is a great need for researchers to work on various types of discourse.

1.2.1 Formulaic Language Units

The amount of research on the topic indicates how widespread and common formulaic language is, and that it is necessary for human communication, with Fillmore (1979: 92) arguing that "a very large portion of a person's ability to get along in a language consists in the mastery of formulaic utterances." Wray (2012: 245) notes that the new generation of grammatical theories puts formulaic language at the center of our linguistic experience, saying that

36 Schmitt and Carter (2004: 3) characterize formulaic sequences as "intentionally all-encompassing, covering a wide range of phraseology", and that is why it is "difficult to identify absolute criteria which define formulaic sequences."

through the realization of templates, "perhaps everything we say is formulaic", which is in opposition to the original Chomskyan grammar. However, there are clearly formulaic sequences that stand out as "more formulaic than others" (ibid). To get a glimpse of the plethora of formulaic language units (or sequences, terms used interchangeably throughout this thesis), this part will aim at briefly presenting the most commonly researched types of units.

It should be noted that formulaic sequences do not only include common collocations, but can also be found in all registers and in highly specialized texts. Therefore, some of the formulaic units can be frequent only in a particular genre or within certain groups (e.g., based on the gender, profession, or age of speakers). In order not to overlook any type of possible formulaic sequences, some researchers argue for an inclusive approach (e.g., Nation and Read 2004). Wray (2002: 47) also acknowledges different taxonomies made by a number of researchers, and states that generally, all of these taxonomies are based on at least one of four features of formulaic units, i.e., form, function, meaning, and provenance[37].

Various categorizations focus on functional-pragmatic use of formulaic units or on their syntactic structure (Wood 2010: 46). One important distinction is made by Raupach (1984: 115), who describes two types of formulaic units: *routines* which are memorized as wholes, such as *How are you?*, therefore expressing a more or less complete function, and *frames* or *patterns* (or *motifs* in French terminology; Longrée and Mellet 2013) which have a free component, such as *Where's + N*, and so they create a structure to be filled with items relevant to the context of communication, saving processing time. Forsyth and Grabowski (2015: 7) refer to these formulaic frames as *phrase-frames* or *p-frames* and define them as "sets of variants of an n-gram[38] identical except for one word in either the initial, medial or final position, e.g., *in the * of*."

Cowie (1988) identifies two other main groups of formulaic sequences: pragmatically specialized, whose meanings reflect their function in discourse (e.g., *Good morning*) and grammatically specialized, whose meanings are

[37] However, these features often overlap, which is what causes problems in proper classification (Wray 2002: 47).

[38] N-grams are understood by Forsyth and Grabowski (2015), as in Fletcher (2002-2007), as sequences of any n words.

referential and which function as invariables in grammatical constructions (e.g., *pass the buck*), while Yorio (1980: 438) focuses solely on the function feature of formulaic sequences, noting that they "make communication more orderly because they are regulatory in nature. They organize reactions and facilitate choices, thus reducing the complexity of communicative exchanges." Therefore, they have the feature of being "group identifying" as "they separate those who belong from those who don't" (Yorio 1980: 438). Therefore, from Yorio's point of view, four main categories can be distinguished:

1) Situational formulas, which fit given conversational contexts, e.g., *You had to be there*;
2) Stylistic formulas, which are specific to particular language registers, e.g., *By way of conclusion*;
3) Ceremonial formulas, which contain language rituals and are required by certain formal situations, e.g., *Ladies and gentlemen;*
4) Gambits, whose function is to organize interactions, e.g., *What do you think?*.

Using the general classifications presented above, pragmatemes can be considered situational formulas according to Yorio (1980), routines according to Raupach (1984), and units that are pragmatically specialized according to Cowie (1988).

Wood (2015: 37) enumerates ten "main areas of focus" in the study of formulaic language, i.e., "collocations, idioms, lexical phrases, lexical bundles, metaphors, proverbs, phrasal verbs, n-grams, concgrams[39], and compounds." This classification is not the only one that can be found, is by no means exhaustive (as, for instance, it leaves out pragmatemes), and some of the distinctions between the units may be blurry, but because these units are researched most often, they require a short description.

---

[39] Or "congrams", as referred to in Wray's (2012) diagram (see p. 57).

Collocations

In the study of formulaic language, many definitions of various formulaic units can be found, and *collocation* is no exception. Most generally, collocations describe syntagmatic relationships among co-occurring words (Wood 2015: 38), or, in Carter and McCarthy's (1988: 163) words, "collocation is an aspect of lexical cohesion which embraces a 'relationship' between lexical items that regularly co-occur." The two main approaches to collocations are as follows: the frequency-based approach, as initiated by Firth (1951), and the phraseological approach, represented in the Soviet phraseological research (e.g., Vinogradov 1947, Amosova 1963, Kunin 1970). In the first, different types of collocations can be distinguished depending on the frequency of co-occurrence of the words: (1) habitual collocation, in which the co-occurrence is quite frequent, e.g., *silly ass*, and (2) idiosyncratic collocation, in which the co-occurrence is less frequent but the unit still functions as a whole, e.g., *sleek supple soul* (Firth 1951 discussed in Wood 2015: 4-5). In the second approach, collocations are viewed as fixed (at least to a certain degree) word combinations of a transparent (again, at least to a certain degree) meaning (Wood 2015: 39). In phraseological research, the classification of collocations according to Mel'čuk (1998: 31) is worth noting: (1) "collocations with support verbs", e.g., *take a step*, (2) collocations in which the meaning of one word depends on its relation to the other word, e.g., *black coffee*, (3) "collocations with intensifiers", e.g., *strong* (but not *powerful*) *coffee*, and (4) collocations in which the meaning of one word strictly connects with the other, e.g., *rancid butter.*

Idioms

Idioms, similarly to collocations, have different definitions, from very narrow to very broad. For a long time idioms have been thought to be the archetype of formulaic sequences, being generally defined as units the whole meaning of which is different from the meaning of the sum of its parts (Wray 2002: 56). For instance, Nattinger and DeCarrico (1992: 33) describe idioms as "complex bits of frozen syntax, whose meanings cannot be derived from the meaning of their constituents, that is, whose meanings are more than simply the sum of their individual parts." As for their holistic meaning, Wray (2002: 57) notes that some idioms can be understood only by using general knowledge (e.g., *pig in a poke*), while others can be understood with a little common sense (e.g., *let the cat out of the bag*).

Nonetheless, across different definitions, the following defining traits can be summarized to describe idioms (Skandera 2004, Wood 2010): length of two words or more, semantic opacity[40], noncompositionality, mutual expectancy (lexicality), and lexicogrammatical fixedness[41].

Rosales Sequeiros (2004: 110) distinguishes idioms from *genuine formulas* (e.g., *Hello*). Although they both look formulaic, idioms have semantic content and can be therefore interpreted like any other concept. In current theories of meaning, three entries are taken into account: lexical, logical, and encyclopedic (e.g., Sperber and Wilson 1995), and according to Rosales Sequeiros (2004), idioms do have the logical entry (for instance, the logical entry of the idiom *to rain cats and dogs* is *to rain a lot*), while genuine formulas lack this (the meaning of formulas such as *Hello* is only conceptual, i.e., there is no logical information about them and one can understand them only through the information under their encyclopedic entry).

Lexical phrases

Nattinger and DeCarrico (1992: 1) describe lexical phrases as "multi-word lexical phenomena that exist somewhere between the traditional poles of lexicon and syntax, conventionalized form/function composites that occur more frequently and have more idiomatically determined meaning than language that is put together each time."

Their taxonomy of lexical phrases is based on the form feature of formulaic sequences, with the units being classified according to: (1) their length and grammatical status, (2) their having a canonical or a non-canonical shape, (3) variability or fixedness, and (4) whether the phrase is continuous (consists of unbroken strings of words) or discontinuous (requires lexical insertions) (Nattinger and DeCarrico 1992: 38). Accordingly, four categories can be distinguished:

---

[40] Some researchers (e.g., Cowie 1988, Wood 1986) argue that semantic transparency is a characteristic to be treated rather as a continuum, "shading by gradual degrees from total non-compositionality to fully regular combination" (Wood 1986: v).

[41] However, some of these criteria can be flexible. For instance, Wood (2010: 44) presents the example of the idiom *teach an old dog new tricks* which can be said in a reversed order: *teach new tricks to an old dog.*

- polywords – short phrases functioning like single lexical units that can be either canonical or not, and allow no variability and no lexical insertions (e.g., *so far so good*),
- institutionalized expressions – units of sentence length, mainly canonical and continuous, invariable (e.g., *give me a break, nice meeting you*),
- phrasal constraints – units of short to medium length, canonical or not, allow variations of lexical and phrase categories, mainly continuous (e.g., *good* ___, as in *good morning* or *good afternoon*),
- sentence builders – thanks to the fillable slots allow constructions of whole sentences, they can be both canonical and non-canonical, continuous and discontinuous, and they allow phrasal and clausal variations (e.g., *my point is that X*) (ibid: 38-44).

Nattinger and DeCarrico (ibid) suggest one more classification which depends on the function of lexical phrases and contains three types: (1) social interactional markers, which maintain conversations (e.g., *Hello, How are you?*) or describe why conversations take place (e.g., *I appreciate your X* to express gratitude), (2) necessary topics, which are used for daily or ordinary conversations (e.g., *My name is X*) and (3) discourse devices, which connect the meaning with the discourse structure (e.g., *as a result, as far as I know*). Wood (2002: 3) also distinguishes the fourth functional group, i.e., fluency devices, with examples such as *you know* or *so to speak*.

Wray (2002: 48) comments on Nattinger and DeCarrico's formal taxonomy that while it appears to be neatly prepared, there are many counterexamples and contradictions, and Nattinger and DeCarrico themselves use labels such as *mostly*, *somewhat*, and *often*, which suggests that their categories are not strict but rather fluid. Wray (ibid) then advises that it would be better if their taxonomy contained subcategories to differentiate the units more carefully. One could add to Wray's suggestions that more formal factors should be taken into consideration as well, such as the autonomy of lexical phrases. The existing taxonomy forms a very heterogeneous set, for instance, there are autonomous phrases (*How are you?*) as well as chunks that need to be filled with additional information (*My name is X*), which may constitute an issue in the further examination of lexical phrases.

Lexical bundles

Lexical bundles are units of three or more words identified with the help of corpus analysis software. They characterize particular types of discourse, so they are more function than meaning units, and they are have been examined a lot in academic writing, with some being characteristic for specific disciplines (Wood 2015: 45). Biber (2006) distinguishes three large categories of lexical bundles (which can be then further divided into function sub-categories): (1) referential bundles, which are the most common units and make reference to real or abstract entities, as well as to textual content (*a little bit of*), (2) stance bundles, which express certainty (*I want you to*), and (3) discourse organizers, which mark relationships between discourses (previous and subsequent ones, e.g., *What I want to do is*, which introduces a topic). Furthermore, Biber also treats pragmatically specialized formulaic sequences (as called by Cowie 1988, e.g., *Good afternoon*, which also constitutes what is called in this thesis a *pragmateme*) as lexical bundles. Another classification often used in lexical bundles research (e.g., Jalali et al. 2015, Jalilifar et al. 2016) is the functional one proposed by Hyland (2008), who distinguishes: (1) research-oriented bundles, used to structure the real world's experiences and activities (*the use of the*), (2) text-oriented bundles, used for organizing the text (*in addition to the*), and (3) participant-oriented bundles, which focus on the text's reader or writer (*may be due to*).

Metaphors

Metaphors are multi-word expressions the meaning of which is not compositional; however, "there is a tension between a literal and a metaphoric interpretation" (Wood 2015: 46). According to Wood (ibid), a metaphor is composed of three parts: the *vehicle* of a metaphor is the word that should not be understood literally, while the *topic* is its referent, and the *grounds* describe the analogy between the two. For instance, in the corpus used for this thesis (for its description see p. 123), in the second episode of the first season of TV series *Ginny and Georgia*, two metaphors are used one after the other: "For a woman, life is a battle. And beauty is a goddamn machine gun." In these metaphors, *battle* and *machine gun* are the vehicles, while *life* and *beauty* are the topics, and the grounds are the analogy between life struggles and a sustained fight in the first case, and between aesthetic qualities of a woman and a weapon in the latter. Furthermore, metaphors constitute one of the types of formulaic units that best represent the fact that formulaic sequences may often serve a poetic purpose.

Proverbs

Proverbs are sentence-length units which are shared by whole communities. As Wood (2015: 47) notes, they can have pragmatic functions such as advice and warning, instruction and explaining, and communicating common experience and observations. For instance, the English proverb *An apple a day keeps the doctor away* is advice on healthy eating, while the Polish *Jak sobie pościelisz, tak się wyśpisz* (lit. *How you sleep depends on how you make your bed*, the English equivalent would be *As you make your bed so must you lie in it*) is a form of warning about facing the consequences of your actions.

Compounds

Compounds are words created by two already existing words. Compounds constitute "special cases in formulaic language study" because they are "more a branch of word formation" (Wood 2015: 47). Depending on how they are written, three types can be distinguished: closed form compounds, written as one word (e.g., *notebook*), hyphenated form compounds, separated by a hyphen (e.g., *daughter-in-law*), and open form compounds, with the two words written separately (e.g., *post office*). As the word becomes more and more lexicalized with time, the spelling of a compound may change, and closed form compounds are the most lexicalized of the three types (Wood 2015: 48). With lexicalized compounds appearing in dictionaries along with single lexemes, it seems that this category is not as relevant for the discussion of formulaic units as others are; moreover, some language speakers may even be unconscious of the relationship between the two words that form the compound, especially when it is a heavy lexicalized one, such as *notebook*.

Phrasal verbs

Phrasal verbs[42] are units in which the verb is combined with a preposition (prepositional phrasal verbs) or particle (particle phrasal verbs), or both

[42] The description of phrasal verbs provided in this subsection refers to English phrasal verbs. However, it has to be noted that this linguistic phenomenon is not unique for English, although it is often thought to be (Marks 2005).

(particle-prepositional phrasal verbs), and their interpretation is always figurative to at least a certain degree (Wood 2015: 49). They are often used in informal speech and sometimes have single-word equivalents of Greek, Latin or French origin that are used in rather formal registers (e.g., *set up* and *establish*), and while it is common to advise people not to use phrasal verbs in formal writing, "there are many situations — even in quite formal texts — when a phrasal verb is the most natural-sounding way of expressing an idea", e.g., *put on* and *don* (Park 2007: 1), which is why this advice should always be carefully received.

Concgrams

According to Wood (2015: 50), what distinguishes concgrams from other two or more word combinations is that they are noncontiguous sequences, i.e., the words that constitute the concgram are separated by other words. Cheng et al. (2006, 2009) provide a broader definition, stating that concgrams are "instances of co-occurring words irrespective of whether they are contiguous, and irrespective of whether or not they are in the same sequential order" (Cheng et al. 2009: 237). Therefore, concgrams in this definition allow both for constituency permutations (e.g., *work hard* and *work very hard*) and positional permutations (e.g., *work hard* and *hard work*). Wray (2012: 246) distinguishes between concgrams as in Cheng et al.'s definition and "more linear" n-grams which only allow for constituency variations.

As mentioned before (see p. 60), Wood's (2015) list of different formulaic language units briefly described above is by no means exhaustive. It lacks units such as binomials, i.e., "coordinated word pairs whose lexical elements share the same words class", e.g., *rights and duties* (Mollin 2014: 1), adjacency pairs, i.e., units consisting of two adjacently positioned utterances, with different speakers producing each utterance (Schegloff and Sacks 1973), e.g., *Good night. -Night!*, an example of a *greeting-greeting* adjacency pair, and, finally, pragmatemes (even though there are units that can be called pragmatemes that are found among the other described units, e.g., some lexical phrases). This section has shown that categories are often fluid, and this may be linked to the difficulties in their identification, which will be discussed in the next section.

1.2.2 Formulaicity criteria: identification of formulaic sequences

As numerous as the classifications and definitions of formulaic sequences are, so are the approaches to their identification. Wray (2002: 19-20) suggests that there are two main ways to collect formulaic sequences, i.e., through an empirical method such as an experiment or a questionnaire, and by searching the collected linguistic material for word strings that can be called formulaic according to previously prepared criteria. This section focuses on the latter approach, as it is also the one used in this thesis research, and discusses a few of the methods of formulaic unit identification.

Firstly, because formulaic sequences are recurrent, one can say that it is likely that a word string that is used frequently can be called formulaic. Therefore, some researchers argue for the use of corpus linguistics in formulaic language research in order to establish the frequency of distribution of words in the text, e.g., Francis (1993: 139) views it as "the only reliable authority" that allows the researcher to base their research solely on evidence. Similarly, Sinclair and Renouf (1998: 151,152) observe that computer systems, unlike humans, do not miss any data and help distinguish the more and less common patterns of usage, and stress that "no description of usage should be innocent of frequency information." However, while Wray (2008: 103) states that researching frequent examples of formulaic sequences is "a good place to start", Sinclair and Renouf (1998) are cautious about the idea that frequency should be the only factor in describing patterns of usage. Furthermore, Wray herself (2002) acknowledges that many apparent formulaic units occur rarely[43], which is true for example for many pragmatemes that are used only in very specific situations, e.g., *Long live the king.* These formulas may be infrequent simply because they express a relatively rare message. Therefore, "we need to know how regularly speakers make use of a particular form *when they need to express a particular message*" (Durrant and Mathews-Aydınlı 2011: 61), which is what Wray (2002: 31) calls the "ratio of message-expression." Wood

43 Wray (2002) notes that just as formulaic sequences may occur rarely, not all frequent units can be considered formulaic. Therefore, she argues for "an independent set of supplementary criteria" (2002: 31) to be applied apart from frequency study.

(2015: 20) adds that "we would agree that it is necessary for a string to be more than just *frequent*, it needs to have a unitary meaning or function, and perhaps a particular way of being mentally stored, retrieved, or produced as well." A solution that may fix the problem of units not being "just frequent" would be to use a different parameter instead, for instance frequency per conversational or situational event, depending on the type of formulaic sequence.

For these reasons, in the frequency-based approach, before the corpora are scanned various specifications are set (e.g., length of word combinations, frequency cutoffs). Generally, frequency cutoffs can be from 10 to 40 occurrences per million words, and that is why this method is usually used with large corpora from specific language registers, generally covering one topic (Wood 2015: 21). Wray (2002: 26) adds that making additional decisions to discard certain identified units may be necessary, e.g., because the search tool does not take into account factors such as changes of the speaker or sentence boundaries, or to eliminate examples which are not interesting from the point of view of the given research. However, the frequency-based approach does not take variability into account. As Nation and Read (2004: 25) note, "[i]t is clear that some of the variations are deliberate attempts to add humour by playing with something that is typically fixed."[44] Cheng et al. (2009: 237) also suggest that the meaning of a collocation depends on the local context, since "when writers and speakers co-select words, they create a new meaning which makes other instances of the same individual words and other co-selections involving these same words irrelevant." Furthermore, basing research data on the frequency itself has other limitations, such as lack of information on the psycholinguistic aspects of the examples or the need for other steps to confirm their functionality.

Another possible method to identify which word strings are formulaic is the use of a native speaker's or an expert's intuition. For instance, some researchers can appoint themselves as arbiters on deciding on what

---

44 It should be noted that creativity in the use of formulaic sequences means the loss of its primary function (i.e., easy mental processing) for various communicative purposes, e.g., humor (Brooke et al. 2015: 98).

is formulaic in their data, because they themselves are members of that speech community (Wray 2002: 20). However, intuition as a research method tends to be treated with suspicion, which is why Nation and Read (2004: 29) describe three conditions to be applied in this method. First, a clear definition of a formulaic sequence must be set by the researcher. Then the researcher communicates this definition to another person who searches for formulaic sequences. Finally, a panel of judges should be formed to decide collectively whether a given unit can be accepted as formulaic. Nevertheless, as Wray (2002: 23) points out, there are limitations to this approach as well; for instance, the corpora cannot be large, the judgment may be inconsistent, and different judges may decide matters differently. Peters (1983) therefore proposes a continuum model for formulaic sequences which relates usage and form, meaning that there are formulaic sequences that are recognized as formulaic by everyone, while others may be formulaic only for the speaker, not necessarily for the hearer[45]. Nowadays, due to the subjectivity of the intuition methods, researchers also turn to statistical methods such as inter-rater agreement measures when studying a judgement variable, i.e., "a variable that involves categorization or evaluation of cases (e.g. concordance lines) by the analyst that might bring an element of subjectivity into the study" (Brezina 2018: 87), which is suitable for formulaic sequences.

There is another method for using native speakers' judgment to measure formulaicity, and that is to test the shared knowledge of a speech community. In this method, native speakers have to complete a word string started by another person in order to verify how many of them complete it in the same way (Van Lancker and Kempler 1987: 56). Unfortunately, there are limits to this method, too, as it can be effectively applied to formulaic units that do not depend on context (Wray 2002: 25).

In all, the differences between frequency-based and intuition approaches are presented in Table 1.

45 Wray (2002: 63) adds that in that case, formulas accepted by the entire speech community do not need to be decomposable, while formulas recognized as such only by the speaker are semantically transparent and grammatically regular.

Table 1. The comparison of the intuition and the frequency-based approaches to formula identification, with characteristics based on Wray (2002: 23)

	Intuition	**Frequency-based computer research**
Amount of analyzed data	Small data sets	Corpora of any size
Alterations of the results	Applicable (for example, due to tiredness of judges or a change of opinion over time)	Not applicable
Variation of opinion	Applicable (due to the number of judges)	Not applicable
Variables	Taken into account (judges can react if they see a linguistic structure that goes beyond the expected border)	Not taken into account (in the computer software, the characteristics have to be preset, which can constitute a problem if the identification factors are not precisely defined; the software cannot point to structures other than programmed)

The psycholinguistic approach examines whether particular sequences have been stored as wholes by individual speakers by measuring reaction time, eye movement, and electrophysiological measures, among others. This approach's main limitation is that it does not clarify which sequences are used by whole communities (Wood 2015: 22-23). The same limitation applies to the approach of identifying formulaic sequences through their phonological coherence, the first step of which consists of searching for the strings "which are not interrupted by unfilled pauses" (Raupach 1984: 116), and which takes into account potential pointers of formulaicity such as intonation pattern, changes in speed of articulation, and overall fluency (Wray 2002: 35).

Because the analyses of both frequency and psycholinguistic factors alone cannot provide satisfactory results, especially in terms of spoken corpora, as argue e.g., both Wood (2015) and Wray (2002), the most suitable compromise in identifying formulaic units is, according to Wray (2002: 28) "the application of common sense." Wray (2002: 43) argues that "it may simply be that identification cannot be based on a single criterion, but rather needs to draw on a suite of features." To this end criteria checklists, combining characteristics typical for formulaic sequences, can be developed to identify formulaic units. For example, Wood (2015: 23-32) describes four different checklists designed by researchers for specific purposes: Coulmas's early (1979) list of criteria, which contained two features being thought to be particularly important for a unit to be considered formulaic, a length of at least two morphemes and phonological coherence (Wood 2010: 40), Peters's (1983) criteria of formulas in children's first language, Wray and Namba's (2003) criteria for gradience of formulaicity, and Wood's (2010) criteria for native speaker judgment. In terms of first language acquisition, Hickey (1993: 32) distinguished nine conditions for identification of formulas, some of which are likely to be useful beyond research on child language (e.g., phonological cohesion, community-wide usage, being an idiosyncratic chunk, repeated use with no change in the form, and situational dependency). In all the different lists proposed by researchers, a few key features can be distinguished. From these we can conclude that formulaic units are: (1) multi-word or polymorphemic, (2) stored in memory as if they were single lexemes, and (3) produced as wholes, with some phonological coherence; they may also be longer and more complex than other output, their form may be invariant, and they may be characterized by their use for specific situational purposes (Wood 2010: 42), which will be further investigated in the analytical part of this thesis (see p. 151).

Other researchers also stress the importance of multidimensional research on formulaic sequences. For example, Durrant and Mathews-Aydınlı (2011: 61) suggest starting the analysis by determining the semantic functions of formulaic sequences and working towards the range of their recurrent forms (for an extensive analysis of formulaic sequences using this method, see Durrant and Mathews-Aydınlı 2011). Nation and Read (2004: 33) stress the importance of what they call "an eclectic approach", i.e., triangulation, or using more than one method of analysis in order to obtain results that can be considered valid. In order to present the idea of triangulation in formulaic language research (i.e., employing two or more methods to identify what is formulaic), the study of Schmitt and Underwood (2004) can be mentioned. In this study, Schmitt and Underwood (2004) first collected the units using intuition, then checked their frequency in a corpus, and finally tested them in a cloze test with initial letter cues to verify whether they were truly predictable.

However, "[r]egardless of the measures used to determine formulaicity, absolute certainty is elusive" (Wood 2015: 32), since formulaic sequences do not seem to be "sufficiently consistent in form (nor do they have a consistent function [...]) for them to be pinned down" (Wray 2002: 43). Therefore, perhaps the identification methods should vary depending on the type of set expression, although more research on the topic is needed in order to be able to reliably identify formulaic sequences.

1.2.3 Formulaic language and language acquisition

Many studies support the hypothesis that formulaic language is an important factor in language (both first and second) acquisition in children (e.g., Peters 1983, Myles, Hooper, and Mitchell 1998, Lieven, Salomo, and Tomasello 2009). Peters (1983) states that one acquires formulaic language either by encountering formulaic sequences in the speech of other people or by using their component parts to create them. In the case of children, it is thought that they acquire formulaic chunks frequently used by adults, adopt them for use, and only later in their cognitive development analyze them by segmenting them[46] (Wood 2015: 68-69). Myles, Hooper, and Mitchell's study (1998: 359) emphasises the time when children start using third-person communication as a period when the segmentation process begins. Wood (2015: 71-72), meanwhile, stresses the double role for formulaic language in child language acquisition: first, it facilitates communication, since the child uses particular formulas in particular pragmatic situations (Bahns, Burmeister, and Vogel 1986), and second, it serves the child as an aid in developing grammar abilities, as formulaic chunks are extracted from input and used to create productive

46 Wray (2002, 2012), however, argues that some chunks are actually never broken down, saying that the decision on whether to break down the sequence depends on "whether the unit has a discernible holistic meaning and/or whether it needs breaking down to make it either comprehensible or useful" (Wray 2002: 266), and that holistic storage includes not only irregular units, but also regular ones. Furthermore, Bolinger (1975: 297) observes that "the fact that we can analyze does not necessarily mean that we do." That is because communicative competence does not entail simply knowing the rules of sentence composition and using it at the appropriate time, but "it is much more a matter of knowing a stock of partially pre-assembled patterns, formulaic frameworks, and a kit of rules" (Widdowson 1989: 135). Some researchers, for instance Van Lancker and Kempler (1987: 55), argue that the analysis of some types of formulaic sequences (so-called "familiar phrases" in Van Lancker and Kempler's terminology which contain idioms, proverbs, speech formulas and greetings) can actually result in the wrong interpretation of the unit.

language. In relation to their use, Bahns et al. (1986) found six categories of formulaic sequences used by children:

- Expressive formulas – e.g., *Shut up*;
- Directive formulas – e.g., *Let's go*;
- Game or play formulas – e.g., *You're out*;
- Polyfunctional formulas – e.g., *What is it?*[47];
- Question formulas – e.g., *What time is it?*;
- Phatic formulas – e.g., *See you later*[48].

However, what seems to be true for child language acquisition does not apply to adult second language learners. In the case of adults, factors such as the knowledge of the first language and different acquisition contexts make it difficult to generalize how they acquire their second language. For instance, in Schmidt's (1983) study, the learners did not analyze the units by segmenting them, while Bolander's (1989) subjects sometimes used formulas to acquire some rules of syntax. Ellis (1996) stresses the role of multi-word expressions in serving adult learners as a database for grammar acquisition. Furthermore, adults are not thought to acquire second language formulaic units as wholes (Wood 2015: 79). Nonetheless, while it appears that in general adult learners use formulas to economize the effort of communication (as a "shortcut in communication", saving processing time and effort to focus on other than linguistic aspects of communication, according to Peters [1983: 3]), the knowledge of formulaic sequences seems to be beneficial for other language skills, such as comprehension, reading time, and spoken speech (e.g., speech speed and pausing, among other factors) (Wood 2015: 74-90); therefore, it can be stated that formulaic language has a significant impact on language fluency, with Wood (2010: 1) even suggesting that "a possible key to speech fluency lies in the mastery of a repertoire of formulaic speech units."

---

47 It is worth noting that some of the categories seem to overlap; for instance, the polyfunctional formula *What is it?* is undeniably also a question formula.

48 It can be observed that Bahns et al.'s classification seems inspired (at least in some degree) by Searle's (1979) speech act theory (for more on which see p. 176).

Schmidt (1992: 358-359) describes fluency as an "automatic procedural skill." Automatization in speech production means that lexical items (including formulaic units) are retrieved from long-term memory, and therefore can be used with less conscious effort (Wood 2010: 5). Nattinger and DeCarrico (1992: 32) note that the advantage of smaller effort permits both the speakers and the hearers to focus on the discourse itself, without narrowing the focus down to individual words, with Wray (2002: 17) adding that especially when a person has to focus on another activity while speaking (e.g., driving a car), it is unlikely that a lot of non-formulaic sentences will be produced. Research on fluency and formulaic language shows that the use of formulas is a key factor behind speech smoothness and speed, with formulaic sequences being usually uttered with fewer pauses than free expressions (Pawley 1986: 107). Furthermore, formulaic language is thought to play an important role in writing, especially in terms of textual cohesion (Wood 2002: 13), and this can also be observed in subtitles, which usually avoid a non-conventional writing style (i.e., one that would contain more novel than set expressions) because it might be a distraction for the viewer.

1.2.4 Pragmatemes in formulaic language

One type of formulaic sequence has not been explicitly discussed in this section so far, and that is pragmatemes. While pragmatemes were described above in more detail (see Chapter 1.1), this subsection focuses on setting them among formulaic language units, beginning with their role in pragmatics.

Pragmatics, according to Crystal (1997: 301), is

> "the study of language from the point of view of users, especially of the choices they make, the constraints they encounter in using language in social interaction and the effects their use of language has on other participants in the act of communication."

Or, in other words, pragmatics is "a dynamic function of language and is applied to the juxtaposition of a linguistic event and a situation, in order to make sense of their coincidence" (Wray 2002: 58). Many studies on formulaic language have shown its role to be vital in pragmatic competence, i.e., achieving particular communication goals. This competence equals "the knowledge and skill necessary for successful and appropriate use of language in communication" (Wood 2015: 93) and includes both pragmalinguistics (the ability to perform language functions, e.g., refusing an invitation) and sociopragmatics (the ability to access the context of that function, e.g., assessing the circumstances in order to choose the appropriate means of language). In terms of pragmatics, formulas are not only recurring sequences; their other important characteristics are that they are used in specific situations and created as a result of a social contract between members of a speech community (Bardovi-Harlig 2012: 207). In other words formulas in pragmatics "are conventional expressions representing ways of saying things agreed upon by a speech community" (ibid: 209). Nonetheless, while Coulmas (1979: 242) argues that "an adequate analysis of the meanings of R[outine] F[ormula]s depends heavily on a proper description of their respective situational contexts", it has to be stressed that not all social verbal communication is formulaic, nor is it equivalently formulaic in every language in a given context (Bardovi-Harlig 2012: 223).

Many researchers (e.g., Coulmas 1979, Wood 2010, Bygate 1988) stress the importance of context as a deciding factor for formulas' meaning and selection. Specific social or cultural situations make it possible not only to understand the meaning of a given formula but also to help the speaker to structure their speech. According to Coulmas (1979: 243), formulas appear in regularly occurring and very specific patterns of communication, therefore helping to create unambiguous communication and a sense of group identity (the same applies also to other formulaic sequences, e.g., to lexical bundles). By using them, the speaker shows their membership in a particular speech community (Bardovi-Harlig 2012: 223). Nonetheless, some researchers suggest that formulas in a given context can only function as a tool to achieve "phatic communion" (Malinowski 1923: 315), implying that they are redundant, but with factors such as behavior and the appropriateness of context, the communicational purpose can be achieved (Wray 2002: 55).

As has been observed throughout this section, there are numerous definitions of formulaic sequences and their types. Similarly, in pragmatic research, the term *formula* can be used in at least three ways. Firstly, to describe conventional expressions used by speech communities in social communication, e.g., *Nice to meet you*. Secondly, to refer to a word string the meaning of which cannot be understood using interlanguage grammar, e.g., *Do you have time?* Thirdly, the term *formula* can be used instead of *semantic formula* (or *pragmatic strategy*), to mean a component of a speech act, such as "an expression of apology", which can be realized by a conventional expression, e.g., *I'm sorry* (Bardovi-Harlig 2012: 207-208). Therefore, because of the abundance of different usages of the term *formula* both in formulaic language research and in pragmatics, for the purpose of this thesis, the term *pragmateme* is used to distinguish the units being studied here from other types of formulaic sequences.

On the identification of formulaic units in pragmatics, Wood (2015: 94) notes:

> In pragmatics research frequency-based research is relatively rare. Formulaic sequences are identified in various ways depending largely on the goals of the research. It is common to either start with the formulaic sequence and work from there or to start with the situation and context, specifically the illocutionary force or the speech acts, and determine the sequences used.

Bardovi-Harlig (2012: 210) adds that the method of starting with preidentified units is common to production studies that focus on investigating their contexts and variations in pronunciation and meaning. In contrast, the method of starting with the context (i.e., the interactional setting, speech act, or illocutionary force) and then identifying formulas is used in studies of comprehension, recognition, or attitude. There are many studies that have identified a number of contexts, both social and linguistic, to the use of formulas, that are based on the analysis of authentic oral and written samples (e.g., Sharifian 2008, Vergaro 2008). Unlike other approaches to formulaic sequences, in the pragmatic approach the method based solely on frequency is rare[49], because usually "the value of the expressions is asserted or assumed" (Bardovi-Harlig 2012: 211). Bardovi-Harlig (2012: 213) notes that the approach that is undertaken depends on the research question(s), and that the establishment of quantitative characteristics of formulas is needed to support arguments such as "compliments are formulaic"

[49] Wong (2010) is one example of a study reporting primarily frequency. However, frequency is more often one of several factors being examined. For instance, Manes and Wolfson's (1981) study identified recurrent formulaic units in a given context and determined their rate of use.

(e.g., Manes and Wolfson 1981), "formulas are not restricted to the expression of politeness" (e.g., Culpeper 2010), or "high-frequency formulas are the social norm in certain contexts and reasonable acquisitional targets for L2 learners" (e.g., Bardovi-Harlig 2009). In all, the need for more research on formulas is evident, and this thesis hopes to fill the gap at least at some level.

1.2.5 Formulaic sequences in translation

As presented by Rosales Sequeiros (2004: 111), successful translation: "a. Resembles the original interpretively (i.e., it shares analytical and synthetic implication with the original); b. Induces sufficient contextual effects; and c. It does so without unnecessary effort."

Furthermore, Gournay (2009: 133) perceives properly understood and rendered idiomatic elements as one of the key elements of successful translation. However, before formulaic sequences are discussed in terms of translation, the notion of the unit of translation (UT) should be first introduced. This is a concept that has been variously defined in Translation Studies (TS). For instance, Vinay and Darbelnet (1995) view the UT as the smallest part of an utterance that is composed of elements that cannot be translated individually. Similarly, the definition suggested by Bogucki et al. (2019: 54) in the dictionary of Polish translational terminology (*Słownik polskiej terminologii przekładoznawczej* [SPTP]) states that the UT is "[n]ajmniejsza jednostka tekstu wyjściowego (lub wypowiedzi) wyodrębniona w procesie tłumaczenia, której budowa i znaczenie nie pozwalają na przekład z zachowaniem sensu w przypadku rozbicia na mniejsze elementy składowe" [the smallest unit of the source text (or the utterance) that is isolated in the process of translation and whose structure and meaning do not allow for its constituent elements to be translated without a loss in meaning]. In this definition, the UT is constructed of a sign or a number of signs that mean something when put together, and in that sense, multi-word formulaic sequences can be considered UTs. Even more so, Bogucki et al. (2019) point to the equivalents of UTs often having different formal characteristics in the ST and the TT, which can also be true for some formulaic sequences (for instance, the Polish equivalent for the English directive pragmateme *You're up!* can be *Twoja kolej* which is informative and lacks a verb). Matthiessen (2001: 116) suggests that a sentence is a "likely candidate" to be the UT. Translation scholars disagree also on whether the UT can be found in the source text (ST; e.g., Vinay and Darbelnet 1995) or rather in the target text (TT; e.g., Huang and Wu 2009). Some even question whether the UT can be found in the text at all, with Ballard (2010: 437) representing the process-oriented approach and stating that "it is only in the act of translation that units become a reality" and that therefore the UT "is initiated by a translator" at the moment when a translation strategy is applied "to a segment or element of the [ST] (which is the base of the unit) with a view to producing a segment or element (the outcome of the unit) that will contribute to the reconstruction of a new entity" (ibid: 439), with this entity being at the end perceived as a text. In this approach, the UT is dynamic and "changes according to the translator's cognitive and processing needs" (Alves and Gonçalves 2003: 11).

Some scholars explicitly point to formulaic sequences as being UTs. For instance, for Teubert (2002: 193) UTs are ST segments such as multi-word units, compounds, collocations and set phrases that are "large enough to be monosemous" and have "only one equivalent in the target language" or more than one synonymous equivalent. Gambier (2022: 100), in terms of the disagreement between translation scholars on the nature of UT, also points to equivalence, noting that "[a]ll those definitions are based, explicitly or not, on the equivalence paradigm." Similarly, Kenny (2009: 306) notes that "if repeated stretches of source text consistently receive the same translation in a target language, then this can be taken as quantitative evidence that there are units of source and target texts between which a relatively stable translation relationship exists."

However, it can be argued that UT segmentation does not have to equal language unit segmentation, and in some cases the UT consists of not only the formulaic sequence but also other elements surrounding it (which will be the case for example for formulaic units with slots). Or, using Bennett's (1994) terminology, formulaic sequences can be considered *translation atoms*, i.e., the smallest segments to be translated as wholes, while the *translation focus* refers to a larger segment, a section of text on which the translator concentrates at any given moment. As suggested by the sociolinguistic approach to formulaic language (see p. 54), formulaic sequences are used in particular contexts. Wray (2012: 249) argues that the "context is more than just the words that collocate with other words. It is about who we are and how we use language to express our identity and manipulate our world." For a translator, this means that they need not only to remember the semantic equivalent[50] of a given expression but also to keep in mind its appropriateness in the situation. Furthermore, they have to take into account the fact that the "pragmatic variables of one society may differ from those of another" (Wray 2002: 55). In regard to translatability of formulaic units, Coulmas (1979: 245-246) stressed that:

> some situations, such as, presumably, *greeting* or *leave-taking* may be universal; others may be common to some societies and language, e.g., *proposing to change from* v- *to* t- *forms of address*; and still others may be restricted to one sole culture, as many rituals, customs, and habits probably are. [...] The time of day may be determining factor in one society[51], and immaterial in another, where the season may be of much greater relevance. Likewise, place, sex, age, familiarity, rank, role relationship, social occasion, etc. may or may not be relevant to the selection of a given R[outine] F[ormula].

Therefore, the use of formulaic language requires more than the knowledge of a language's grammar; it requires encyclopedic knowledge of the target language (TL) and culture. That is why there is a possibility of different interpretations of formulaic sequences, as there can be different types of encyclopedic information used to interpret them (Rosales Sequeiros 2004: 106,109). Furthermore, the translator should not prematurely conclude that there exists a fully equivalent formula even if the situation it is used in is considered universal (Coulmas 1979: 246). The characteristics of formulaic

---

50 While formulaic sequences are more often rendered holistically than semantically in translation, there are modern translation trends in which foreignization is a strategy used deliberately to induce a particular (e.g., shocking) effect on the recipients of translation (Rosales Sequeiros 2004:106).

51 For instance, in Polish, there is no literal equivalent for *Good afternoon*. Poles say *Dzień dobry* (lit. *Good day*) or *Dobry wieczór* (*Good evening*), depending on whether the sun has already set and it is dark or not. Therefore, the time when the pragmateme can be uttered changes greatly between winter, when the sun sets around 6 p.m. and summer, when the sunset is after 9 p.m.

sequences can lead to many problems, such as translation errors due to the lack of knowledge on the part of the translator. Given the already troublesome nature of formulaic units, it is particularly interesting how they are rendered in those translation modes that pose a number of difficulties on their own. That is why the next part of this thesis is devoted to audiovisual translation.

CHAPTER 2

Audiovisual Translation

In the last thirty years, audiovisual translation (AVT) has become increasingly popular: both in the communications industry, with the amount of audiovisual content growing immensely worldwide, and in academia. Among researchers, after rather slow beginnings caused by the specificity of AVT, it has shifted "from the margins to the centre of the academic debate" (Díaz-Cintas interviewed by Bogucki 2020: 11), and therefore is no longer "an ugly duckling at the periphery of TS" (Remael et al. 2012: 13). But today, the question whether audiovisual translation studies (AVTS) is "a mature field of studies in its own right" (ibid) or a sub-discipline within TS remains without a definite answer. While this thesis does not aim to push this discussion in either direction, one thing is certain: AVT is not a translation as such in the sense of simple language conversion, as there are more complex factors that need to be considered in studying (and practicing) AVT than the factors present in the standard textual translation (i.e., linguistic layer, contextual elements, discourse types, culture, etc.), such as the multimedia nature of AVT and the impact of technology. With this in mind, some key concepts presented by TS should be properly adapted for AVTS, with Gambier (2014) listing nine such concepts: text, authorship, sense, translation, translation unit, translation strategy, translation norms, relationships between written and oral, and accessibility. Therefore this section focuses on many aspects of AVT that differ from those of regular translation.

According to Reiss (1971/2000), there are four types of texts: informative (e.g., a scientific report), expressive (e.g., a lyric poem), operative (e.g., an advertisement), and audio-medial (i.e., a written text destined to be spoken or sung). The last category was later changed to *multi-medial* in order to incorporate texts such as comics, that is, texts which do not have acoustic elements but do have visual ones (Trosborg 1997: 278); this type of text depends on a non-linguistic medium. In multi-medial texts, language is only a part of a complex of elements (Reiss 1971/2000: 49). While Reiss's typology is well-based, it does not reflect the nuances of texts that exist in today's world. To focus more on the multi-medial texts, Snell-Hornby (2006: 85) suggests a further categorization of this text type and distinguishes four classes of multi-medial texts, i.e., multimedial texts (often called *audiovisual*), which can be saved on different electronic media and involve both vision and sound (e.g., a movie), multimodal texts, which also involve different types of verbal and non-verbal expression (sound and image), but are not saved on any electronic media (e.g., an opera), multisemiotic texts, which use various graphic, verbal and non-verbal, sign systems (e.g., comics), and audiomedial, which are texts written to be read out loud (e.g., a political speech). Today, one could slightly modify Snell-Hornby's description of audiovisual texts, as they no longer have to be saved on traditional media (such as CDs or even flash drives) and can be instead put in the cloud, i.e., be virtually available and stored (for more elaborate discussion on defining the cloud, see for example: Bolaños-García-Escribano and Díaz-Cintas 2020: 521-524).

Having positioned audiovisual texts in the text typology, it is now possible to answer the question posed in the title of this subsection. Audiovisual translation (AVT) is the transfer of a source semiotic complex (consisting of image, non-verbal and verbal sound, music, and any noise) into a target semiotic complex (Tomaszkiewicz 2006: 100). If one takes into consideration the well-known translation typology by Jakobson (1959: 223), who distinguishes intralingual translation (rewording), which is the interpretation of verbal signs with other verbal signs in the same language, interlingual translation (translation proper), which consists of transferring verbal signs from one language into another, and intersemiotic translation (transmutation), which is the interpretation of verbal signs by means of nonverbal signs, AVT is a unique type that combines intersemiotic and interlingual (or intralingual, if one includes media accessibility into the field of AVT; this topic is further elaborated on in "Types of AVT" subsection, see p. 85) transfer, as there are more factors that need to be taken into account than solely the textual layer. Gambier (2014: 47-48) also stresses different semiotic codes in audiovisual material, which is presented in Table 2.

Table 2. "The semiotic codes in the production of meaning" (reproduction from: Gambier 2014: 48)

	Audio channel	**Visual channel**
Verbal elements (signs)	*linguistic code:* dialogue, monologue, comments/ voices off, reading *paralinguistic code:* delivery, intonation, accents *literary and theatre codes:* plot, narrative, sequences, drama progression, rhythm	*graphic code:* written forms such as letters, headlines, menus, street names, intertitles, subtitles
Non-verbal elements (signs)	special sound effects/*sound arrangement code* *musical code*	*iconographic code*
	paralinguistic code: voice quality, pauses, silence, volume of voice, vocal noise such as crying, shouting, coughing, etc.	*photographic code:* lighting, perspective, colours, etc. *scenographic code:* visual environment signs *film code:* shooting, framing, cutting/ editing, genre conventions, etc. *kinesic code:* gestures, manners, postures, facial features, gazes, etc. *proxemics code:* movements, use of space, interpersonal distance, etc. *dress code:* including hairstyle, make-up, etc.

All of the non-verbal and verbal elements in a piece of audiovisual material can be in different relationships, such as redundancy, autonomy, complementarity, contradiction, criticism, distance, or help (ibid: 48). Furthermore, verbal elements themselves can have different functions, i.e., allocative, when used to identify a character, performative, when they help to achieve something, explicative, when they add information that cannot be obtained from the observation of the visual layer, selective, when used to help the interpretation of a particular shot, and demarcative, when used to organize the plot (ibid: 49). These features of AV material contribute to the fact that AVT is a very complex process. The complex relations between the visual and the audio will be further explored in the analytical part of this thesis (see p. 209); as with pragmatemes, visual context may be indispensable in some cases (e.g., *Fresh paint*) and key to proper understanding in others (e.g., if a police officer appears on the screen entering a room and shouts *Clear!*, it means "the room is empty, you can safely enter", but if the scene shows two people having a conversation, *Clear!* may mean "I understand").

2.1 History of AVT: then and now

Along with the birth of cinema, the need for AVT was born. Even though the first movies, that is, silent movies, were thought to be universal, Gambier (2014: 45) points out that this universality was just a myth, and there were, in fact, many different kinds of sounds in silent movies, e.g., a narrator telling the story behind a curtain. That is why it was common to hire additional actors who were acting as interpreters; they read or improvised dialogues seen on the screen in the TL (Palion-Musioł 2012: 96). For instance, in Japan, a *benshi* (Japanese: *orator*, Martínez Sirés 2016), an interpreter for movie purposes, or a *film explainer* (O'Sullivan and Cornu 2018) was someone whose task was not only to read the translated dialogues but also to use different voice tones and accents in often added dialogues in order to differentiate characters in the movie and explain cultural elements in real time if necessary (Loska 2007: 59, 62-63)[53]. Furthermorse, from the visual standpoint, intertitles, or title cards, i.e., printed texts inserted in the middle of a movie ss(De Linde 1996), were also one of the first movie elements subject to translation.

Nonetheless, according to most scholars AVT as we know it appeared along with sound films around the beginning of the 1930s (Palion-Musioł 2012: 96). The first translation practices included inserting intertitles of dialogues in the TL or replacing the soundtrack with explanatory sequences in the TL; however, the reception of such translations was rather hostile (Zanotti 2018). Therefore, other methods started to be implemented, such as producing multilingual versions, dubbing, and subtitling (Perego and Pacinotti 2020). Firstly, multilingual versions of movies were made with actors being imported from different countries to perform in the TL (Barnier 2004), and although this practice was common particularly in 1930 and 1931 in Hollywood and

[53] The practice of film explaining has not entirely disappeared; it still can be observed in some form at film festivals (O'Sullivan and Cornu 2018).

for a whole decade in Germany (1929-1939), it was later abandoned as it generated high costs (Perego and Pacinotti 2020). In 1930 dubbing and the remake (adaptation of a movie by the change of the language and the plot to a certain extent) emerged, and in 1934, subtitling was first used (Gambier 2014: 46).

With the new form of translation, a new field of study was slowly developing. The first publication about AVT is thought to be *Le dubbing* written by Valentin Mandelstamm, which was published in the early 1930s in the *Cinés* journal (Franco and Orero 2005). In contrast, seemingly the first piece on subtitling, *Le sous-titrage de films* by Simon Laks, was published around twenty years later, in 1957 (Díaz-Cintas 2009), but due to its limited distribution, was not widely discussed. According to Díaz-Cintas (ibid: 2), it was a time of "acute lethargy" regarding the field; there were almost no academic publications on subtitling and few on dubbing. AVT remained understudied until the 1990s, which was the "golden age" of AVT (ibid: 3). A hundred years after the cinema was born (as 1995 marked its 100th anniversary), studies on AVT began to bloom. With further advancements in technology, globalization, and digitalization of multimedia texts, the research in this field is steadily increasing (Sung-Eun 2014: 380), and although studies on screen translation (that is, dubbing and subtitling) are still the most prominent in the field, other, younger AVT types are now gaining more and more academic interest (Perego and Pacinotti 2020). After this brief overview, it is now possible to present the categorization of AVT types.

2.2 Types of AVT

At first, the term *audiovisual translation* was not in use; it was proposed around 1995 (Gambier 2014: 46), but before that, papers used terms as simple as *film translation* or *cinema translation* (Díaz-Cintas 2009: 6). Later, with the expansion of television and video games, terms such as *language transfer*, *translation for the media*, *multimedia translation* (a term still used by some scholars, e.g., Tryuk 2009), *versioning* (often used by professionals in the field), *screen translation* (which refers to all products distributed via screen but disregards certain translation types such as surtitling for the stage), and finally *audiovisual translation* were suggested (Szarkowska 2009: 10). With the emergence of the term *audiovisual translation*, attention was brought to the multisemiotic dimension of various AV types (Gambier 2014: 46). Because this term seems to convey the diversity of this translation type and is the one that is most often used in reference to subtitling, 'AVT' will be used in the present thesis. Nonetheless, it should be noted that with the advancement of technology and the development of the industry, new terms used by practitioners in the field have emerged. One of them is media localization, i.e., adapting a product (in this case, most often a videogame, which requires a lot more than translating the text, but can also refer to a commercial, a TV show, or another medium) to a specific locale. In addition to translation, in the process of localization, it is also important to adapt the design and overall graphics (e.g., fonts) and modify the product so that it feels like it was created specifically for a given market[54].

As to what types of translation AVT includes, various typologies can be found (e.g., Greco and Jankowska 2020, Perego and Pacinotti 2020). Gambier (2014) proposes the division of AVT into two main groups: translation between codes but within the same language and translation between languages. Gambier's further division is shown in Table 3.

Table 3. Division of AVT based on Gambier (2014)

Translation between codes, within the same language	**Translation between languages**
1. Intralingual subtitling for language learning 2. Intralingual subtitling for accessibility 3. Intralingual dubbing	1. Script/scenario translation 2. Free commentary 3. Interpreting 4. Surtitling 5. Interlingual subtitling 6. Dubbing 7. Voice-over
• Live subtitling • Audio description (AD)	

[54] Source: https://gala-global.org/knowledge-center/about-the-industry/language-services. Accessed on July 25, 2022.

As can be observed from Table 3, Gambier (2014) is one of the researchers who use the term AVT as a hyperonym which subsumes practices of translating audiovisual material into a different language for an audience that does not understand the source language, and the "linguistic mediation" (Díaz-Cintas and Massidda 2019: 2) of audiovisual material aimed at making it available to audiences that are sensorily impaired, such as the blind, the partially sighted, the deaf, and the hard-of-hearing. In AVT for the sensorily impaired, language transfer is rarely implied, "as it is typically intralingual, thus the shift is of a semiotic rather than linguistic nature" (Deckert and Bogucki 2018: 67). As for terminology used in the field, these types of transfer are modes of media accessibility (MA), which is thought to be closely related to AVT by some researchers (e.g., ibid) and more generally, a part of AVT by others, such as Gambier (2014) and Díaz-Cintas (2020), who defines accessibility as "making audiovisual programmes available to people that otherwise could not have access to them, irrespective of whether the barriers are sensory or linguistic" (ibid: 24), therefore encompassing the two transfers under one term because the aim of the two is the same, i.e., to facilitate access to entertainment and information. In order to present the spectrum of AVT understood as a hyperonym, all the types suggested in Gambier's table (2014) will now be briefly discussed.

In the first group, the difference between intralingual subtitling for language learning and for accessibility is the way these two modes are processed. In the case of intralingual subtitling for language learning, various noises such as telephones ringing or doors slamming are not conveyed in subtitles because the purpose of these subtitles is to help sociolinguistic understanding, whereas in the intralingual subtitles for accessibility, which are often called subtitles for the deaf and the-hard-of-hearing, SDH in short (Díaz-Cintas and Massidda 2019), both verbal and non-verbal audio material is rendered into text so that the deaf and the hard-of-hearing can recognize the full sound experience of the movie. In some environments, especially in the United States, both types of intralingual subtitles are called *[closed] captions* (*closed* because they cannot be turned off by the viewer, in opposition to *open captions* which can be turned off at any given moment). While it is worth noting that according to Gambier (2014: 49) the terms *closed captions* and *intralingual subtitles* cannot be considered synonymous since intralingual subtitles can often be in fact turned off on TV channels or DVDs (or, most recently, on video-on-demand online streaming platforms), to avoid confusion with interlingual subtitles, in this dissertation, the term *captions* will be used to refer to intralingual subtitles.

Intralingual dubbing, or *revoicing*[55], is used in two situations. First, when a dialect, slang, or an accent which may be difficult for the target audience to understand is used (e.g., *Harry Potter*, even though its source language (SL) was English, was dubbed in the United States). Second, if the original soundtrack was recorded in noisy surroundings, there might be a need to re-record some parts in a studio later (ibid).

Live (or real-time) subtitling, or *respeaking*, is used for live broadcasts. In this type, the subtitler notes the words which are being spoken (by exact quotation or by rephrasing them) in real time. Today, new technologies, especially voice recognition software, are more and more used for this task. This subtitling can be inter- or intralingual (Greco and Jankowska 2020).

Finally, audio description (AD) is an AVT type that can be both intra- and interlingual and is a common practice in both cases. It is used to give access to AV material primarily to the blind and the visually impaired but also to the elderly and people with cognitive difficulties (Mazur 2020). It consists of reading the information about what is happening at a given moment on the screen or stage, or what is presented in a museum (audio guides for tourists). The information read should not interfere with the sound or musical effects included on the soundtrack.

As for the second group of AVT, script/scenario translation is a procedure done to present the plot to people working on a movie (e.g., technicians or actors) or to gain financial support for co-production. Depending on the purpose of such translation, the procedure should be performed accordingly. For instance, if the director is seeking a cast member, the translation should provide essential information for the candidate actor so that they can decide whether they would like to work on that project (Cattrysse and Gambier

55 The term *revoicing* may be used in different ways, including as a synonym for dubbing, but Chaume (2020: 105) argues that is rather "a hypernym that also includes intralingual post-synchronisation (…); voice-over (…); narration; fandubbing, fundubbing and gag dubbing (…); simultaneous film interpreting; and audio description."

2008), whereas if the director wants to present the script to potential sponsors, the translation should be concise but informative.

Free commentary is mainly used in programs for children, documentaries, and corporate videos. One of the oldest types of AVT, it consists of text adaptation for the target audience with the use of comments, clarifications, omissions, and additions. It is usually synchronized not with the original soundtrack but with the image on the screen (Gambier 2014).

Interpreting as an AVT type can be performed in different ways depending on a given situation; it can mean interpreting that is consecutive (usually prerecorded), simultaneous (often performed in the case of live broadcasts), or in sign language. Some authors, such as Greco and Jankowska (2020), consider live subtitling to be a form of interpreting for AVT as well.

Surtitling can be compared to subtitling but is used in live settings, that is, in operas and theatres. The surtitles are lines of text placed either on the back of the seats or above the stage. In contrast to subtitles, the surtitles usually are not prepared in advance since it is assumed that the performers (actors or singers) never perform in exactly the same way on every occasion. That is why the translator must always be present to insert the surtitles during the show properly, and hence "turns into a performer" (Carrillo Darancet 2020: 174).

In this dissertation, separate subsections will be devoted to dubbing, voice-over, and interlingual subtitling since these AVT types are the most prominent in television and cinema. For this reason it is important to describe them and their constraints in more detail, and the most space will be devoted to subtitling, as it constitutes the focal point of the present dissertation.

2.2.1 Dubbing

Dubbing, or "adapting a text for on-camera characters" (Gambier 2014: 51), is "replacing the original soundtrack containing the actors' dialogue with a TL recording that reproduces the original message, while at the same time ensuring that the TL sounds and the actors' lip movements are more or less synchronized" (Díaz-Cintas 2003: 195). Lip-synchronization is not however the only factor important in dubbing. Gambier (2014) notes two more: time-synchronization and isochronism (matching the length of the dubbed text and the original). Some authors (e.g., Chaume 2020) also point to kinesic synchrony, i.e., matching the translation and the body movements and body language of the actors on screen. In the industry, dubbing is a "team effort" (Chaume 2020: 104) which involves more people than just a translator, such as dubbing assistants who work on segmenting the text, actors or voice talents who perform the dubbing under the direction of a dubbing director, a sound engineer to edit the soundtrack, and, finally, people responsible for quality control. A distinct phenomenon observed since the 1990s is fandubbing, a home-made version of this AVT mode which is done non-professionally by fans[56] who translate the dialogues and then record the audio with their own voices (Perego and Pacinotti 2020).

Thanks to dubbing, the viewer can easily focus on the visual aspects of the movie and fully enjoy elements such as costumes and scenography as they receive the translation in audio (in contrast to subtitling). Even if they turn their eyes away from the screen, they are still able to follow the plot because they can hear the dialogues in their own language. Furthermore, because each actor has their own distinct voice, there is no difficulty in distinguishing who is speaking at the moment, in contrast to voice-over. However, dubbing may leave the audience with a sense of artificiality. Especially in live-action movies, differentiating between the dubbed and the original version can be possible due to both different lip-synchronization and the sound of the movie recorded in a studio (Belczyk 2007).

According to Chunbai (2009), the translator has to follow two principles when preparing a target text for dubbing: immediate comprehensibility and pragmatic equivalence with the principle of relevance. The first principle refers to prioritizing the viewer's understanding over surface fidelity, while the second one stresses that the translation "should be able to make the target audience smile, laugh and cry as the original does with the help of non-linguistic media and of graphic, acoustic, and visual kinds of expression" (Chunbai 2009: 153). Thanks to the application of these principles, the audience does not have to make unnecessary effort in order to understand the dubbed movie they are watching.

Furthermore, Chunbai (2009) also distinguishes three constraints that need to be taken into account in dubbing: 1) the irreversibility of utterances, 2) matching lip movements, and 3) matching gestures and movements.

[56] While this is a common definition of fandubbing, it seems that in different countries this phenomenon can look different. Furthermore, in addition to *fandubbing*, terms such as *fundubbing* and *gag dubbing* have emerged (for more information on the topic see e.g., Baños 2020).

As stated in the introduction to this subsection, lip-synchronization is one of the most important factors of dubbing that scholars (e.g., Díaz-Cintas 2003, Gambier 2014, among others) point to. Chaume (2004: 36) explains that "the criterion for good synchronization is met when the original actor appears to be actually speaking the translated dialogue, in other words, when the translation is made invisible." However, only in close-up shots is total lip-synchrony crucial; it would be vain to expect to see all TL phonemes matched with SL lip movements (Chaume 2004). That is why the "synchronization of the duration of the translation with the screen characters" (Chaume 2012: 69), i.e., isochrony, is a more important criterion in well-made dubbing. It should also be noted that synchrony in dubbing should be considered not only on a textual level but also on the visual one. Chaume (2012) gives the example of dubbing into Spanish where *omelette* can become *pie* if the dish does not appear on the screen; similarly, the French pragmateme of choosing a cheque as the payment method in *Je veux payer par chèque, s'il vous plaît* could be translated into Polish with the use of a more common payment method in Poland, i.e., a card, as *Chciałbym zapłacić kartą*, as long as the situation of the payment itself is not shown on the screen. Therefore, the occurrence of pragmatemes in dubbing would be an interesting topic for future research.

Due to synchronization of various kinds being so important, usually a number of changes to the original text have to be made. For example, the text has to be made longer or shorter, or certain elements have to be added, e.g., different conjunctions (Tomaszkiewicz 2006). With all these changes in mind, Tomaszkiewicz (2006) argues that dubbing is rather an adaptation, not a translation *sensu stricto*.

Voice-over

Voice-over, or *half-dubbing*, according to Gambier (2014: 51), is an AVT type in which the translated text is read (usually by a journalist or an actor) while the original soundtrack volume is significantly reduced. While it is primarily associated with the translation of documentaries (Orero 2009), voice-over is applied to a plethora of fictional programs in some countries[57] (e.g., Poland;

[57] Furthermore, Matamala (2019) notes the trend of employing voice-over for programs on the border of fiction and non-fiction (i.e., reality shows) in countries that have not widely used it before. Therefore, is a phenomenon that should be further observed.

see the subsection on audience preferences, p. 99). However, scholars such as Tomaszkiewicz (2006) argue that voice-over for documentary films and voice-over for fiction films should be considered two different AVT types because they have different characteristics. Voice-over for documentary films is a commentary made by a third-person narrator who explains to the viewer what they are currently seeing on the screen and makes remarks on the topic (Kuhn and Westwell 2012: 446-447). In that sense, the term *voice-over* can also be used to refer to any unseen commentator heard during any AV material, and that is the definition usually provided by film studies, while in TS, *voice-over* “refers to situations in which a voice giving a translation is heard simultaneously on top of original voice” (Mailhac 1998: 222). In order to avoid confusion, in this thesis, the term *translated narration* will be used to refer to the monologue commentaries made in productions such as documentaries, and *voice-over* will be understood as a translation read on top of the original soundtrack in fiction films (as inspired by Tomaszkiewicz 2006).

Despite voice-over’s low production costs, there seem to be no scholars who praise it as a perfect AVT type. On the contrary, its flaws are widely known. One of the biggest disadvantages to voice-over is the confusion caused by the overlap with the diegetic sound, especially in scenes where multiple characters are speaking. As Belczyk (2007: 9) notes, following the plot in these cases may become not only a puzzle but even a “nightmare”.

As in many AVT types, synchrony is vital to a well-done voice-over. Matamala (2019) distinguishes four types of synchrony that need to be considered in voice-over: voice-over synchrony, literal synchrony, kinetic synchrony, and action synchrony.

Voice-over synchrony refers to a concept similar to isochrony, described in the subsection devoted to dubbing (see p. 89), with the difference that voice-over should begin “some words after the original utterance” and finish “some words before the latter ends” (Matamala 2019: 68). In Tomaszkiewicz’s terminology, this trait is called the “postsynchronisation of voice-over” (2006: 118) and is not a necessity, especially when dialogues are fast-paced. Furthermore, voice-over synchrony can be further divided into full isochrony, meaning that at least one word at the beginning and one word at the end of the SL utterance are heard, initial isochrony, with at least one word heard at the beginning of the utterance, and final isochrony, with at least one word heard at the end of the utterance (Sepielak 2016).

Literal synchrony refers to literal translation without the original voice overlapping the translation. However, this is not a common practice, since literal transfer often results in the translation having an artificial feeling (Matamala 2019).

Kinetic synchrony aims at matching the utterances with what can be seen on the screen, in particular movements and gestures, while the focus of action synchrony is the synchronization of sound with the images on the screen. According to Tomaszkiewicz (2006), the latter is especially important in the translation of documentaries, but one can think of various examples similar to the one provided in the subsection on dubbing (see p. 89) and say that the same synchrony may be key to the translation of certain pragmatemes in fiction films.

2.2.3 Subtitling

As stated previously (see p. 86), subtitles can be either intralingual or interlingual, but in this dissertation, starting here, the term *subtitling* will, if not stated otherwise, be used to refer to interlingual subtitles, as they are the primary focus of this research. Subtitling is "moving from oral dialogue in one or several languages to one or two written lines" (Gambier 2014: 50). Nonetheless, it is often stressed that any linguistic information, not only dialogues but also parts of the visual image (e.g., signs or graffiti) and soundtrack, e.g., song lyrics, should be conveyed in subtitles (Díaz-Cintas 2009). Therefore, subtitling is a translation of a polysemiotic text which is constituted by three parallel meaning-producing semiotic channels: two non-verbal (the image and the sound) and one verbal (the dialogues)[58]. Furthermore, subtitling is a diasemiotic translation in the sense that the translation crosses over from speech to writing (Gottlieb 2004). Due to the complex nature of subtitles, their production is fraught with a number of challenges that need to be discussed in this subsection.

[58] Nonetheless, Ramos Pinto (2022) notes that verbal elements are those which are primarily translated in subtitles, while other meaningful resources such as visual and aural elements are often disregarded, which can be detrimental to the viewer's reception and, as a result, to the commercial success of a movie.

With the first subtitles being made way before the digital revolution, the first subtitlers worked with nothing but a "paper and pencil" (Bywood 2020: 505) and various manual techniques were used to add subtitles to the film, including thermal processes, among others (for a detailed description of subtitles' technical history see, e.g., Ivarsson 2009). Since the rise of the desktop PC, however, the subtitler's job has become linked to modern technology. The first subtitling computer software dates back to the same time as the introduction of the PC in the workplace, but the evolution of subtitling computer programs we know today began at the end of the 1990s when external VHS players were no longer needed and were replaced by built-in movie-player software (ibid). The next stage of development came with the Web 2.0 era, when more software was introduced, including popular freeware such as Subtitle Workshop (ibid). Today, the shift we are observing concerns subtitling with the use of cloud computing (Bolaños-García-Escribano and Díaz-Cintas 2020). With the advance of technology, the subtitler's job has become more efficient, as subtitlers have at their disposal automatic tools that facilitate speech recognition, speech alignment, extracting dialogues from screenplays and splitting them into labeled subtitles, and other capabilities (Bywood 2020). Nonetheless, subtitlers still have to be carefully trained and skilled, with Gottlieb (1994: 101) commenting on their versatile abilities as follows: "the subtitlers must possess the musical ears of an interpreter, the stylistic sensitivity of a literary translator, the visual acuteness of a film cutter, and the esthetic sense of a book designer."

Subtitling, as well as being much less expensive than dubbing (since fewer people need to be involved in the process), has a number of other advantages. It allows the viewer to fully enjoy the actors' acting skills, including how they pronounce their lines. For instance, Belczyk (2007: 8) comments that not even the best dubbing actors can imitate Marlon Brando's mumbling in *The Godfather*. Furthermore, thanks to the original soundtrack, and therefore the SL, being left untouched, viewers who know or are learning the SL may enjoy the pronunciation and learn new words, semantic structures, and whole sentences with the visual context, which is often essential to the understanding of linguistic structures. To facilitate the process of learning languages using subtitles, an intriguing tool was introduced to the market in 2019. Learning Languages with Netflix, or Language Reactor[59] (after the rebranding in the summer of 2021), is a Google Chrome extension (which is planned for inclusion on other browsers at the time of writing) which allows its users to watch a movie or a TV show available on Netflix (and on YouTube) with simultaneous subtitles in two languages[60]. This main feature, among many others, is supposed to make language learning a more effective, interesting, and pleasant experience, according to the tool's developers[61] (further description of this tool is presented in the "Methods" section, see p. 123).

Nevertheless, subtitling also has a number of disadvantages. Firstly, the viewer's attention is always focused on the bottom of the screen, as this is where the subtitles are usually placed. This may lead to the scenography and parts of the plot going unremarked, especially by a person who is a slow reader. Secondly, the placement of subtitles on the screen always diminishes the visual impression; if done correctly, the subtitles should not cover any important visual information; however, a part of the screen, to be exact up to two twelfths of the screen, according to the generally accepted norms (Díaz-Cintas 2020), is always covered. Nonetheless, while the placement of subtitles at the bottom of the screen is customary, it should be noted that eye-tracking research on the dynamic placement of subtitles is being conducted, e.g., Fox 2016, and it is possible that in the future the industry practice concerning subtitle placement will change. Furthermore, with the advance of virtual and augmented realities and the growing popularity of 360° videos[62], as well as vertical videos on social media, technical rules concerning subtitling need revision.

Despite the possible disadvantages of subtitling, it still remains one of the most popular solutions to cater to the foreign audience's need for having

---

59 See https://www.languagereactor.com/. Accessed on July 25, 2022.

60 Bilingual subtitles have been in use for a long time, but with a different purpose. For instance, they appear in cinemas in countries such as Belgium, where there are French- and Flemish-speaking communities, and at international film festivals to attract a wider audience (Díaz-Cintas 2020).

61 Source: https://chrome.google.com/webstore/detail/language-reactor/hoombieeljmmljlkjmnheibnpciblicm. Accessed on March 2, 2022.

62 Some experiments with the audience have already been conducted for these new content types, e.g., Brown and Patterson 2017.

foreign AV content translated. To consider subtitles well-made, apart from the linguistic point of view, four criteria have to be met: readability, assimilability, discreetness, and naturalness (Belczyk 2007). In terms of readability, subtitles should not exceed two lines[63] (spatial coordinate) and should be displayed on the screen long enough so that the viewer can read and understand them (temporal coordinate). As for the temporal coordinate, the task of deciding the starting and ending moments of when the subtitle is displayed on the screen is called spotting, and it "has to mirror the rhythm of the film and the performance of the actors, and be mindful of pauses, interruptions and other prosodic features that characterise the original speech" (Díaz-Cintas 2020: 154). Common practice suggests a duration of at least one second and a maximum of six seconds, without crossing a shot change, for the subtitle to be displayed (ibid). Within both temporal and spatial coordinates, the subtitle is usually shorter than the original uttered sentence, which is also due to the change of the medium (from a spoken form to a written one). Therefore the translation must be concise, often omitting inessential information. This happens to such an extent that Bogucki (2004: 72) calls translational loss "practically an occupational hazard" in subtitling. While the matter of translational loss is a great concern in TS, there is no single answer to the question of what it means to lose something in translation. Kabara (2015: 166) points to two major concerns, namely "loss of source text meaning and loss of source text «poeticness»." In terms of the textual part, Tomaszkiewicz (2006) estimates that 30-40 percent of the original text is lost in subtitling, while Antonini (2005) finds that, among European languages, the word count reduction can be of 40-75 percent. However, apart from the fact that the reduction in quantity of words does not have to equal the reduction in meaning[64], more comprehensive studies on the topic are needed to fully

63 While the maximum of two lines is still a required practice in the industry, authors such as Díaz-Cintas (2020) point to the fact that this rule is broken constantly in the cybersubtitles, which may suggest that the adage of well-made subtitles being unnoticeable to the audience should be considered outdated.

64 Furthermore, Kabara (2015: 177) argues for well-made subtitles being able to bring to the source text qualitative growth by allowing it "to reach a wider audience" who then "makes inferences to interpret the text calling upon broader background knowledge resources that include both the target culture and the source culture."

understand the word loss in subtitling. As to what can be omitted, Coelho (2007: online) comments that "the translator needs to take into account that the film viewers also receive non-verbal information from the images", so the information that can be inferred from visual context may be omitted. Similarly, repetitions are often omitted in subtitling as this does not affect meaning. In contrast, in terms of *poeticness* (Kabara 2015), elements such as politeness patterns (including greetings) or stylistic effects are hard to preserve in subtitling due to the technical restrictions of this translation type (Bogucki 2004). What is more, apart from the technical constraint concerning the length of a subtitle, Bogucki (ibid: 86) advocates for the principle of relevance to be always utilized in subtitling, explaining that since "the aim of the target text is to aid the audience in comprehending and appreciating a filmic message", the translation product should be maximally simplified, "so that the message it conveys gets across to the intended recipient, yet the process of taking it in is not too strenuous." After all, nobody but AVT scholars goes to the cinema saying "Let's go to the cinema, I want to see some subtitles", as was noted jokingly by Jan Pedersen in his presentation at "Languages and The Media" Conference in Berlin in 2022.

The second criterion, the assimilability of subtitles, means that thanks to the proper division of subtitles, information can be assimilated quickly, that is, the viewer is able to understand the meaning of the subtitle directly upon reading it (Belczyk 2007). According to Tomaszkiewicz (2006), an average viewer reads at a rate of 150-180 words per minute, and therefore, the length of displaying the subtitle on the screen should be between 1.5 and 6 seconds, keeping in mind the rule that the subtitle should appear a quarter of second before the line is uttered and disappear before the change of a scene. Regarding the third criterion, subtitles should also be discreet, i.e., not distract the viewer from what is happening on the screen and not cover any important visual information (Belczyk 2007). That is why it is widely accepted that subtitles can be of a maximum of the two-thirds length of the screen, with 32-40 characters per line (Tomaszkiewicz 2006). However, every supplier has its own guidelines as to the maximum number of characters in a subtitle. For instance, the BBC's limit is 37 characters per line[65], while

[65] Source: https://bbc.github.io/subtitle-guidelines/index_r1.html. Accessed on March 2, 2022.

Netflix does not set a limit for the majority of languages but suggests using not more than 42 characters per line[66] (for a more elaborated discussion on the number of characters in subtitles see the subsection "AVT for big streaming companies: the example of Netflix", p. 103).

Lastly, the criterion of naturalness means that stylistically, subtitles should imitate an oral conversation in the TL. While this trait is fundamental, Belczyk (2007) notes that if a choice has to be made between the readability and naturalness of a subtitle, readability should always be considered more important. The naturalness of subtitles cannot exceed certain limitations either. As Gottlieb (1994: 106) notes, the audience would "be taken aback by reading the oddities of a spoken discourse" if there were no shift between the spoken and the written language. After all, spontaneous (however artificial [scripted] in fiction films; the phenomenon called "prefabricated orality" by Chaume 2004: 168) spoken language is full of particularities such as pauses, self-corrections, false starts, ellipses, grammatical errors, slips-of-the-tongue, and lack of cohesion, with multiple people often talking at the same time (Gottlieb 1994). In the last case, the spotter (either the translator or the technician) has to decide whose line will have to be deleted. Similarly, the prosodic features of speech are not entirely represented in subtitles, with exclamation marks and italics only being their "faint echoes" (ibid: 102), which may be particularly interesting in the reception of pragmatemes in subtitling since prosody is a vital factor for these units to function as pragmatemes (Banyś 2020). Hence, subtitling is a fragmentary translation (Gottlieb 1994), meaning that to fully grasp the meaning, the audience has to combine the subtitles with the visual image and the original acoustic sound.

With all of the above peculiarities in mind, "language professionals tend to disagree as to whether subtitling is indeed translation" (Gottlieb 2004: 219). For instance, Toda (1997), a famous Japanese subtitler, considers subtitling to be a transfer of the dialogue's *essence* rather than its direct translation, while Díaz-Cintas (2020: 167) agrees that subtitling is indeed a "unique translational type" and "an unusual form of translation." Maybe that is why not

---

[66] Source: https://partnerhelp.netflixstudios.com/hc/en-us/articles/215274938-What-is-the-maximum-number-of-characters-per-line-allowed-in-Timed-Text-assets-. Accessed on March 2, 2022.

only professionals are drawn to it, since fansubbing, i.e., "the activity of fans subtitling for fellow fans" (Massidda 2020: 189), is a popular phenomenon that dates back to the 1980s when Japanese anime programs, unavailable in the West, were first translated and distributed by fans in the US. Since then, especially after computer software became largely available in the 1990s, fansubbing has flourished both as a community-based activity, for instance in the Czech Republic, Italy, and elsewhere, and as an individual practice, for instance in Poland (Luczaj and Hoły-Luczaj 2014). On top of that, fansubbing is not the only phenomenon of what Díaz-Cintas (2018) calls *cybersubtitles*, i.e., different cases of volunteer subtitling encountered on the web. Apart from fansubtitling, the core of cybersubtitles also consists of *guerilla subtitles*, produced for activism and political causes, and *altruist subtitles* created and crowdsourced for positive initiatives such as TED[67] and Khan Academy[68] (ibid).

2.3 Audience preferences

Due to the high cost of production, the first Hollywood sound films were displayed only in their SL, i.e., English. This phenomenon led some people, such as Louis B. Mayer, a renowned film producer, to believe that English may become the universal language of all cinema (Wedel 2012). However, that idea soon proved to be wrong and for the purposes of foreign distribution, different AVT modes had to be implemented. In the beginning, subtitles for movies were made mainly in three languages: French, German, and Spanish. These language versions could also be distributed in Portugal and the Netherlands, where these languages were not widely used, but where a lot of people spoke or understood Spanish, in the first case, or German, in the latter (Palion-Musioł 2012). Then other language versions of subtitles appeared, but with many people in the 1930s still being illiterate, dubbing started gaining more popularity in countries with higher illiteracy rates. All the new ideas connected to the invention of sound films and further film distribution seem to have played roles in forming cultural preferences concerning favorite AVT modes in different countries. Nonetheless, there are still other reasons that

---

67 See https://www.ted.com/. Accessed on July 25, 2022.

68 See https://www.khanacademy.org/. Accessed on July 25, 2022.

led different countries to favor different AVT modes. For instance, censorship used to be a key element in choosing a given AVT mode. Historically, dubbing was the primary choice in fascist countries such as Germany and Italy, while in communist Eastern Europe, it was the voice-over. With both of these modes, manipulation and censorship are more manageable than in the case of subtitles. Furthermore, economic aspects were also taken into consideration, with subtitling being the least expensive mode to produce and dubbing being the most expensive one (Díaz-Cintas 2009).

To this day, the best known classification of countries according to their AVT mode preferences is the one suggested by Gottlieb (1998), who distinguishes three types of countries: dubbing countries (usually bigger ones, where the official language is either Spanish, French, German, or Italian), subtitling countries (non-European and small European countries, e.g., Denmark, Portugal, and Israel), and voice-over countries (Eastern and Central European countries, e.g., Poland, Slovakia, Hungary, and Russia). Furthermore, a fourth group that can be described consists of countries that display AV content in English without translation (i.e., mainly English-speaking countries). In this group, when faced with non-English content, there seems to be no preference for one AV mode over another, "although a certain degree of bias for subtitled produce can be observed" (Díaz-Cintas 2009: 196). Nonetheless, this bias is changing, since English-speaking countries seem to be turning to dubbing as Netflix original productions in languages other than English become increasingly popular, along with their dubbed versions[69] (Bolaños-García-Escribano et al. 2021).

However, as of today, over 25 years have passed since Gottlieb's original typology; therefore it can only be considered a signpost in indicating countries' true preferences for AVT. Since then, many articles have been published (and still are being published) on the topic (e.g., Szarkowska and Laskowska 2015, Matamala, Perego and Bottiroli 2017), disputing Gottlieb's

[69] According to the data presented by Solsman (2022), the most watched TV show on Netflix (based on total hours viewed in the first 28 days from the release date) is the Korean TV series *Squid Game*. Another non-English production, *Money Heist / La Casa de Papel* (part 5) placed third on the list. Among other high-ranking shows are: French *Lupin*, Colombian *Café con Aroma de Mujer*, Spanish *Elite*, and Mexican *Dark Desire*.

original claims. For instance, Díaz-Cintas (2009) describes Slovenia and Romania as subtitling countries, Hungary, Slovakia, Bulgaria, and the Czech Republic as dubbing ones, and the Baltic countries among those preferring voice-over. In addition, with the growing popularity of online streaming services, which often offer different AVT modes to choose from, the distinction between dubbing/subtitling/voice-over countries seems now more fluid than ever. Díaz-Cintas, interviewed by Bogucki (2020: 14), calls drawing sharp lines between subtitling and dubbing countries "convenient" but "certainly misleading", while Chaume (2012: 7) comments on the issue as follows:

> The AVT landscape is no longer black and white. The distinction between dubbing and subtitling countries has become blurred. Former dubbing countries now have significant subtitling industries and have witnessed the growth of their voice-over market. In turn, audiences in former subtitling countries are becoming more used to dubbing, and former voice-over countries are moving towards dubbing and subtitling. The important question for audiences is that the single option of either dubbing or subtitling or voice-over should give way to a variety of audiovisual texts that might be dubbed, subtitled, voiced-over, subtitled for the deaf, or audiodescribed for the blind. The more options we have, the better for the consolidation of a freer, multilingual, and diverse audience.

Regarding the recipients of translations analyzed in this dissertation, i.e., French and Polish speakers, their preferences vary too. Firstly, in France[70], according to Shevenock's 2022 study[71], 61 percent of people prefer dubbing, 22 percent subtitling, and 17 percent of people tend to watch content without translation. Dubbed versions of foreign content are also set as default when watching Netflix in France. As for Poland, the preferences are not so evident.

---

70 While no similar research data have been found on other French-speaking countries, it can be assumed that dubbing is the generally preferred AVT mode for French speakers (for example, see this article from Quebec: https://www.lorientlejour.com/article/1210910/le-public-prefere-le-doublage-au-sous-titrage.html, accessed on July 25, 2022).

71 Source: https://morningconsult.com/2022/04/25/subtitles-dubbing-streaming/. Accessed on July 25, 2022.

Poland has always been (in)famous for a particular type of voice-over, where a single (usually male) voice can be heard in the TL, with the SL still being heard at a lowered volume. Even though foreign movies shown in cinemas are always subtitled or dubbed, with the dubbed films usually those made for children, Poles got so used to watching TV with voice-over in their own homes that when Netflix released the first season of their blockbuster TV series *Stranger Things* (which happened the same year Netflix launched in Poland, 2016) with dubbing and subtitles only, the Polish audience was not happy about it, to say the least, calling the dubbed version "horrible" and "dreadful"[72], which supports many older studies showing that Poles prefer voice-over to any other AVT mode (e.g., Canal Plus's study described in Bogucki, 2004, BBC Prime's study in Subbotko, 2008, and TNS OBOP's study in Garcarz, 2007). Since then, Netflix has been successfully employing voice-over for foreign content on the Polish market. However, more recent studies, such as Szarkowska and Laskowska (2015) and Deckert and Bogucki (2018), challenge the position of voice-over in Poland. In Szarkowska and Laskowska's 2015 study of hearing, hard of hearing, and deaf people's preferences, when asked whether they prefer watching AV content with subtitling or voice-over, 77.25 percent of their hearing participants favored subtitling over voice-over (6.88%)[73]. Interestingly, the results were not dependent on the age of participants, which may indicate that the audience's preferences about AVT are not set in stone and that the growing availability of subtitles thanks to streaming platforms such as Netflix impacts those preferences. Meanwhile, Deckert and Bogucki (2018) studied the opinions of students majoring in sociology, Italian, and English on a number of factors regarding subtitling, voice-over, and dubbing, including the faithfulness of the given translation mode, its suitability to different AV material types, the audience's cognitive effort, and making choices regarding translation mode. Their study shows a number of interesting results that describe the complexity of the Polish AVT milieu well. However, the most relevant one for the topic of this section is the

---

72 Source: https://qz.com/1231253/netflix-finds-dubbing-doesnt-work-in-poland-and-other-local-tv-nuances/. Accessed on July 25, 2022.

73 Other responses included not having any preference (5.29%) and saying the choice depends on the situation (10.58%) (Szarkowska and Laskowska, 2015).

fact that although the majority of students perceived subtitling as the most faithful type of AVT (66.26%), the preferred choice of the mode depended heavily on the AV text type, with subtitling being favored for feature films and TV shows (65.24% and 54.27%), dubbing for animated films (87.12%), and voice-over for documentaries (66.67%).

Therefore, as Pedersen (2018: 84) puts it, "AVT has gone from being a national choice to being an individual choice", so labels such as "subtitling country", "dubbing country", or "voice-over country" are not entirely correct anymore, unless one is talking about historical preferences. While "there does not appear to be an optimal mode of audiovisual translation" (Deckert and Bogucki 2018: 78) and often several factors play a role in the final choice, including, but not limited to, tradition and knowledge of SL, the studies mentioned here are indicative of the growing popularity of subtitling in Poland and, therefore, can also be used to support Díaz-Cintas's view (2009: 199) that "[t]he mode that has undergone the greatest growth, and that will continue to grow in the foreseeable future, is subtitling." Again, that is one of the reasons why this dissertation focuses on subtitles, with a particular look into French and Polish examples.

2.4 AVT for big streaming companies: the example of Netflix

For the purposes of this research, TV series and films available on Netflix were chosen. Therefore this subsection will be devoted to the phenomenon of Netflix, both in terms of the development of AVT and in general, because with the constant launches of platforms that follow Netflix's business model (the so-called "Netflixification" of media [Minzheong 2021]), such as Hulu, Amazon Prime Video, Disney+, HBO Max, and others, it is evident that the impact of the original platform on the approach to AV content is both significant and permanent (Jenner 2014).

The "Netflix revolution" (Osur 2016: 2) started inconspicuously, since at first Netflix was nothing but a DVD rental service. Launched in 1997, it quickly became a novelty in the rental business by launching a website where people could order their DVDs to rent and have them sent by mail (Jenner 2014, Osur 2016). Taking it a step further, Netflix soon "placed 10,000 titles from its 90,000 film library on-line in 'Watch Instantly' mode" (Cunningham and

Silver 2012: 1581), which was the beginning of the service we know today. In 2007, the online video-on-demand (VOD) feature was introduced to Netflix's users, allowing them to watch their preferred content on the computer, a year later on Xbox 360 and Blu-ray, and in 2009 on PlayStation 3 and smart TVs (Comparitech[74]). This progress, along with the introduction of Netflix as a mobile application for Android and Apple devices in 2010, led to scholars debating whether Netflix had just become the new generation of television, or *TVIV* (Jenner 2014). With over 220 million paid subscribers worldwide as of the second quarter of 2022, according to Statista[75], Netflix has changed the media landscape. Meanwhile, the data shown in the Future of TV survey revealed that 27 percent of Americans planned to cut their cable television subscriptions by the end of 2021[76], which is an increase in comparison to previous years. A similar trend can also be observed in other countries. For example, in the United Kingdom, as of 2018, more people subscribed to online streaming services (15.4 million) than to traditional pay-tv services (15.1 million)[77], whereas in Poland, where 19.4 percent of people consider canceling their cable TV subscription according to a 2020 study[78], some cable TV providers started offering a Netflix subscription if one subscribes to their standard cable TV offer[79].

Another undeniable factor in Netflix's success is that it was the first paid VOD service to launch globally, gradually expanding to different countries

74 Source: https://www.comparitech.com/blog/vpn-privacy/netflix-statistics-facts-figures/. Accessed on July 25, 2022.

75 Source: https://www.statista.com/statistics/250934/quarterly-number-of-netflix-streaming-subscribers-worldwide/. Accessed on July 25, 2022.

76 Source: https://www.businesswire.com/news/home/20210112005291/en/New-Survey-Shows-27-Percent-of-U.S.-Households-Plan-to-Cut-Cable-TV-Subscriptions-in-2021. Accessed on July 25, 2022.

77 Source: https://www.cordbusters.co.uk/streaming-tv-uk-more-popular-than-cable/. Accessed on July 25, 2022.

78 Source: https://www.komputerswiat.pl/aktualnosci/internet/co-piaty-polak-planuje-zrezygnowac-z-kablowki-na-rzecz-streamingu-chcemy-placic-mniej/vk67079. Accessed on July 25, 2022.

79 Source: https://panwybierak.pl/blog/netflix-od-kablowki-czy-warto/. Accessed on July 25, 2022.

from 2010 to 2016, when it became available worldwide[80] (Britannica[81]). Nevertheless, VOD technology and global impact are not the only factors that made Netflix revolutionary. Today, Netflix is known not only as a VOD service but as a production company that produces and distributes original content. Although nowadays, other VOD services such as Hulu stream their own productions too, Netflix was a pioneer in doing so, as back when the first productions were released by the company, other VOD services offered mostly television content, i.e., films and TV series that had been previously presented elsewhere, on cable TV or in cinemas, or had been available as DVDs (Jenner 2014). *House of Cards*, the first season of which was released in 2013, was the first Netflix original production, and today, as of April 2022, over 1,500 titles (out of over 17,000 titles available across the world in Netflix's library) are so-called Netflix originals (Comparitech). Currently, the company's original content constitutes its focal point, and the worldwide success of Netflix and its original productions would not be possible without proper localization. Most Netflix originals, unlike some other content available in the Netflix library, are translated into many languages[82]. For instance, the blockbuster TV series *Stranger Things* was dubbed into nine languages and subtitled in 22, including Hebrew, Thai, and Korean, among others (Quartz[83]).

---

80 As of the time of writing this dissertation, Netflix is not available in Syria, North Korea, China, Russia, or Crimea (source: https://help.netflix.com/fr/node/14164. Accessed on July 25, 2022).

81 Source: https://www.britannica.com/topic/Netflix-Inc. Accessed on July 25, 2022.

82 Nonetheless, with Netflix productions often being based on other productions (e.g., *He's All That*, the 2021 remake of the 1999 *She's All That* and the TV series *Lucifer*, whose first three seasons were produced by Fox, with later seasons by Netflix), a question that may arise is the continuity of translation. In theory, this issue should be solved by either employing the same translator who worked on the original version to work on the remake or sequel (which is rarely the case), or by adding proper annotations for the translator. The same issue applies to TV series for which the continuity of terminology throughout episodes is essential. For instance, if in a TV series there is a restaurant one can enter only by saying a secret sentence (a unique pragmateme), and this situation is repeated in different episodes, the sentence should be translated the same every time; otherwise, there is no continuity. While one can certainly think of examples of lack of continuity either in TV series and films and their remakes or in sequels, more research is needed to discuss it as a phenomenon.

83 Source: https://qz.com/1107696/how-netflix-translated-stranger-things-so-it-worked-globally/. Accessed on July 25, 2022.

While the shift started by Netflix largely concerns marketing, programming strategies, and viewing practices (Jenner 2014), the new technology and its impact on the approach toward AV content are also crucial elements of the phenomenon of the platform's influence. Therefore, this dissertation will not describe practices that appeared in relation to VOD services, such as binge-watching, however interesting they may seem (for more on that topic, see, for example: Jenner 2018, Osur 2016). Instead, the technology aspect will now be described in more detail, especially how Netflix changed AVT practices.

Ever since the worldwide expansion of Netflix and its original productions, AVT has been at the center of Netflix's attention. In 2019, 63 percent of Netflix subscribers were located outside of the US (Iqbal 2020). With the massive amount of available content, the growing need for AVT and media localization services is evident. Due to Netflix's transnational strategy, all Netflix originals have to be translated before the first broadcast, which is always on the same date all over the world (Jenner 2018). This strategy not only creates an immense amount of new content to be translated but also puts pressure on when the translation has to be completed. As a result, the industry has been experiencing "the shortage of talent"[84], so much so that in 2017, Netflix launched the first-ever test for media translation professionals via an online platform called Hermes. The purpose of Hermes was to employ professional freelance translators who would ensure good subtitling quality. The idea behind the platform was to address the problem that in the case of working with third parties, i.e., localization vendors (as Netflix had done before), it was possible to "measure the company's success through metrics like rejection rates, on-time rates, etc.", but it was not possible to "measure the individual" (Netflix Technology Blog)[85], while with a standardized test, Netflix could work with individuals and match specific projects to them according to their results. The test's main advantage was that it was supposed to be highly scalable and not replicable thanks to thousands of question

[84] According to Jim Bottoms, Europe Executive Director at MESA, "[g]iven the way the market is growing, there are already capacity shortages and this is likely to get worse in the short term." Source: https://slator.com/talent-crunch-hits-media-localization-as-amazon-netflix-accelerate-market-growth/. Accessed on July 25, 2022.

[85] Source: https://netflixtechblog.com/the-netflix-hermes-test-quality-subtitling-at-scale-dccea2682aef. Accessed on July 25, 2022.

combinations. Hermes checked the participants' knowledge of English, and their ability to translate idioms, identify errors, and produce well-made subtitles (ibid). Therefore, not only were the participants' translation abilities tested, but so too were their skills in using industry-standard software and ability to work under pressure, since a specific time was given to complete each test task (Jenner 2018). However, the platform was closed one year after its launch, in 2018, with Netflix claiming that the great response all over the world had permitted the company to reach its capacity for all of the sought language pairs. Some time later, a Netflix representative admitted that the company had overestimated its own ability to train such a large number of translators (Bond 2018). Today, Netflix continues to work both with freelance translators and localization vendors.

Despite the fact that Netflix's AVT landscape features dubbing, voice-over, and subtitling (as well as audio description, closed captions, and SDH subtitles in terms of MA), the present thesis will now focus on the last mode, since subtitles constitute the focal point of this research. For all of the AVT modes featured on Netflix, the company provides detailed guidelines for its vendors. They are available and open to the public on the Netflix Partner Help Center website[86]. The guidelines for written texts are called "Timed Text Style Guides" (TTSG), and apart from the general TTSG, there are separate guidelines concerning subtitle templates (this topic will be elaborated on further in this subsection), subtitling timing, and supplementals and marketing assets. Furthermore, there are separate guidelines for 47 languages (as of July 2022) that are considered supplementary to the general file.

Before further discussing Netflix's TTSG, a short introduction to AVT norms and guidelines may be made. As described by Toury (1995) and later further developed by Hermans (1999), norms are recurring patterns of behavior and the values or ideas behind them that are shared by a community. In translation, as in everyday life, norms guide decision-making so that communication can be successful. Norms can be codified by a local authority, as in the case of the British Ofcom norm, or by international bodies, as in ISO EN 17100 (Pedersen 2020). Guidelines, on the other hand, "can be defined

86 Source: https://partnerhelp.netflixstudios.com/. Accessed on July 25, 2022.

as the document that sets out the norms that govern the behaviour of practitioners in a community, be it a country, a company[87], or those working for a certain commissioner or client" (Pedersen 2020: 419). In short, guidelines are expressions of norms. Norms and guidelines develop over time and change along with cultural and technological development. However, it seems that a significant shift in norm perspective was caused by the appearance and growing popularity of VOD platforms. As Pedersen (ibid) notes, VOD norms are usually based on guidelines for English captioning, which, among other things, favor higher reading speeds, which may impact the reception of subtitles in countries where viewers are not used to reading subtitles. Nonetheless, the one-size-fits-all solutions first adopted by booming VOD companies seem to be changing as constant updates are gradually being added to local norms, as is the case with Netflix (Pedersen 2018).

As for Netflix's general TTSGs, they are to be followed[88] by all translators who work for Netflix (either as freelancers or via official vendors). The most important general instructions stipulate, among other things: line treatment (2 lines maximum) and how they should be broken, subtitle duration (between 5/6 of a second and 7 seconds per subtitle event), and positioning[89]. Furthermore, Netflix is open to developing its guidelines, as under every TTSG, both general and local, there is a detailed change log and a button allowing translators (or apparently any person affiliated with Netflix) to provide feedback on particular guidelines.

In his paper on AVT norms and guidelines, Pedersen (2020: 417) calls describing the norms of every country and every company a "Herculean task" and a "Sisyphus job" since norms and guidelines are subject to change.

---

87 While guidelines are proper to a smaller entity, it is worth mentioning attempts to create universal standards such as the *Code of Good Subtitling Practice* (Ivarsson and Caroll 1998) or *A Proposed Set of Subtitling Standards in Europe* (Karamitroglou 1998), and national standards such as the Danish *Retningslinjer for undertekstning i Danmark* (Bjerre Rosa and Øveraas 2019).

88 Whether the guidelines are actually followed in practice is a question on its own. While "a brief scan" done by Pedersen (2018: 97) suggests that they are, extensive research on the subject is lacking.

89 Source: https://partnerhelp.netflixstudios.com/hc/en-us/articles/215758617-Timed-Text-Style-Guide-General-Requirements. Accessed on July 25, 2022.

Similarly, this thesis cannot discuss all particular guidelines suggested by Netflix. It would be both irrelevant to the conducted research and possibly inapplicable in the future due to the fact that guidelines may change. Nonetheless, since the research conducted in this thesis focuses on French and Polish as TLs, a closer look at the TTSGs of these languages may prove to be useful in the analysis. Therefore, Table 4 presents a quantitative comparison of French and Polish TTSGs.

Table 4. Quantitative analysis of French and Polish TTSGs[90].

	French	Polish
Length (number of words)	2,894	2,258
Number of subsections	24	22
Number of updates (from 15th May 2016 until July 2022)	46	29
Presence of target language (TL) examples	Yes	Yes

Both TTSGs are structured similarly. However, the French TTSG is a little bit longer than the Polish one, both in the word count and the number of subsections. The main differences can be observed in the much longer abbreviation section in the French TTSG, and that in the French version guidelines for the translation of brand names has a separate subsection (in the Polish TTSG, equivalent information appears as a bullet point in the "Special Instructions" subsection). Furthermore, the French TTSG devotes a whole subsection to female forms of job titles and professional functions, whereas this matter is nowhere treated in the Polish TTSG, despite the fact that feminative forms are also considered a relevant topic in Polish linguistics (see e.g., Szpyra-Kozłowska 2020, Latos 2020, Tomala 2021). More changes have also been added to the French TTSG; however, this can be explained by Pedersen's (2018) argument that the more common the TL is, the more active users providing feedback to the TTSG will there be; hence more changes to the guidelines.[90]

[90] Based on: https://partnerhelp.netflixstudios.com/hc/en-us/articles/216787928-Polish-Timed-Text-Style-Guide, https://partnerhelp.netflixstudios.com/hc/en-us/articles/217351577-French-Timed-Text-Style-Guide. Both accessed on July 25, 2022.

Interestingly, with regard to how TTSGs are divided between languages, it seems that "the company focuses more on linguistic differences than on national norms" (Pedersen 2018: 92). This is observable in the French TTSG, where references to Canadian French appear twice: first, in the guidelines for translation of brand names, and second, in the subsection on punctuation. Nonetheless, in some cases, separate TTSGs are devoted to different language variations (e.g., Brazilian and European Portuguese).

Lastly, both in the French and Polish TTSGs the maximum number of characters per subtitle event is 42 (as is the case in all TTSGs besides Japanese, Korean, Russian, Simplified and Traditional Chinese, and Thai). Reading speed[91] is also considered to be the same: 17 characters per second (cps) for adult programs and 13 cps for children's programs. These guidelines have been considered particularly debatable both by AVT scholars and by practitioners. For instance, Krzysztof Kowalczyk, the vice president of the Polish Association of Audiovisual Translators (Stowarzyszenie Tłumaczy Audiowizualnych, STAW), interviewed for the purpose of this thesis, claims that even subtitles that exceed the required reading speed (up to 22 cps) are often allowed, which, if done by an unskilled translator, may result in a translation that contains all, often including unnecessary, information from the dialogue, and that may be particularly strenuous to read. He then notes the difference between Netflix's and national norms (in Poland, the established norm for a subtitle event is 14-15 cps). Furthermore, Romero-Fresco (2015) estimates that with a reading speed of 17-18 cps, viewers focus primarily on subtitles (80% time spent on text) and not so much on the image, which may affect the overall reception of the AV content. However, a newer study done by Szarkowska and Gerber-Morón (2018) does not confirm Romero-Fresco's claim. On the contrary, in their study, which used eye-tracking and participant questionnaires as methods, Szarkowska and Gerber-Morón found that not only do viewers seem to adjust their reading to the speed of the subtitles but also that their enjoyment is generally higher when subtitles come faster.

91 While the term "reading speed" is commonly used (including in Netflix guidelines), some scholars such as Díaz-Cintas (2020) suggest "subtitle display rate" to be a more accurate term since it is not the viewer's reading speed being measured but rather the maximum rate that a subtitle event should not exceed.

Purposely absent from the discussion above is the use of templates, which may constitute a separate topic on its own. According to Netflix's Subtitle Template Timed Text Style Guide, a template "is an edited, positioned, researched, annotated and checked subtitle file, timed to shot and audio, matching the SL of the associated content (unless it is a pivot file) which is intended to serve as a basis for downstream interlingual subtitling."[92] In short, templates are properly prepared SL bases for further translation into multiple TLs. They are to contain not only SL text but also time stamps and annotations explaining important contextual information such as jokes and puns, relationships between characters, spatial coordinates, cultural references, and nuances, among other factors. For instance, heavily culture-based pragmatemes like the Polish *95 do pełna, proszę* (lit. *95 full tank, please*, with "95" meaning the most popular type of petrol used in Poland) should be carefully annotated in templates[93]. With these technicalities in mind, one can trace back the origins of templates to dialogue lists which generally include dialogue exchanges but may also include annotations (Díaz-Cintas 2001), which are simple text files, unlike timed and segmented template files which are in a subtitle format.

Even though templates have been in use for around thirty years now, as the practice is believed to have begun with the rise of the DVD in the mid-1990s (Oziemblewska and Szarkowska 2020), they are still subject to debate among AVT scholars and practitioners. Some praise the advantages of templates: they help to meet the enormous demand of the market for subtitles in a reduced time, cost-effective manner, facilitate quality control, and increase safety in regard to piracy concerns (Georgakopoulou, 2006). Georgakopoulou (2019: 137) even goes on to call templates "the Holy Grail of subtitling" and "one of the greatest innovations in the subtitling industry at the turn of the century." But despite many apparent advantages, subtitlers generally seem to blame templates for both lowering fees in the industry and reducing the quality of subtitling, as shown by Szarkowska in her 2016 study. Another common

---

92 Source: https://partnerhelp.netflixstudios.com/hc/en-us/articles/219375728-Timed-Text-Style-Guide-Subtitle-Templates. Accessed on July 25, 2022.

93 While it is certain that pragmatemes with a strong cultural base should be noticed and annotated in templates, it should be further investigated whether also annotating other types of pragmatemes (e.g., of idiomatic meaning) would be worthwhile.

practice subject to even greater scrutiny is pivot translation, i.e., translating non-English content through an intermediary language, most often English, templates into other languages. According to Netflix, "[a] Pivot Language Dialogue List (PLDL) will be commissioned for any content for which the source language is not English."[94] The scope of using English templates for translating originally non-English content has not been widely investigated; however, preliminary research on the topic suggests that the majority of non-English content is now translated through English into other languages. For instance, a study done by Dallı (2023) found that only 2 percent of Korean dramas available on Netflix were translated into Turkish by subtitlers specializing in Korean. The rest did not specify Korean in the language pairs they work with. Therefore, the author concludes that "pivot subtitling is more than just a practice; it is *the* practice" (ibid: 97). On Netflix, pivot language templates have their own guidelines in order to ensure quality. Like regular templates, they are mandated to be timed, positioned, and carefully annotated. In this case, annotations are particularly important due to distortions that may be introduced by the language change, as Netflix's guidelines explain: "for example, always ensure you add context and explain as much as possible about the source language file so that the Polish translation represents the Japanese in an equivalent way, not the English pivot file."[95] Nonetheless, research has shown it not to be wholly effective. Studies done by both Oziemblewska and Szarkowska (2020) and Dallı (2023) reveal that annotations are scarce in pivot templates, and if they are present, they tend to comment on the obvious instead of explaining language and contextual differences in detail (for instance, one respondent in Oziemblewska and Szarkowska's study shared the following example of an unnecessary annotation: "Vietnam: a country in Asia" [Oziemblewska and Szarkowska 2020: 17]). Dallı then presents the possible effects of poorly annotated (or completely unannotated) pivot templates, with changes in politeness being an example.

---

94 Source: https://partnerhelp.netflixstudios.com/hc/en-us/articles/360001610707-Legacy-Workflow-Pivot-Language-Dialogue-List-SOW. Accessed on July 25, 2022.

95 Source: https://partnerhelp.netflixstudios.com/hc/en-us/articles/219375728-Timed-Text-Style-Guide-Subtitle-Templates#h_01EXJ1B1VSKZP6HAM6SW1F480V. Accessed on July 25, 2022.

No matter the opinion on the use of templates, it is clear that they "became the cornerstone for the globalisation of the subtitling industry" (Georgakopoulou, 2019: 137) and are now "an inseparable part of modern subtitling workflows" (Oziemblewska and Szarkowska 2020: 1). While Oziemblewska and Szarkowska (2020) argue against the use of pivot templates, Dallı suggests that mistakes could be avoided should the annotations be comprehensive and subject to extensive quality control. In all, one could say that today, well-made templates are key to well-made subtitles, as in 2001 "the provision of good dialogue list [made] the difference between a high-quality product and an inferior one" (Díaz-Cintas 2001: 200).

Finally, as mentioned previously, Netflix and technology are two inseparable terms. The technological advance in AVT has always been prompted by the appearance of new film technology, such as VOD services. In terms of subtitling, the advance is visible in the development of new subtitling software, particularly cloud-based (Díaz-Cintas and Massidda 2019). Cloud-based systems, although in use since the late 1990s (Bolaños-García-Escribano and Díaz-Cintas 2020), are becoming more and more popular for AVT. Believed to have started with YouTube's online caption feature launched in 2008 (ibid), subtitling[96] cloud-based systems now offer a plethora of professional features and range from commercial, such as OOONA, to proprietary, such as Netflix Originator[97] (Bolaños García-Escribano 2021). In the cloud, not only can subtitling be done, but so can proofreading, quality control, and post-production, thanks to features such as managing system, burning subtitles and images, sharing one's translation with other entities, and (semi-) automated technical and linguistic checks (Díaz-Cintas and Massidda 2019). What is interesting is that although computer-assisted translation (CAT) tools are still not widespread in AVT, some cloud-based systems managed

---

96 While this thesis focuses on subtitling, it has to be stressed that cloud-based systems are now being implemented for other AVT modes as well, e.g., ZOO's Cloud Dubbing (Bolaños-García-Escribano and Díaz-Cintas 2020).

97 Kowalczyk (2021, interview) said that not all subtitlers are obliged to work with Netflix Originator (however, if they do, they are bound to work with templates). Some subtitlers who prepare subtitles for Netflix via national vendors still work on provided dialogue lists or prepare translation by ear, all of which may influence the quality of the final translation product.

to implement CAT tools such as translation memories (TMs) and glossaries; however, there is still a lot to be done in terms of integrating CAT tools into subtitling software (ibid, Díaz-Cintas 2022). What is more, the machine translation (MT) feature has been part of subtitling software for some time now. Despite the rather unsuccessful attempts at applying MT to subtitling in the first decade of the millennium, such as the MUSA (MUltilingual Subtlitling of multimediA content) project and the later SUMAT (An Online Service for SUbtitling by MAchine Translation) project (Bolaños-García-Escribano and Díaz-Cintas 2020), MT is now an integral part of some AVT tools, starting from desktop software such as Subtitle Edit version 3.5.7, which uses automatic translation, through Google engines (Díaz-Cintas and Massidda 2019), to cloud-based tools such as OOONA, which allows its users to machine-translate their templates with Amazon Translate, and Netflix Originator, which bases its MT on its own engine. However, while these tools are available for subtitlers to use, it is uncertain how many of them actually make use of them in their projects. In the aforementioned interview with Kowalczyk (2021), he observed that while vendors around the world insist on using MT, it is still an uncommon practice when the TL is neither a schematic nor a highly-resourced one, such as Polish[98]. Therefore, to fully understand the quality of the final product, one would have to take into consideration how exactly the subtitles are prepared and what the further quality control process looks like. To do this, more research on industry practices around the world is needed.

2.5 Subtitling translation techniques

In Translation Studies (TS), terms such as translation strategy, technique, method, and procedure coexist. There are many ways of defining these terms, and some of them are often used interchangeably (see, for instance, Hatim and Munday 2004). *Encyclopedia of Translation Studies* (Baker and Saldanha 2009: 282) speaks only of translation *strategy* and notes the disagreements

[98] Nonetheless, the widespread use of MT in AVT seems to be a matter of time. Therefore, Díaz-Cintas and Massidda (2019: 1) suggest that "[t]o be successful in this ecosystem, translators need to adapt and adjust to the new changes so that they can harness state-of-the-art technologies to their advantage rather than risking being replaced by them."

concerning its precise definition, adding that "a variety of other terms can be used to mean the same thing." Meanwhile, the dictionary of Polish translational terminology ([SPTP], Bogucki et al. 2019) distinguishes translation strategies (with a comment that this term is often ambiguous and used interchangeably with notions such as *technique* and *procedure*) and translation procedures (or techniques, treated synonymously). While a lot more can be said about various ideas on these notions, due to the spatial limitations of the present thesis, it is important to present and follow one approach.

According to Tardzenyuy (2016: 48), translation strategy is a holistic, pre-translation decision "that is taken by the translator before engaging in the actual translation." This definition is close to the one of a global strategy proposed by Hejwowski (2004), who distinguishes between global and local strategies, describing the former as applicable to the entire text or significant passages and the latter as applicable to individual issues encountered in the translation process. SPTP (Bogucki et al. 2019: 123) adds that before the global translation decision is taken, the translator has to specify a number of factors, including the text type, its recipients, and goals (as well as the recipients and goals of the translation). SPTP (ibid) distinguishes two main translation strategies: foreignization and domestication, as famously proposed by Venuti (1995), who was inspired by Schleiermacher (1813). The first strategy consists of keeping unfamiliar elements of the source culture in the translation, and therefore "sending the reader abroad" (Venuti 1995: 20), while the second suggests eliminating these elements from the translation, "bringing the author back home" (ibid)[99]. A third strategy noted by SPTP (2019) consists in a compromise of the first two: it is called neutralization and aims at the substitution of foreign elements by more universal ones.

In contrast, translation technique is not a holistic but "a practical method by which a translation strategy is operationalized" (Tardzenyuy 2016: 48). Therefore, translation techniques do not apply to the text as a whole but are used when a translator is faced with a particular translational dilemma

99 It has to be noted that Venuti's approach to the proposed strategies was not neutral; rather, he considered them to be an ethical issue which may impact the power balance between the source and the target culture. For more information on Venuti's approach and criticism of it, see, for example, Myskja (2013).

(Bogucki et al. 2019), and so correspond to the *local strategy* in Hejwowski's (2004) terminology. Having briefly defined these terms, from now on, in this thesis, the term *translation strategy* will be used to refer to the holistic decision made before the translation process itself begins, while *translation technique* will refer to particular choices made to solve specific translational challenges, even when other authors use different terminology in their works, in order to avoid confusion (for a more extensive discussion on translation procedures, techniques, and strategies, see, for example, Gil-Bardají 2009).

In the field of TS, many typologies of translation techniques have been presented, but Vinay and Darbelnet are considered pioneers in this subject. In 1958, they published their *Stylistique comparée du français et de l'anglais*, a contrastive linguistics piece on French and English usage, which presented "the first classification of translation techniques that had a clear methodological purpose" (Molina and Hurtado, 2002: 499). According to Vinay and Darbelnet, translation challenges could be solved with the use of seven techniques (or *procedures* in their terminology): borrowing, calque, literal translation, transposition, modulation, equivalence, and adaptation. Since it was published almost 65 years ago, Vinay and Darbelnet's classification not only has inspired a plethora of other researchers to explore the topic of translation techniques further, but also has sparked considerable discussion in the field (for more information on its criticism see, e.g., Chaves-Fernández and Sevilla-Morales 2021). In this time many other typologies have been developed, for instance, by Baker (1992), Newmark (1988), and a very detailed one suggested by Chesterman (1997), who distinguishes ten syntactic, nine semantic, and nine pragmatic techniques ('strategies' in his terminology). Taking into account the nature of subtitling and the language units studied in the present thesis, Chesterman's pragmatic techniques should be listed. These are: cultural filtering (domestication of cultural elements), explicitness change, information change (either addition or omission of information), interpersonal change (alters the formality, emotiveness, and technical lexis levels), illocutionary change (changes of speech acts), coherence change (changes in text structure), partial translation (summary, transcription, and the like), visibility change (adding elements drawing attention to the translator's presence), transediting (major rewriting or/and reordering), and other pragmatic changes, such as the choice of dialect (ibid).

An interesting take on the issue of translation techniques is presented by Molina and Hurtado Albir (2002) whose approach is dynamic and functionalist. In their definition, translation technique is seen as a materialized solution for a translation problem[100]; therefore, it operates on micro-units of a text and "affects the result of translation" (ibid: 509.) Furthermore, translation technique in this approach can only be classified by making a comparison with the ST unit, and, by nature, is discursive, contextual, and functional[101] (ibid). Unlike Vinay and Darbelnet (1958), Molina and Hurtado Albir (2002) stress that their taxonomy is characteristic to translation, not to comparing languages. They distinguish eighteen techniques (ibid[102]):

1) Adaptation – replacing a cultural element from the source culture with one present in the target culture.
2) Borrowing – incorporating an element from the SL to TL without changes or with a change in spelling.
3) Calque – translating a foreign element literally.
4) Literal translation – translating an element word for word (when "form coincides with function and meaning", ibid: 510).
5) Established equivalent – using an element generally recognized as equivalent in the TL.
6) Discursive creation – establishing "a temporary equivalence that is totally unpredictable out of context" (ibid).
7) Generalization – using a term more general in the TL.
8) Particularization – using a term more precise in the TL.
9) Description – replacing an element with its description.
10) Amplification – adding information explaining the ST element.

[100] In Molina and Hurtado Albir (2002) view, both strategies and techniques are related to problem solving in translation; however, while techniques point at the final result of translation, strategies are connected to the process of translating itself.

[101] Molina and Hurtado Albir (2002) do not evaluate techniques in terms of their appropriateness.

[102] In the original article, the techniques are presented in an alphabetical order; here, the order was changed so that similar (or likely to be confused) techniques were explained one after the other.

11) Linguistic amplification – adding linguistic elements (common in dubbing and consecutive interpreting.)
12) Linguistic compression – synthesizing linguistic elements (common in subtitling and simultaneous interpreting.)
13) Reduction – suppressing the ST element.
14) Substitution (linguistic, paralinguistic) – changing linguistic elements for paralinguistic, such as gestures or intonation (or vice versa).
15) Compensation – changing the place of an element (either a piece of information or a stylistic effect).
16) Modulation – changing the focus, point of view, or cognitive category (can be lexical or structural).
17) Transposition – changing a grammatical category.
18) Variation – affecting linguistic variation (changing tone, dialect, style, etc.)

Because, according to Molina and Hurtado Albir (2002), translation technique is "an instrument of textual analysis, that, in combination with other instruments, allows us to study how translation equivalence works in relation to the original text" (ibid: 498), this approach will be among others used to examine the translation of pragmatemes in this study (see p. 210).

What is more, it seems that in recent years, typologies of translation techniques have become more specialized and now focus on solving a particular problem rather than being considered applicable to all translational difficulties. These narrower typologies are especially important for the present thesis, as it focuses on a specific linguistic issue itself. An example of translation techniques related to particular translational difficulties is the taxonomy suggested by Hejwowski (2015), who describes separate typologies for the translation of cultural elements, linguistic allusions, and idioms. As has been presented in Chapter 1 (see p. 29), some pragmatemes are idiomatic. Therefore, Hejwowski's typology concerning the translation of idioms is particularly relevant for this research, and it consists of six techniques:

1) Use of an idiom that has the same form and meaning
2) Use of an idiom that has a similar meaning but a different form
3) Use of a non-idiomatic expression
4) Syntagmatic translation

5) Creation of a new idiom
6) Omission

While most of Hejwowski's techniques are self-explanatory, a further explanation of the use of a non-idiomatic expression and the creation of a new idiom is needed since both of these techniques suggest a solution that is not fixed in the language. Moreover, the wording "creation of a new idiom" can be controversial on its own as nobody can instantly create a unit that would meet the criteria of an idiom, i.e., be frequently used and understood in a language. However, in this concept, the non-idiomatic expression does not imitate a phraseological structure, while the new idiom imitates in one way or another an already existing idiom.

The units studied in this thesis, i.e., pragmatemes, refer to a particular culture in various degrees; they are culture-bound elements[103]. When a situation in which a pragmateme is used is typical only for the source culture and no similar reference exists in the target culture, the translator is faced with a challenge, as a "referential vacuum" (Rabadán, 1991: 164) occurs. For these cases, a few typologies have been suggested by various researchers, with the ones proposed for AVT being the most relevant for the purposes of the present thesis. Gottlieb (2009) compares three (along with his own) taxonomies of translation techniques for culture-bound elements: one designed for subtitling by Nedergaard-Larsen (1993), another one also based on a subtitling study by Pedersen (2003), and a more general one (in terms of the text type) by Leppihalme (1997). The comparison is made based on the degree of source text fidelity. To briefly present the scope of numerous ideas on translation techniques, Gottlieb's comparison is reproduced in Table 5.

The classifications enumerated above may provide a valuable insight into the translation of cultural elements; however, all of them have their limitations. Leppihalme's study (1997) is centered solely on allusions, Pedersen's (2003) techniques listed in Gottlieb (2009) are a part of an unpublished pilot study, Nedergaard-Larsen (1993) bases her conclusions on the analysis of not

103 In literature, culture-bound elements are also called cultural references, realia, or ECRs, i.e., extralinguistic cultural-bound references (Díaz-Cintas and Remael 2007).

Table 5. The comparison of translation techniques related to the translation of culture-bound elements; reproduced from Gottlieb (2009: 3)

	Nedergaard-Larsen (1993)	**Leppihalme (1997)**	**Pedersen (2003)**	**Gottlieb (2009)**
Maximum fidelity	Identity	Retention	Non-translation	Retention
		Retention with explicitation	Explicitation	
High fidelity	Imitation Direct translation		Literal translation	Literal translation
Low fidelity	Explicitation Paraphrase	Replacement by SL element	Generalisation	Specification
				Generalisation
	Situational adaptation Cultural adaptation	Replacement by TL element	Cultural substitution	Substitution
Minimum fidelity	Omission	Omission with sense transfer Total omission	Omission	Omission

more than four films, and Gottlieb (2009: 32) himself notes that the numbers of examples included in his study are "indeed rather small." Therefore, the nine techniques for cultural references in subtitling proposed by Díaz-Cintas and Remael (2007: 202-207) will be now further elaborated on, as this classification is based on extensive studies made by Díaz-Cintas (2003) and Santamaria Guinot (2001).

1) Loan – full incorporation of the source text unit into the TL and text when no translation exists in the TL (e.g., *spaghetti*).
2) Calque – literal translation; this may be problematic due to technical constraints, which often do not allow for any further explanation of foreign concepts even if those are needed (unlike the possibility of explaining in brackets or footnotes in other text types).
3) Explicitation – "meeting the target audience half way" (ibid: 203), specifying (with a hyponym) or generalizing (with a hypernym or superordinate), with the latter being a much more frequent choice; in some cases, translation may also be a form of explicitation.
4) Substitution – type of explicitation occurring when despite the existence of an equivalent term in the target culture, a hypernym or a hyponym is used due to spatial constraints (e.g., *goulash* and *stew*).
5) Transposition – replacing the source culture concept with a target culture concept, used when other techniques are not possible either because of the likelihood of lack of understanding or because of spatial limitations; produces best results when the two concepts are not very different so that the two cultures do not clash in the oral-visual realm of TL subtitles and SL audio.
6) Lexical recreation – inventing a neologism, especially when one is created in the source text.
7) Compensation – in case of translational loss, overtranslation or addition is done in another place in translation.
8) Omission – sometimes necessary due to either space limitations or terminology.
9) Addition – another form of explicitation; done if the lack of understanding of a passage may cause serious problems to understanding a program as a whole.

Apart from the application of Molina and Hurtado Albir's (2002) techniques typology, in the present research, translations of the pragmatemes occurring in the corpus will be analyzed from the point of view of the last taxonomy since it is based on practical research and suitable to analysis of pragmatemes considered as cultural elements. Furthermore, pragmatemes will also be analyzed with the account of Hejwowski's typology since their meaning may be idiomatic. Both of the classifications seem complementary, with one referring to extra-linguistic notions of culture, and the other to the linguistic layer; however, it is hypothesized that a separate classification, tailored for the translation of pragmatemes in subtitling, will be needed. In that case, a new classification will be proposed in the analytical part (see p. 234).

What is more, both Hejwowski's (2015) and Díaz-Cintas and Remael's (2007) classifications refer to lexical units, which recalls the discussion on pragmatemes as translation units (see p. 77). However, since the SL of the translations analyzed in this research is English, it should be noted, as also discussed by Gottlieb (2009: 27), that "[e]specially when translating works from a dominant culture, it may be difficult to determine whether a certain element is specific to that culture, or whether it is well-known in the target community", and therefore, a large number of pragmatemes, despite being cultural elements, may not "constitute a translation problem because both the source and target cultures belong to the same cultural macrosystem (the West)" (Lorenzo et al. 2003: 289) and be simply preserved in translation, which, on the other hand, may raise questions regarding comprehensibility of subtitles and prominence of English (Díaz-Cintas and Remael 2007).

Chapters 1 and 2 provided the theoretical foundation necessary for this study, covering the topic of pragmatemes and situating it within the formulaic language research, as well as addressing translation techniques and audiovisual translation, particularly subtitling. Building on the discussions from these chapters, Chapter 3 will now present a detailed description of the methods used in this research.

Methods

In order to study pragmatemes, sufficient, homogeneous linguistic material has to be gathered. Therefore, this section is devoted to the methods behind the collection of pragmatemes for further contrastive and translational analysis. Firstly, it is described how the corpus is chosen and gathered. Then the search of pragmatemes within the corpus, which implies the use of a list of units prepared in advance, is discussed. Finally, the description of the tables of pragmatemes and their translations, which will be the basis for the analysis, is provided.

3.1 Preparing the corpus

As this study aims to focus on pragmatemes that are uttered in everyday life[104], the linguistic material for the analysis has to be carefully chosen to represent real-life language[105]. However, before the gathered material is discussed in detail, it should be noted why the methods offered by corpus linguistics were selected to be used in this research.

Corpus linguistics is "the study of language based on examples of real-life language use" (McEnery & Wilson 2001: 1), which utilizes large numbers of electronically encoded texts of different modes and genres. Thanks to the use of electronic means in the analysis, complex calculations can be carried out. Therefore, it is possible to move away from the studying particular instances in isolation and to study many similar texts at once, thanks to which actually

104 This study focuses on the everyday language prevalent among the general population, deliberately avoiding any examinations of sociolects (language unique to specific social groups), professiolects (language unique to specific professional groups), or idiolects (language unique to individuals). However, pragmatemes examined in this thesis might also constitute a part of a discourse not typical in everyday interactions, but rather prevalent across all people, such as the language used in courtrooms.

105 For the discussion on the limitation of studying real-life language in this thesis see p. 268.

occurring data can be reflected on, repetitive linguistic patterns can be identified, hidden meanings can be uncovered, and sounder generalizations can be made, among other characteristics that could not be revealed by analyzing a single text (Baker 2006, Bruti 2020). Because in corpus linguistics, an enormous amount of data is analyzed, accusations of *armchair linguistics*, such as the one that intuitive hypothesizing is not reliable, can be avoided (Fillmore 1992). Nonetheless, the quantitative results of corpus investigations should not exist in a void either; in the words of Fillmore (1992: 1), "the two kinds of linguists [i.e., one who works with a corpus and one who speculates] need each other, [o]r better, (…) the two kinds of linguists, wherever possible, should exist in the same body." That is why corpus examinations should always be followed by some manual processing. This way, examples that one could miss on their own can be found through computer processing, while important judgments (e.g., the intended cognitive experience of the reader; ibid) which do not directly stem from the corpus alone can be made.

Within corpus linguistics, two main approaches can be distinguished: corpus-based and corpus-driven. In the first, hypotheses and theoretical claims are made before conducting the study, and corpus data are used to verify them (Tognini-Bonelli 2001), making it a deductive approach, while in the second, observation of corpus data "leads to a hypothesis, which in turn leads to the generalization in terms of rules of usage and finally finds unification in a theoretical statement" (ibid: 17), which makes it an inductive approach. While it may seem that these two approaches are direct opposites, Bruti (2020: 383) notes that the distinction has recently become subtler and that "in actual facts, many studies merge them, often starting from corpus-driven reflections and moving on to corpus-based investigations." However, in some fields, one approach may be more frequently used than in others; for instance, in AVT, the majority of studies are corpus-based (researchers investigate corpora to examine the translation of a particular phenomenon or a set phrase; ibid).

According to Baker (2006), methods of analyzing corpora have been in use since the nineteenth century, with the earliest corpora being analyzed manually in the absence of computer technology (e.g., an 11 million word German corpus by Käding 1897), but it is with the general availability of personal computers in the 1980s that studies utilizing corpus-based approaches became truly popular, so much so that nowadays, “the centrality of corpora to contemporary lexicography, Natural Language Processing and European linguistics at least is undeniable” (Kenny 2006: 45). Apart from dictionary creation, corpus methods have been used in many areas of linguistic research such as language description (e.g., Sinclair 1991), interpretation of literary texts (e.g., Louw 1997), and language teaching (e.g., Johns 1988), among others. Corpus linguistics has also been useful for TS (following in Baker’s [1993] footsteps, e.g., Kenny 2001b) and AVTS (e.g., Bywood et al. 2013).

Furthermore, according to Kenny (2006: 46), “a (semi-) automatically searchable corpus of electronic texts is the ideal resource to use” if one is studying highly predictable units of a significant frequency, which pragmatemes are. However, the pragmatemes studied in this dissertation are in the majority a part of everyday conversations[106], and while large written-text corpora are widely available in many languages, gathering naturally occurring data that would represent real-life conversations has never been an easy task, which results in a much smaller number of available spoken corpora (Mikhailov, Tommola, and Isolahti 2010). While corpora of transcripts of conversations recorded in informal settings do exist (e.g., Spoken British National Corpus 2014 [Brezina et al. 2018], *Spokes* search engine for Polish conversational data [Pęzik 2014]), compiling such corpora is time-consuming and expensive, and it is also connected to privacy and naturalness issues: to make a transcript of a spoken conversation, one has to ask for permission from all the parties involved to be able to record them, and because of that, the participants may behave differently than they would if they were not aware of being recorded, which is known as the observer’s paradox (Gut 2020). That is why spoken corpora often consist not only of actual everyday conversations but also of “transcripts of interviews, movie and television scripts, subtitles downloaded from DVDs, etc.” (Kitao 2012: 53).

In spoken corpora, the majority of the material is collected from various interviews and speeches broadcast on television (ibid), which do not necessarily demonstrate how pragmatemes are used in everyday conversation. Furthermore, because this study focuses on three languages, English,

106 See Footnote no. 104.

French, and Polish, and translations from English to French and Polish, the corpora in these languages have to be comparable in size and content. To study the translations, it would be preferable for the corpora to be not just parallel corpora (understood here as corpora containing comparable texts[107]), but rather corpora with actual translations of the source texts. Due to the unavailability of such specific corpora (to my best knowledge), I decided to gather them on my own.

The corpora of this thesis were gathered from captions (ST subtitles) and subtitles (translations) of TV series. TV series available on Netflix were chosen for multiple reasons, including these: firstly, the importance of Netflix in the landscape of VOD platforms (for more on this topic, see Subsection 2.4, p. 103), secondly, the availability and accessibility of the newest productions with official translations into many languages (which is not something one can be sure of when using other subtitle corpora such as OpenSubtitles[108]), and thirdly, the possibility of quick corpus building using Language Reactor (LR). LR, formerly known as Learning Languages with Netflix[109], is a tool (as of today, an extension only for the desktop version of Google Chrome) independent from the Netflix company, that allows its users to display content on Netflix with two lines of subtitles in two different languages simultaneously (and in its premium version, with three lines of subtitles, one of these being machine translated subtitles in a chosen language[110]).

107 As Lefer (2020: 257-258) notes, the term *parallel corpora* "is sometimes used to refer to comparable texts in two or more languages, especially texts that belong to comparable genres or text types and deal with similar topics", acknowledging the existing ambiguity of the term, which can be also used to refer to corpora that include source-texts aligned with their translations.

108 Source: https://www.opensubtitles.org/, accessed on December 27, 2022. Furthermore, in comparison to OpenSubtitles, building a corpus based on Netflix content allows the researcher to look into the visual layer of the analyzed material, while OpenSubtitles contain only subtitle text files.

109 Source: https://languagelearningwithnetflix.com/, accessed on December 27, 2022.

110 While the human translations displayed by LR are the official ones provided by Netflix, the machine translated subtitles are provided by LR; however, it is unclear whether LR developers use an already existing machine translation engine or whether they created their own: I have tried contacting the LR team on this matter many times, but, unfortunately, without a response.

After rebranding in the summer of 2021, the software provides new features separate from Netflix, such as displaying simultaneous lines of subtitles in different languages on YouTube, adding machine-translated subtitles to your own video, having any text machine translated and read out loud, and learning foreign language phrases with *PhrasePump* exercises, among others (see Figure 2). The purpose behind all LR's features is to facilitate learning foreign languages in an engaging and enjoyable manner, which is reflected in users' opinions[111].

However, for the present research, only one feature of this tool is crucial: the export of captions and subtitles into text files.[112] Once the LR extension has been installed, two main buttons are added in the Netflix display window: the purple LR button at the bottom of the page that allows the user to choose the language of subtitles, turn on machine translation, slow down or speed

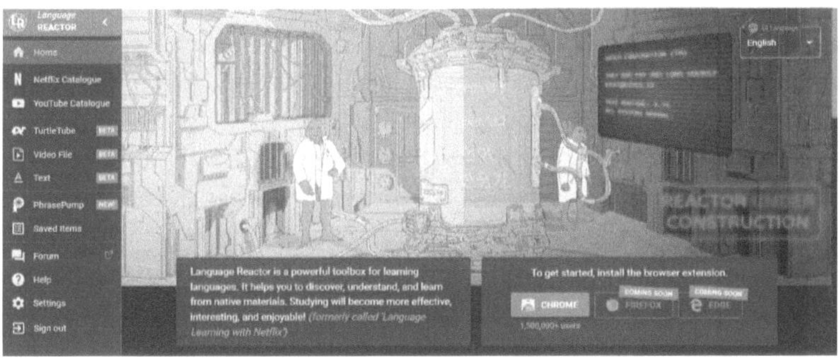

Figure 2. A screenshot of the main LR page, with its key features on the left panel[112]

---

111 See, for instance: https://chrome.google.com/webstore/detail/language-reactor/hoombieeljmmljlkjmnheibnpciblicm. Thanks to multiple features of the tool, users often share their own ways of using LR on the tool's forum (https://forum.languagelearningwithnetflix.com/) and elsewhere, which I discussed in detail in my presentation *Nauka języków obcych przy użyciu dwujęzycznych napisów do filmu* (Eng. *Learning Foreign Languages with the Use of Bilingual Subtitles*) at the *Języki obce – klucz do dialogu* (Eng. *Foreing Languages – Key to Dialogue*) conference organized by the Silesian University of Technology on the 19th November 2021.

112 Source of the screenshot: own. Source of the page: https://www.languagereactor.com/, accessed on December 27, 2022.

Figure 3. A screenshot presenting the updated Netflix display with LR turned on[113]

up the watched content, change the font of the subtitles, among many other things, and the sidebar that allows the user to follow the chosen captions or subtitles one after the other in the form of a list. The updated Netflix display with LR extension is presented in Figure 3.

It is in the sidebar that the export feature is available. Upon clicking on the right arrow located in the upper-hand right corner of the sidebar, the export window is displayed and the user is allowed to download subtitles in two languages (and, in the premium version, also with machine translation), with or without timestamps, and with or without highlighting of saved words (if the user is signed up and has saved any words to remember) into an Excel file or a print-ready HTML page (which can later be saved, for example, as a PDF file). Figure 4 shows the export window.

Because in the later stage of the research, the corpus will be analyzed with the use of corpus linguistics software that can analyze only .txt files, each episode was downloaded as a separate Excel file (see Figure 5) with the use of LR, and then the captions from the second column of the Excel files were copy-pasted into Notepad++ to create a single .txt file that contained captions from all the TV series in a given language. These .txt files (one for the English corpus, one for the French, and one for the Polish) could then

[113] Source: own.

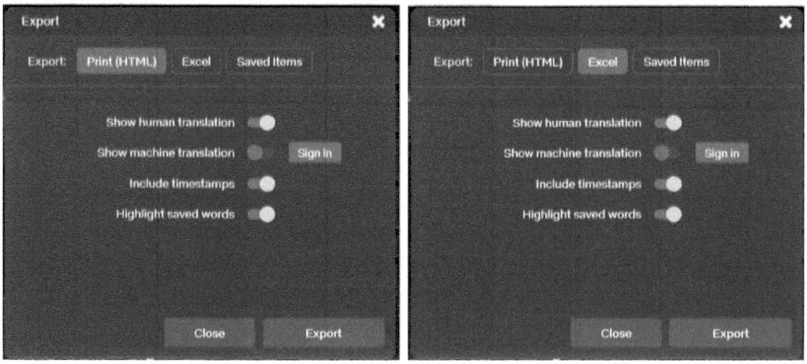

Figure 4. A screenshot presenting the export feature of LR[114]

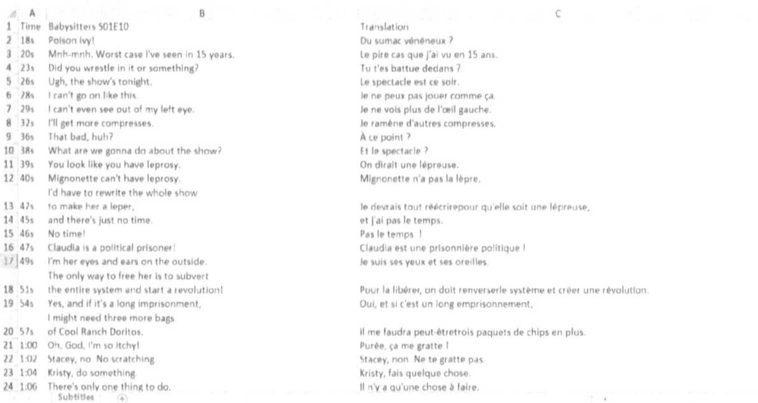

	A	B	C
1	Time	Babysitters S01E10	Translation
2	18s	Poison ivy!	Du sumac vénéneux ?
3	20s	Mnh-mnh. Worst case I've seen in 15 years.	Le pire cas que j'ai vu en 15 ans.
4	23s	Did you wrestle in it or something?	Tu t'es battue dedans ?
5	26s	Ugh, the show's tonight.	Le spectacle est ce soir.
6	28s	I can't go on like this.	Je ne peux pas jouer comme ça.
7	29s	I can't even see out of my left eye.	Je ne vois plus de l'œil gauche.
8	32s	I'll get more compresses.	Je ramène d'autres compresses.
9	36s	That bad, huh?	À ce point ?
10	38s	What are we gonna do about the show?	Et le spectacle ?
11	39s	You look like you have leprosy.	On dirait une lépreuse.
12	40s	Mignonette can't have leprosy.	Mignonette n'a pas la lèpre.
13	42s	I'd have to rewrite the whole show to make her a leper,	Je devrais tout réécrirepour qu'elle soit une lépreuse,
14	45s	and there's just no time.	et j'ai pas le temps.
15	46s	No time!	Pas le temps !
16	47s	Claudia is a political prisoner!	Claudia est une prisonnière politique !
17	49s	I'm her eyes and ears on the outside.	Je suis ses yeux et ses oreilles.
18	51s	The only way to free her is to subvert the entire system and start a revolution!	Pour la libérer, on doit renverserle système et créer une révolution.
19	54s	Yes, and if it's a long imprisonment,	Oui, et si c'est un long emprisonnement,
20	57s	I might need three more bags of Cool Ranch Doritos.	Il me faudra peut-êtretrois paquets de chips en plus.
21	1:00	Oh, God, I'm so itchy!	Purée, ça me gratte !
22	1:02	Stacey, no. No scratching.	Stacey, non. Ne te gratte pas.
23	1:04	Kristy, do something.	Kristy, fais quelque chose.
24	1:06	There's only one thing to do.	Il n'y a qu'une chose à faire.

Subtitles

Figure 5. A screenshot of the Excel file containing timestamps, captions, and subtitles[115]

be analyzed with the corpus linguistics software (see Subsection 3.3, p. 139); nonetheless, the separate Excel files containing TV series episodes individually, downloaded directly with LR, were kept for further translational analysis (see Chapter 5, p. 209)[114,115].

---

[114] Source: own.

[115] Source: own.

With the method behind gathering the corpora having been presented, it is now possible to discuss what they contain. Table 6 lists all the TV series used in this research's corpora.

In total, the English corpus[116] contains 770,836 tokens, the French[117] 664,508 tokens, and the Polish 138,516 tokens.

Table 6 presents the TV series that were chosen for this research. It also contains their genre types which need further explanation. Initially, the scope of this research was to cover only TV series that would illustrate everyday language in situations resembling the ones occurring in the daily life of an average person. That is why most of the TV series in English are recently produced dramas (the oldest of them streamed for the first time in 2017), with plots that are set in the present day to avoid language that could be considered outdated or archaic. However, the genre and plot type were not up to the researcher's choice in terms of TV series in French and Polish. Due to the desired comparability of the corpus, the shows used for this research had to have subtitles available in the languages under study. Therefore, the shows in French and Polish listed in Table 6 are all that was available on Netflix with English and Polish (in the first case) and French and English (in the second) subtitles at the time of assembling the corpus, that is, as of September 2021[118]. Because the amount of Polish content with English and French translations available on Netflix is clearly and understandably lower than the content in the other two languages, eight movies were added to the corpus in order to

116 "The English corpus" is used here to refer solely to the corpus of SL captions (similarly for "the French corpus" and "the Polish corpus"). The corpus of translations was also gathered; however, the translations are used only for the analysis of the SL pragmatemes, not the whole texts.

117 "The French" refers here to the French language (as the corpus also contains Belgian TV series).

118 It has to be stressed that the overall amount of French and Polish content available on Netflix is greater; however, even though the translational analysis in this dissertation covers only translations from English to French and Polish, only shows in French and Polish that have translations available into English, French, and Polish were chosen so that this research can be continued and extended in the future with the comparable corpus already assembled. This would not be possible, did the Polish and French corpora contain shows without available translations.

Table 6. The list and a short description of TV series and movies used for gathering the corpora of this dissertation

Lang.	No.	Original title [English translation]	Genre	Year	No. of episodes
ENG	1.	*Atypical*	Comedy drama	2017, 2018, 2019, 2021	38 (seasons 1,2, 3, and 4)
	2.	*The Baby-Sitters Club*	Comedy drama	2020	10 (season 1)
	3.	*Dash & Lily*	Rom-com	2020	8 (season 1)
	4.	*Dead to Me*	Comedy	2019, 2020	20 (seasons 1 and 2)
	5.	*Emily in Paris*	Rom-com	2020	10 (season 1)
	6.	*Firefly Lane*	Drama	2021	10 (season 1)
	7.	*Ginny and Georgia*	Comedy drama	2021	10 (season 1)
	8.	*Good Girls*	Crime comedy drama	2018, 2019, 2020, 2021	50 (seasons 1,2, 3, and 4)
	9.	*Never Have I Ever*	Comedy drama	2020, 2021	20 (seasons 1 and 2)
	10.	*Sweet Magnolias*	Romantic drama	2020	10 (season 1)
	11.	*You*	Psychological thriller	2018, 2019	20 (seasons 1 and 2)
TOTAL					**206**
FR	1.	*Caïd* [*Dealer*]	Thriller	2021	10 (season 1)
	2.	*Dérapages* [*Inhuman Resources*]	Drama	2020	6 (season 1)
	3.	*Disparu à jamais* [*Gone for Good*]	Mystery	2021	5 (season 1)
	4.	*Dix pour cent* [*Call My Agent!*]	Comedy drama	2015, 2017, 2018, 2020	24 (seasons 1,2, 3, and 4)
	5.	*Family Business*	Comedy	2019, 2020	12 (seasons 1 and 2)
	6.	*Glacé* [*The Frozen Dead*]	Mystery	2017	6 (season 1)

(Continued)

Table 6. (Continued)

Lang.	No.	Original title [English translation]	Genre	Year	No. of episodes
	7.	*Into the night*	Sci-fi drama thriller	2020	12 (seasons 1 and 2)
	8.	*La Mante*	Thriller	2017	6 (season 1)
	9.	*La Révolution*	Supernatural drama	2020	8 (season 1)
	10.	*Le Bazar de la Charité*	Drama	2019	8 (season 1)
	11.	*Le chalet* [*The Chalet*]	Slasher	2018	6 (season 1)
	12.	*Lupin*	Mystery thriller	2021	10 (seasons 1 and 2)
	13.	*Marianne*	Horror	2019	8 (season 1)
	14.	*Marseille*	Political drama	2016, 2018	16 (seasons 1 and 2)
	15.	*Mortel*	Supernatural drama	2019, 2021	12 (seasons 1 and 2)
	16.	*Mytho* [*Mythomaniac*]	Drama	2019	6 (season 1)
	17.	*Plan cœur* [*The Hook Up Plan*]	Comedy	2018, 2019	15 (seasons 1 and 2)
	18.	*Unité 42* [*Unit 42*]	Crime	2017	10 (season 1)
	19.	*Vampires*	Horror	2020	6 (season 1)
	20.	*Zone Blanche* [*Black Spot*]	Thriller	2017, 2019	16 (seasons 1 and 2)
TOTAL					**202**
PL	1.	*1983*	Crime drama	2018	8 (season 1)
	2.	*Kajko i Kokosz* [*Kayko and Kokosh*]	Animation	2021	14 (seasons 1 and 2)
	3.	*Otwórz oczy* [*Open Your Eyes*]	Supernatural	2021	6 (season 1)
	4.	*Rojst 97* [*The Mire*]	Crime drama	2021	6 (season 2)
	5.	*Sexify*	Comedy drama	2021	8 (season 1)
	6.	*W głębi lasu* [*The Woods*]	Mystery	2020	6 (season 1)
	7.	*Prime Time*	Thriller	2021	1 (movie)
	8.	*Bartkowiak*	Crime drama	2021	1 (movie)
	9.	*Dawid i Elfy* [*David and the Elves*]	Family movie	2021	1 (movie)

(*Continued*)

Table 6. (Continued)

Lang.	**No.**	**Original title [English translation]**	**Genre**	**Year**	**No. of episodes**
PL	10.	*Hiacynt* [*Operation Hyacinth*]	Crime Drama	2021	1 (movie)
	11.	*Jak pokochałam gangstera* [*How I Fell in Love with a Gangster*]	Action film	2022	1 (movie)
	12.	*Miłość do kwadratu* [*Squared Love*]	Rom-com	2021	1 (movie)
	13.	*W lesie dziś nie zaśnie nikt 2* [*Nobody Sleeps in the Woods Tonight Part 2*]	Horror	2021	1 (movie)
	14.	*Wszyscy moi przyjaciele nie żyją* [*All My Friends Are Dead*]	Black comedy	2020	1 (movie)
TOTAL					**56**

extend it[119]. Furthermore, because the TV series that constitute the French and the Polish corpora were not chosen but rather included by necessity, the variety of genres is wider than in the English corpus. Therefore, in comparison to the English corpus, both in the French and Polish corpora, there is a smaller fraction of TV series depicting everyday life. Instead, a few series deviate from portraying a typical ordinary life of the general population. Examples include the slasher series *Le Chalet* (*The Chalet*), series set in different historical periods such as *La Révolution*, set around the time of the French Revolution, and the series *1983*, set during the Cold War, and even one animation (*Kajko i Kokosz* [*Kayko and Kokosh*]). While it must be acknowledged that because

119 Unfortunately, even after the movies were added to the corpus, the final number of words is substantially smaller than in the case of English and French. This limitation will be taken into account in the present analysis. Nonetheless, every year, a large amount of Polish content is uploaded to Netflix, and therefore in the future, this research will merit being repeated with a larger pool of data.

of these differences, the language in the English, French, and Polish corpora may vary in terms of register or usability, it is also hypothesized that thanks to the similar time of production of the TV series, these differences will not greatly hinder research on pragmatemes[120]. Furthermore, to avoid archaic language and focus on pragmatemes used nowadays, the lists of pragmatemes were compiled from many different sources to be used in the next stage of the research. The next subsection discusses in detail the methods and reasons behind the preparation of these lists.

3.2 Preparing the list of pragmatemes

As presented in the section devoted to pragmatemes (see Chapter 1.1), these are units that are not easy to define, let alone to assign a one-fits-all formula (for instance, one cannot say that all pragmatemes are a combination of nouns and verbs). Due to their lack of a fixed syntactic structure, searching for pragmatemes using corpus linguistics software must be done a different basis. In this research, the method of starting with the preidentified pragmatemes was chosen, because it is noted by Bardovi-Harlig (2012) that such an approach is common in studies of formulaic sequences that focus on investigating their contexts and variations. Therefore, the preparation of the pragmatemes list constituted a pivotal stage in finding pragmatemes in corpora. Three lists of pragmatemes were created: in English, French, and Polish. To ensure that the units in the lists are indeed fixed in a language, reliable sources such as dictionaries, phrasebooks, and academic publications were used, although it has to be noted that as of today, a dictionary of pragmatemes *per se* does not exist. However, units that can be considered pragmatemes can be found in dictionaries of phrases and phraseological units, in phrasebooks designed for learning languages by everyday conversations, and so on. The resource closest in content to a pragmatemes dictionary is Blanco and Mejri's (2018: 193-204) *Index des*

120 This hypothesis is based on the fact that over time, language undergoes changes, reflecting evolving societal norms and technological advancements. Nowadays particularly, in the second decade of the 21st century, which is characterized by rapid technological development, our language is subject to swift transformation. These changes affect our language, and so the language of TV writers, even if they remain unconscious of it.

pragmatèmes which contains 865 French units. However, the units in their list are pragmatemes that accord with Blanco and Mejri's (2018) definition, therefore, not all of them will align with the definition presented in this dissertation. Similarly, not all phrases in a phrasebook will be pragmatemes. That is why all the chosen sources had to be carefully examined in order to find and list only those units that would be aligned with the pragmateme definition proposed in Subsection 1.1.7 (see p. 49). All the sources used to prepare the list of pragmatemes in the languages of the analysis are listed in references on p. 293.

In total, 45 sources[121] were used. Bilingual sources were often used to find pragmatemes in two languages simultaneously. With such a variety of sources, several observations regarding the identified pragmatemes emerge. First, the list of the gathered pragmatemes contains not only units applicable to routine, everyday situations in the lives of the general population such as *How are you*, but also units specific to particular professions or social contexts, such as *Hetta!*[122] (a Polish command used to make a horse turn right) or *Idźcie w pokoju Chrystusa*[123] (Eng. *Go in the peace of Christ*, a formal goodbye used at the end of a mass), and units used in different registers (e.g., in Polish, the informal *No to chlup!*[124] and the formal *Zdrowie pana/pani*[125], both used in the situation of raising a toast). Second, across the sources, some pragmatemes were exclusively noted with the word "please" (applies also to the French "s'il vous plaît" and the Polish "proszę"), as if they were not in use without it, e.g., the pragmateme *Sign here* appeared in the sources used only with the word "please", either as *Sign here, please*[126] or *Please sign here*[127]. Furthermore, a lack of uniformity was noticed concerning punctuation in certain pragmatemes across different sources, with some pragmatemes appearing with different

121 With the sum of all the sources in mind, it has to be stressed that the largest source of Polish pragmatemes that was used, i.e., Chlebda's work, although a publication of ten volumes, was counted as one source.

122 Source: Chlebda, W. (2016). *Podręczny idiomatykon polsko-rosyjski*, vol. 8.

123 Source: Chlebda, W. (2010). *Podręczny idiomatykon polsko-rosyjski*, vol. 5.

124 Source: Widawski, M. (1997). *Nowy słownik slangu i potocznej angielszczyzny*

125 Source: Platkow, A. (1974). *Rozmówki francuskie*

126 Source: Bernacka, A., Motyliński, R. (2005). *Rozmówki angielskie*

127 Source: Baltrušaitytė, J. (2008). *Lithuanian-English, English-Lithuanian dictionary & phrasebook*

ending punctuation depending on the source. For instance, *See you later!* was cited in Boudjedid-Meyer (1998), while in Bernacka and Motyliński (2005), it appeared as *See you later* (without any punctuation). This variance not only complicates automated corpus searches but also fails to offer insights into the discussion on significance of prosody in pragmatemes (see Banyś 2020). Third, some ostensible pragmatemes proved to be false, especially in bilingual sources. For instance, the unit *A pleasant journey!*[128] appears to be a literal translation of the Polish *Przyjemnej podróży!*, rather than the equivalent in use, which contains a verb: *Have a pleasant journey*[129]. Similarly, *Acceptez-vous des cartes de credit ?*[130] is a literal translation of the Polish *Czy akceptują Państwo karty kredytowe?* and the English *Do you accept credit cards?*, and seems to appear only in bilingual resources for learning French, while the French pragmateme in use is *Prenez-vous la carte ?* (lit. *Do you take the card?*). Fourth, in situations when multiple pragmatemes exist for a given context, often only one is featured in the sources. For example, French sources note only *Est-ce que cette place est libre ?*[131] (lit. *Is this place free?*) to ask whether a seat is taken, but do not include a synonymous pragmateme *Est-ce qu'il y a quelqu'un ici ?*. Similarly, while *Are you all right?*[132] is present in English sources, *Are you ok?* or *Are you okay?* are not found. Fifth, across the sources, there seemed to be no consistency regarding the approach towards different grammatical forms. For instance, while sources identified pragmatemes such as *Nice to meet you*[133] and *It was nice meeting you*[134], equivalents such as *Nice meeting you* and *It was nice to meet you* were absent from them. Sixth and last, certain pragmatemes identified in the sources may sound archaic to native speakers (e.g., *Je suis*

128 Source: Häublein, G., Jenkins, R., Staniszewska-Kowalak, D. (1997). *Angielsko-polski słownik tematyczny*

129 The Corpus of Contemporary American English (COCA) does not note any instances of *A pleasant journey!* used without any preceding verb.

130 Source: Drzymała, P. (1991). *Francja: informacja turystyczna, rozmówki polsko-francuskie, mini-słownik*

131 Source: Jedlińska, A., Szwykowski, L., Tomalak, J. (1979). *Słownik turystyczny francusko-polski, polsko-francuski*

132 Source: Häublein, G., Jenkins, R., Staniszewska-Kowalak, D. (1997). *Angielsko-polski słownik tematyczny*

133 Source: Pawlikowska, B. (2010). *Blondynka na językach: angielski brytyjski*

134 Source: Bartnicki, K. et al. (2003). *Duży słownik polsko-angielski*

charmé de vous voir.[135] [lit. *I am charmed to see you.*]) or may no longer align with modern reality (e.g., *Ten czek nie ma pokrycia*[136] [Eng. *The check bounced*] no longer corresponds to the typical Polish reality since checks have become obsolete in Poland, while *Proszę nie odkładać słuchawki*[137] [lit. *Please do not put down the handset*, meaning "do not hang up"] seems to be used less and less frequently since due to the evolution of phones, hanging up no longer involves using a physical plastic handset.

As it has just been discussed in the previous paragraph, several shortcomings concerning the sources can be identified and, therefore, the research done in this thesis will not cover all pragmatemes that would have been noted by native speakers[138]. However, it is imperative not to undervalue the significance of the pragmatemes that were successfully identified through the referenced sources. After the careful examination of all units presented in the sources, the English list contains 890 pragmatemes from 32 sources, the French 642 pragmatemes from 13 sources (one of which is the list devoted solely to pragmatemes by Blanco and Mejri [2018]), and the Polish 1015 pragmatemes from 32 sources (one of which is Chlebda's [2006-2019] series of ten volumes)[139]. Furthermore, because many pragmatemes only occur in written form (e.g., signs such as *Wet paint* or polite formulas such as *Merci de votre attention* [Eng. *Thank you for your attention*][140]), a separate category was created, which comprises 315 written pragmatemes in English, 525 in French, and 488 in Polish (the sources used to find these pragmatemes were the same as for the spoken ones). From the pragmatemes collected, it is visible that it is not necessarily the number of sources that is important, but the specificity

135 Source: Platkow, A. (1974). *Rozmówki francuskie*

136 Source: Bernacka, A., Motyliński, R. (2005). *Rozmówki angielskie*

137 Source: Hoszowska, B. (1997). *Porozmawiajmy o interesach - po angielsku: business English dla przedsiębiorców i menedżerów oraz ich sekretarek*

138 And it seems that neither does any research on phraseological units.

139 It has to be noted that the final list of pragmatemes includes units that were merged and considered as one. These were pragmatemes that differed only in politeness (e.g., the use of *tu* and *vous* in French), gender (e.g., the Polish *pan* referring to a man and *pani* referring to a woman), and British/American spelling (e.g., *All those in favo(u)r*).

140 The pragmateme in question is used in written communication, while its equivalent in spoken communication is *Je vous remercie de votre attention*.

of content present in the sources. For instance, the Polish list contains the most considerable number of pragmatemes mainly thanks to Chlebda's ten-volume *Podręczny idiomatykon polsko-rosyjski* (2006-2019) which is devoted solely to phraseological units, while the French list, despite being based on a noticeably smaller number of sources, contains a number of pragmatemes comparable to that of the others thanks to the extensive work on the topic of Blanco and Mejri (2018).

Upon observing the pragmatemes in the lists, it was possible to distinguish what is called here *pragmatemic patterns*, i.e., repeatable sequences of words and slots that occur in many of pragmatemes. The list below presents a few examples of such patterns:

a) in English:
   - Thank you for + -ING VERB (e.g., *Thank you for calling*, *Thank you for coming*, *Thank you for inviting me here today*);
   - See you + TEMPORAL EXPRESSION (e.g., *See you later!*, *See you soon!*, *See you one of these days!*);
   - Please + VERB (e.g., *Please hold.*, *Please fill in your registration form.*, *Please charge this to my room.*) and VERB +[TOKEN], please (e.g., *Sign here, please.*, *Follow me, please.*);

b) in French:
   - À + TIME (e.g., *À lundi !*, *À demain !*, *À plus tard !*);
   - bon + NOUN (e.g., *Bon retour !*, *Bon voyage !*, *Bon vol !*);
   - En cas de + NOUN[,] INFINITIVE VERB (e.g., *En cas de malaise, consulter un médecin*, *En cas d'affluence ne pas utiliser les strapontins*, *En cas d'incendie briser la vitre*[141]);

c) in Polish:
   - Czy mogę prosić + PREPOSITION + NOUN (e.g., *Czy mogę prosić o pański paszport?*, *Czy mogę prosić o rachunek?*, *Czy mogę prosić do tańca?*);

141 It is important to note that the examples illustrating this pattern are written pragmatemes. Written pragmatemes were also included in the search for pragmatemes within the corpora, given that subtitles often convey the meanings of written signs visible on screen.

- Do + NOUN (e.g., *Do nogi!*, *Do hymnu!*, *Do usłyszenia!*);
- Dziękuję za + NOUN (e.g., *Dziękuję za przybycie.*, *Dziękuję za telefon.*, *Dziękuję za zaproszenie.*)

Finally, with the lists of pragmatemes and the lists of pragmatemic patterns prepared and saved in a separate Excel file, the next stage of the research could begin, namely the search for pragmatemes in the corpora, which is further discussed in the next subsection.

3.3 Searching for the pragmatemes in the corpora

With the corpora saved in three separate .txt files (one file per language), which is the format necessary for the corpus linguistics software used, the lists of pragmatemes also had to be properly formatted. First, all capital letters were changed to lowercase by applying the regular formula "=LOWER(CELL)" to all cells in the Excel file. This had to be done so that the software did not find only the capital letter variants of pragmatemes. For instance, had the search been conducted only for *How are you*, examples such as *Johnny, how are you* would not have been found. Final punctuation marks were removed with the "Find and Replace" dialog in Excel for two reasons: to avoid any possible software errors often caused by different functions of punctuation marks such as a dot or a question mark, and to ensure that all variants of pragmatemes are found (although Banyś [2020] stresses the importance of prosody in pragmatemes, the examination of sources of the list of pragmatemes has already shown inconsistencies in punctuation in pragmatemes and therefore, one cannot state that *Hello.* is less pragmatemic than *Hello!*). Finally, for the pragmatemic patterns, slots were properly annotated in accordance with the annotation method used in the software[142] (e.g., <N> for nouns).

The corpora files and the pragmateme lists having been prepared, the search for the units in the corpora could begin. For that purpose, Unitex[143], a corpus processing suite, was chosen. Unitex is a French software that allows

142 The used software, Unitex, offer automatic identification of the morphological structure of the text during the preprocessing stage, that is why the corpora did not undergo any other morphological tagging.

143 Source: https://unitexgramlab.org/fr. Accessed on December 27, 2022.

its users to analyze texts in 23 languages (as of 2022) and offers many tools useful for corpus analysis, including text alignment, lexicon-grammar tables, building and applying electronic dictionaries, and pattern matching with regular expressions, among others. The function used to find pragmatemes in the corpus was the "Locate Pattern" one (see Figure 6).

Figure 6. A screenshot presenting the "Locate Pattern" dialog in Unitex[144]

With this function, it is possible to find occurrences either by typing a regular expression (e.g., with the regular expression <A><N>, i.e., every adjective followed by a noun, one can find examples such as *sunny day* or *cute dog*) or by using the graph function. Such a graph should contain all the information on what is supposed to be found. Therefore, to find pragmatemes from the list, a graph was created where all the pragmatemes from the Excel file were copied and pasted. This is how the simple graph depicted in Figure 7 was created.

144 Source: own.

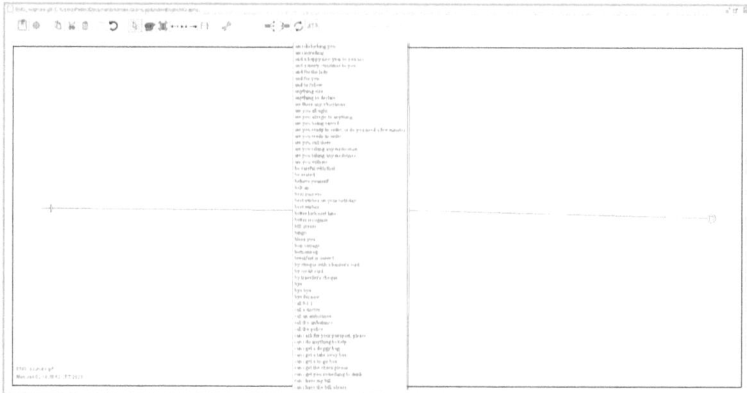

Figure 7. A screenshot of the graph created in Unitex containing the list of pragmatemes[145]

Thanks to this method, many pragmatemes could be found at the same time and presented in one concordance list, without having to be typed and searched for one unit after the other. The frequencies of the units were then written down in a separate Excel file. However, when a unit was of high frequency, it was also separately searched for in Unitex using the regular expression tab in order to ensure that the counted frequency was correct. Figure 8 presents an example of the concordance dialog.

The concordance lists created as the result of the search with the use of the lists of pragmatemes prepared from various sources were then manually consulted by myself in order to dismiss all occurrences of units that cannot be considered pragmatemes. For instance, a search of "after you" would show pragmatemic results such as "Please, after you" and "After you", but also regular units such as "Do not drive your Maserati home *after you* finish." Therefore, each occurrence was manually examined before it was counted as a pragmateme.

145 Due to the large number of units in the graph, only a part can be presented. Source: own.

Figure 8. A screenshot of the concordance list: a part of the result of the search with the use of the graph presented in Figure 7[146]

The next stage of the research consisted of searching for pragmatemes in the corpus with the use of pragmatemic patterns. The graph function was used again. This time, pragmatemic patterns were used to create complex graphs (see Figure 9).

With the application of graphs containing pragmatemic patterns such as the one presented in Figure 9 in the "Locate Pattern" function to the corpus file, the concordance list was created automatically and then carefully consulted. This careful examination of the results of the patterns had to be conducted because it was assumed that not all occurrences that are in accordance with a given pattern were, in fact, pragmatemic. Lastly, manual examination of the corpora enabled me to find examples of pragmatemes that might have been absent from the initial list of pragmatemes due to the fact that they belong to the language of youth that is particularly subject to rapid changes. Examples include the French pragmateme *Wesh* or the Polish

146 Source: own.

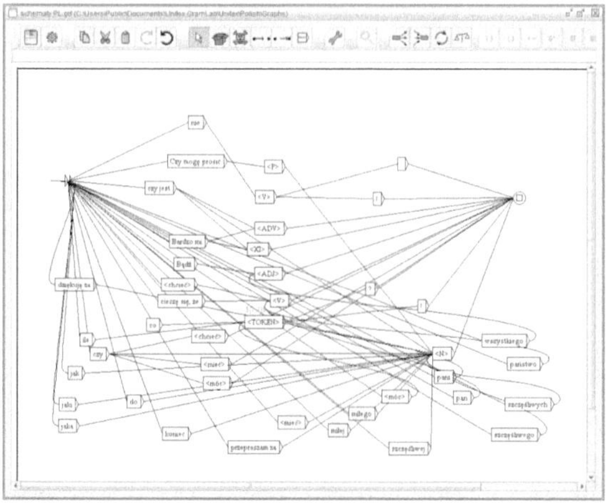

Figure 9. Example of a complex graph: a screenshot of the graph containing Polish pragmatemic patterns[147]

Hejka. These pragmatemes were then also submitted to the automatic corpus search to check their frequency in the corpus.

The above method of using Unitex to find pragmatemes in corpora and determine their frequency was applied to all three corpora in the languages of the analysis (English, French, and Polish). The pragmatemes that were found in the corpora were then assembled into tables presenting their frequency and other characteristics, which is described in the next subsection.

3.4 Assembling the tables of pragmatemes and their translations

For further linguistic (see p. 151) and translational (see p. 209) analyses, two Excel files were created. The first one, depicted in Figure 10, is devoted to linguistic parameters of pragmatemes found in the English, French, and Polish corpora (with separate tabs for each language). The table contains only pragmatemes that appeared in the corpora more than once, since unique units are not considered representative and would be of questionable value in the translational analysis.

147 Source: own.

148 Source: own.

1	Pragmateme	No. of words (complexity	Freq: tota	Freq: false	Freq: true (ENG-SL	Expected no. of occurrences per million words	No. Variant	Imperativ	Ellipsi	Verbles	Questio	Deixis	Deixis type	Speech act	Type	Charged type explanation (examples)
2	After you	2	44	38	6	8	3	No	No	Yes	No	Yes	personal	directive	Loaded	
3	Afternoon	1	42	35	7	9	2	No	Yes	Yes	No	Yes	temporal	expressive	Plain	
4	All cash	2	7	5	2	3	1	No	No	Yes	No	No	none	directive	Plain	
5	All done	2	7	3	4	5	3	No	Yes	Yes	No	yes implic	elliptical	directive	Plain	
6	All set	2	15	11	4	5	3	No	No	Yes	No	No	none	representative	Plain	
7	Another round	2	6	2	4	5	4	No	No	Yes	No	No	none	directive	Plain	
8	Anyone here	2	4	1	3	4	2	No	Yes	Yes	Yes	Yes	spatial	directive	Plain	
9	Anything else	2	43	39	4	5	1	No	Yes	Yes	Yes	yes implic	elliptical	directive	Charged	"Do you want anything else" (ordering) / "OK, and?"
10	Can I get you anything else?	6	3	0	3	4	1	No	No	No	Yes	Yes	personal	commissive	Plain	
11	Is that all?	3	13	7	6	8	2	No	No	No	Yes	Yes	discourse	directive	Charged	"Do you want anything else" (ordering) / Response whe someone apologizes
12	Are you all right	4	10	0	10	13	3	No	No	No	Yes	Yes	personal	directive	Plain	
13	You all right	3	21	10	11	14	3	No	Yes	Yes	Yes	Yes	personal	directive	Plain	
14	Are you OK	3	136	0	136	176	8	No	No	No	Yes	Yes	personal	directive	Plain	
15	You ok	2	202	136	66	86	8	No	Yes	Yes	Yes	Yes	personal	directive	Plain	
16	Are you there	3	5	0	5	6	2	No	No	No	Yes	Yes	personal	directive	Charged	On the phone, when the connection is bad / "Have you arrived" (e.g. as a text)
17	Arms up	2	2	0	2	3	1	Yes	Yes	Yes	No	yes implic	elliptical	directive	Plain	
18	Careful, it's hot	3	2	0	2	3	2	Yes	Yes	No	No	yes implic	elliptical	directive	Plain	
19	Be quiet	2	14	10	4	5	2	Yes	No	No	No	yes implic	in the verb	directive	Plain	
20	Quiet	1	70	61	9	12	5	Yes	Yes	Yes	No	yes implic	elliptical	directive	Plain	
21	Bingo	1	8	6	2	3	1	No	No	Yes	No	No	none	representative	Charged	shouted in a game / "that's it, exactly"
22	Bottoms up	2	2	0	2	3	2	Yes	No	Yes	No	No	none	directive	Loaded	
23	Break a leg	3	6	2	4	5	2	Yes	No	No	No	No	none	expressive	Loaded	
24	Bye	1	200	4	196	254	9	No	No	Yes	No	No	none	expressive	Plain	
25	All right, bye	3	3	0	3	4	1	No	No	Yes	No	No	none	expressive	Plain	
26	Okay, bye	2	18	0	18	23	3	No	No	Yes	No	No	none	expressive	Plain	
27	So long	2	39	36	3	4	1	No	No	Yes	No	No	none	expressive	Loaded	
28	Peace out	2	2	0	2	3	2	No	No	No	No	No	none	expressive	Loaded	
29	Peace	1	30	28	2	3	1	No	No	Yes	No	No	none	expressive	Plain	
30	Call 911	2	4	1	3	4	3	Yes	No	No	No	yes implic	in the verb	directive	Plain	
31	Call an ambulance	3	2	0	2	3	2	Yes	No	No	No	yes implic	in the verb	directive	Plain	
32	Call me [NAME]	3	13	0	13	17	8	Yes	No	No	No	Yes	personal	directive	Plain	
33	Call me	2	98	91	7	9	5	Yes	No	No	No	Yes	personal	directive	Plain	
34	Call me back	3	19	9	10	13	9	Yes	No	No	No	Yes	personal	directive	Plain	
35	Call the cops	3	14	10	4	5	2	Yes	No	No	No	yes implic	in the verb	directive	Plain	
36	I'll call you later	4	4	0	4	5	1	No	No	No	No	Yes	personal	commissive	Plain	
37	I gotta call you back	5	2	0	2	3	2	No	No	No	No	Yes	personal	commissive	Plain	

Figure 10. A screenshot of a part of the Excel table with linguistic parameters of pragmatemes[148]

Apart from linguistic characteristics such as whether the pragmateme is imperative, a question, verbless, elliptic, what speech act it performs, whether deictic markers are present, and what type of a pragmateme it represents (linguistic parameters of the analysis are discussed in detail in Chapter 4, see p. 151), in the table presented in Figure 10, pragmatemes are also noted for their frequency in the corpus, the number of words they consist of, and the number of variants they represent. A variant is understood here as a pragmateme of a different graphic form (including punctuation marks, e.g., *Take care!* and *Take care.* are considered to be two variants of one pragmateme) and a pragmateme with an additional word of politeness (e.g., *After you.* and *After you, please.*) Furthermore, an additional column entitled "Charged explanation" is added to charged pragmatemes to briefly explain their ambiguity. For instance, the explanation for *I'm fine, thank you* is "I'm okay" / "I don't need anything else." All these parameters are further discussed in the linguistic analysis of pragmatemes, see p. 151.

A full count of the pragmatemes together with their variants in the list of English pragmatemes yields 290 in the English corpus, 186 in the French, and 106 entries in the Polish. In the English list, 125 units (43.1%) were exact pragmatemes that were also found in the list of pragmatemes prepared beforehand. This means that the majority of units, 165 (56.9%), were not present in the list of pragmatemes, and were found either as a result of pragmatemic patterns (44 units), or by a similarity to units in the list of pragmatemes, e.g., the pragmateme *You all right* found in the corpus is similar to *Are you all right* found in the list of pragmatemes (82 units), or in the manual search (39 units). Figure 11 presents the percentage distribution in the English pragmatemes found in the corpus.

As for the pragmatemes found in the French corpus, the ratio of pragmatemes from the original list to those found by other means is different than in the English corpus. Here, 128 units found in the corpus were contained in the list of pragmatemes, while 58 units either were similar to the listed ones, resulted from the application of pragmatemic patterns, or were found manually. The exact percentage of these types is depicted in Figure 12.

Similarly to the search bases of the French pragmatemes, units found in the Polish corpus were also predominantly present in the list of pragmatemes, with 77 units identified with the use of the predefined list compared to 31

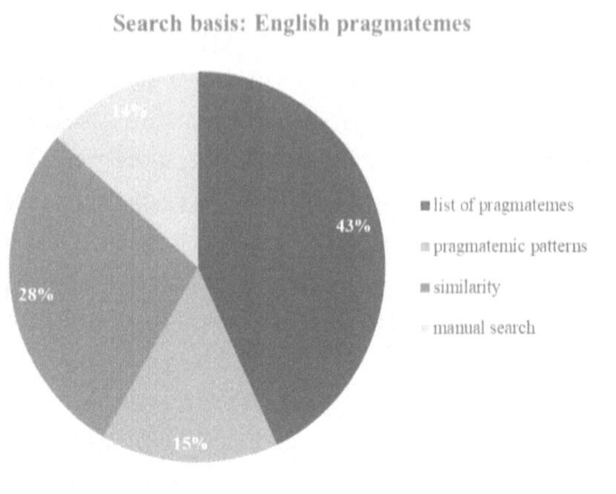

Figure 11. English pragmatemes found in the corpus: the percentage distribution of the search basis

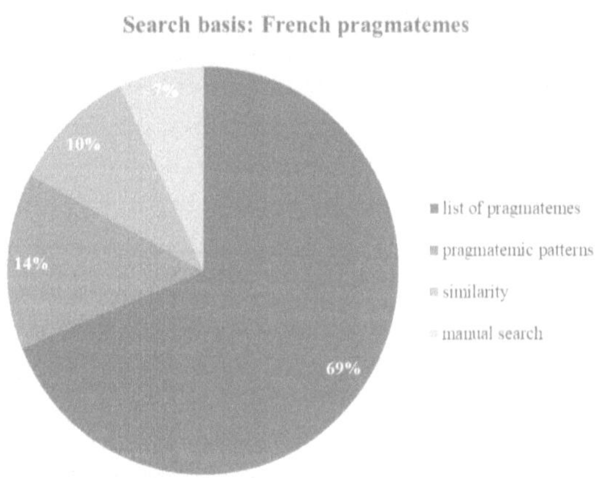

Figure 12. French pragmatemes found in the corpus: the percentage distribution of the search basis

units identified with pragmatemic patterns, through similarity, or manual search. Figure 13 presents the exact percentage of different search bases for the pragmatemes found in the Polish corpus.

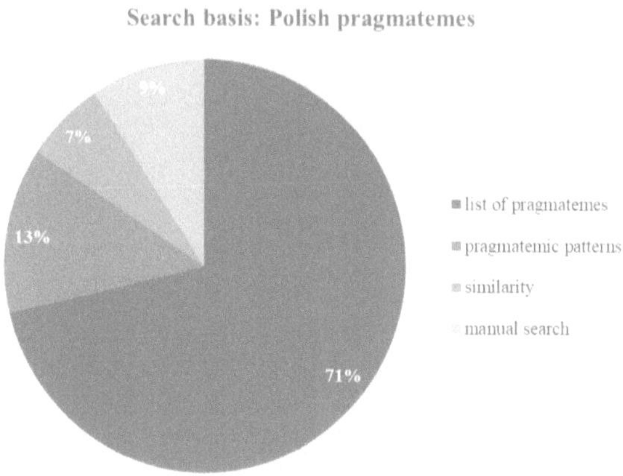

Figure 13. Polish pragmatemes found in the corpus: the percentage distribution of the search basis

All in all, the analysis of the bases of the search for pragmatemes confirms what has been already stated in Subsection 3.2 (see p. 134), where the lists of pragmatemes were presented: it is not the number of sources that matters, but the quality. English was the only language in which a dictionary of phraseological units *per se* was not used. In comparison, in French, an index of pragmatemes composed by Blanco and Mejri (2018) was implemented, while in Polish, a ten-volume publication on phrasemes was employed (Chlebda 2006-2019). The corpus search confirmed the reliability of these sources. However, the use of dictionaries and phrasebooks also proved helpful in the search for English pragmatemes. After all, it is thanks to the assemblage of the pragmatemes from these sources that pragmatemic patterns were created and that similar units were found, as they had their basis for comparison in those sources. Figure 14 summarizes the percentage distribution of the search bases for pragmatemes in all three languages.

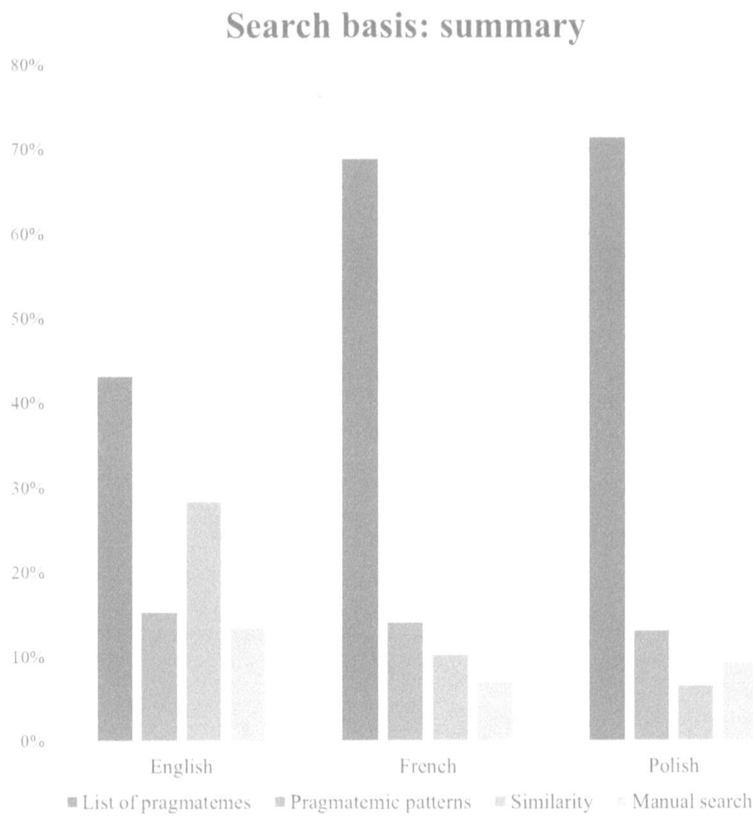

Figure 14. Search basis for pragmatemes found in the corpus: summary

The second Excel table prepared for its use in further analysis contains pragmatemes and their translations. Due to the length of the doctoral project[149], the focus of the translational analysis (see p. 209) is on English pragmatemes

[149] Studying translations from French to English and Polish and from Polish to English and French would not only require additional time but would also mean other factors should be taken into consideration, such as the fact that on Netflix, translations from SLs other than English are usually done through English nonetheless.

	A	B	C	D	E	F
1		SOURCE	TIME	ENGLISH (CC)	FRENCH SUBTITLE	POLISH SUBTITLE
2	After you	You S01E03	40s	After you.	Après toi.	Idź przodem.
3		EiP S01E05	21:10	After you. [No, please, I insist.]	Après toi. [Non, j'insiste]	Idź przodem, [nalegam.]
4		GG S04E12	3:44	After you.	Après toi.	Idź przodem.
5		NHIE S02E06	20:50	After you.	Après vous.	Panie przodem.
6		Atypical S03E10	24:32	After you, sir, and what a lovely pair of truck nuts.	Après vous, votre camion a une bien belle paire.	Proszę przodem. Piękne włochate zawieszki.
7		You S01E01	44:16	Please, after you.	Je t'en prie, après toi.	Idź przodem.
8						
9	Afternoon	SM S01E02	10:52	Afternoon, Mr. Littlefield.	Bonjour, M. Littlefield.	Panie Littlefield.
10		SM S01E04	34:19	Afternoon, Mr. Van.	Bonjour, M. Van.	Dzień dobry, panie Van.
11		SM S01E04	34:00	Afternoon.	Bonjour.	Dzień dobry.
12		SM S01E04	38:31	Afternoon, y'all.	Bonjour à tous.	Dzień dobry.
13		GG S01E01	25:17	Afternoon, Mrs. Boland.	Bonjour, Mme Boland.	Dzień dobry.
14		GG S02E11	28:24	Afternoon, Tara.	Bonjour, Tara.	Dzień dobry.
15		GG S03E08	16:34	Afternoon, ladies.	Bonjour, mesdames.	Dzień dobry.
16						
17	All cash	DtM S01E09	14:19	All cash.	Cash.	Gotówką.
18		DtM S01E09	17:12	All cash.	En cash.	Gotówką.
19						
20	All done	NHIE S02E06	2:23	Okay, all done.	Voilà, j'ai fini.	Dobra, gotowa.
21		Atypical S02E02	2:52	It's all done.	Tout est fait.	Nie trzeba.
22		Atypical S04E05	29:40	All done.	C'est fini.	Zrobione.
23		GG S03E05	29:47	All done.	C'est fini.	Gotowe.
24						
25	All set	GG S04E12	31:52	All set in here.	Ça y est, j'ai fini.	To już wszystko.
26		GG S03E01	23:46	All set, Lucy.	Ça ira, Lucy.	Nie trzeba, Lucy.
27		GG S03E07	10:05	All set.	On a ce qu'il faut.	Nie trzeba.
28		GG S04E03	35:21	All set.	C'est fait.	Już mam.
29						

Figure 15. A screenshot of the Excel table with pragmatemes found in the English corpus and their translations[150]

and their translations to French and Polish. Therefore, the table depicted in Figure 15 contains pragmatemes found in the English corpus.

The columns in the second Excel file represent the pragmateme, the source (name of the TV series [shortened if need be], number of the season, and number of the episode), the time when exactly the pragmateme is uttered, captions in English, and French and Polish subtitles. The information was copy-pasted from the separate Excel files downloaded with the use of LR (see p. 123). If a subtitle contains more information than the caption with the pragmateme, an additional caption is added in square brackets. For instance, in the case of the Polish subtitle *Idź przodem, [nalegam]*, the word "nalegam" is added from the sentence originally uttered after the pragmateme: *No, please, I insist.* Therefore, the cell with the English caption is as follows: *After you. [No, please, I insist.]* so that the part separate from the pragmateme is clearly visible.

With the two tables explained, it is now possible to analyze the pragmatemes, which is the topic of the next two sections, starting with the linguistic analysis in Chapter 4.

Therefore, a study on pragmatemes and pivot translation could be an interesting topic to research in the future.

150 Source: own.

Linguistic analysis of pragmatemes

As discussed in Chapter 1 (see p. 27), researchers studying the phenomenon of a pragmateme have mostly focused on its key components such as the name, definition, and typology (e.g., Blanco and Mejri 2018, Kauffer 2019, Kecskés 2010). However, not many linguistic analyses have been done on the topic. And there is an even smaller number of studies on pragmatemes that have been conducted from a contrastive point of view. So far, the most extensive contrastive study on a concept similar, but not fully equivalent to what is understood here as pragmatemes, is the dictionary collated by Krzyżanowska, Grossmann, and Kwapisz-Osadnik (2021) that contains 50 French *formules expressives de la conversation* [*expressive conversational formulas*] and their Italian and Polish equivalents, with a linguistic description of factors such as speech acts, variants, register, prosody, frequency, syntactic, lexical, and semantic status, and a short contrastive discussion on differences between each French entry and its Italian and Polish equivalents.

The present study endeavors to further enhance the description of pragmatemes, asserting that in order to investigate a phenomenon effectively, one must possess a precise comprehension of the subject. Through meticulous examination of common linguistic attributes, a more comprehensive understanding of the nature of pragmatemes may be attained. Therefore, this chapter is devoted to the linguistic analysis of 286 English, 186 French, and 106 Polish pragmatemes[151] found in the study's corpora. To determine the linguistic characteristics of pragmatemes and examine whether there are any similarities in pragmatemes across the languages under study, the units are analyzed based on the following traits: frequency, complexity, variantivity, imperativeness, presence of verbless forms, presence of question forms, ellipsis, deixis, speech acts, and pragmateme types.

---

[151] Each pragmateme is studied as one lexical entry, no matter their respective frequency in the corpus.

4.1 Frequency

Due to the fact that the studied corpora contain a different number of tokens in the different languages (770,836 in English, 664,508 in French, and 138,516 in Polish), in order to be able to compare the frequencies of pragmatemes found in these corpora, each number of occurrences was normalized per one million words. This normalization was done by multiplying the number of occurrences of a pragmateme by one million and dividing the result of this multiplication by the number of tokens in the corpus in which the pragmateme was found. Figure 16 presents the percentage distribution of the normalized frequencies of pragmatemes found in the corpora.

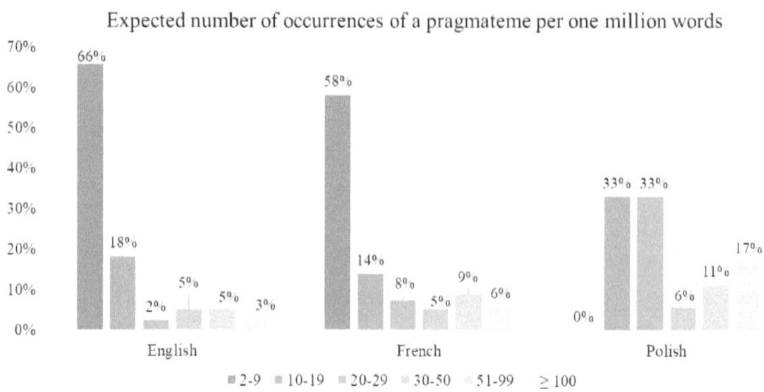

Figure 16. Percentage distribution of the expected number of occurrences of pragmatemes found in the corpora per one million words

Compared to the Polish corpus, the English and French corpora contain a larger number of pragmatemes of a substantially lower frequency, with the median for English being six expected occurrences and for French eight, compared to 22 for Polish, which can be explained by the sample sizes (for a discussion on the study's limitations see Conclusions section, p. 263). Furthermore, while the majority of English (65.7%) and French (58.1%) pragmatemes are expected to occur between two and nine times per one million words, a higher frequency is found for Polish pragmatemes, with the smallest expected number of occurrences being 14.

Throughout this section, in addition to standard column charts depicting percentage distribution (e.g., Figure 16), an alternative method visualizing numerical data is also used, namely the mosaic plot, also known as Marimekko or Mekko chart[152]. A mosaic plot represents frequency information through the size of different areas (Brezina 2018). Unlike column charts such as Figure 16, mosaic plots are constructed with the use of exact counts of pragmatemes within specific categories and languages, rather than percentages. Furthermore, the mosaic plot also displays proportions among different categories (ibid), which is particularly important when analyzing categories of varying sizes (as in this study, where a different number of pragmatemes is found in each of the languages of the analysis). Figure 17 presents the mosaic plot illustrating the number of occurrences per one million words of pragmatemes in the corpora.

In terms of the mosaic plot in Figure 17, it is evident that the English area is the widest, since the largest number of pragmatemes is found in this language. The heights of the areas represent the proportion of outcomes (different normalized frequencies) within each language of the analysis. For instance, the rectangles in the lightest shade visually highlight what has already been discussed in this subsection, i.e., the prevalence of pragmatemes occurring two to nine times per one million words in English and French, and the lack of these low frequency pragmatemes in Polish.

Furthermore, as can be noted both from the percentage distribution chart and the mosaic plot, the Polish corpus has the largest percentage of pragmatemes expected to occur over 100 times per one million words. The exact reason for this phenomenon is difficult to determine; some possible explanations may point to the sources chosen to prepare the initial list of pragmatemes or may suggest that the linguistic material in Polish TV series is more formulaic than that in English and French.

---

152 These names are in use because the charts resemble prints that are known for being associated with the Finnish fashion company Marimekko (Nelli 2014).

153 All of the mosaic plots presented in this thesis were created using Kutools, a Microsoft Excel extension that allows the user to access many advanced features more easily, without requiring complex statistical formulas.

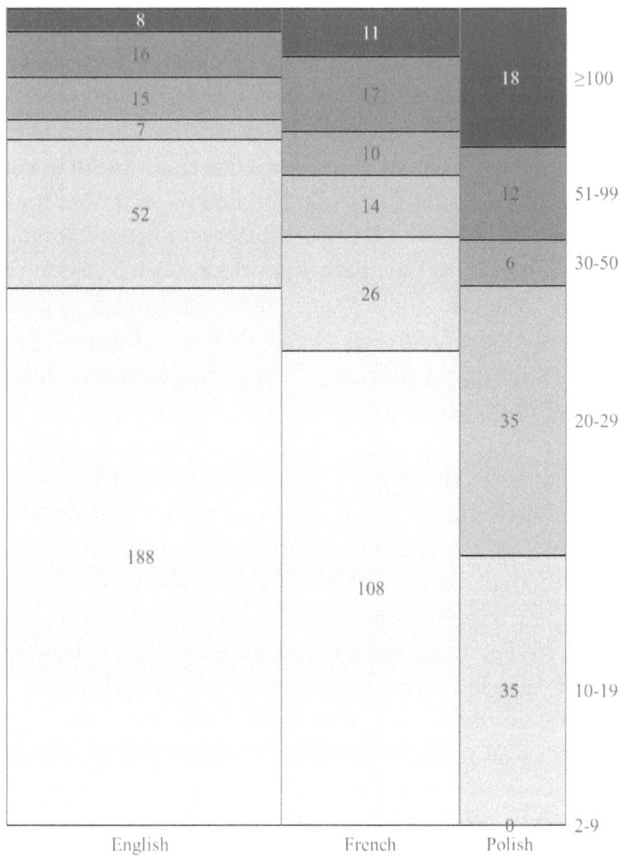

Figure 17. Mosaic plot for the expected number of occurrences of pragmatemes found in the corpora per one million words according to the language of the analysis[153]

4.2 Complexity

In this study, complexity refers to the number of words the pragmateme is composed of. In the analyzed corpora, the majority of pragmatemes in all three languages were not complex and were composed of two words on average, with the median being three words for English and French pragmatemes, and two for Polish pragmatemes. Figure 18 presents the exact percentage distribution of the number of words of the pragmatemes that were found.

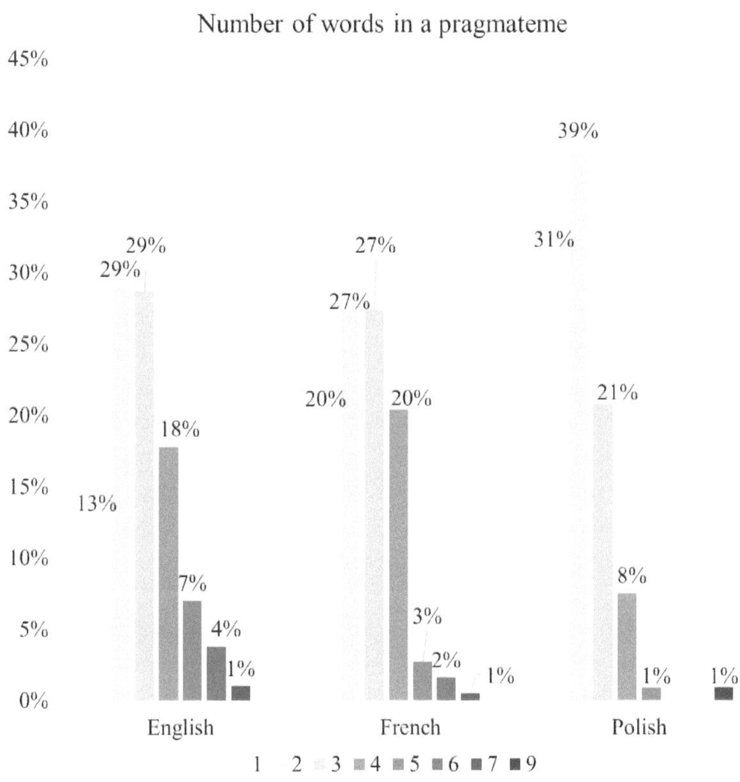

Figure 18. Percentage distribution of the number of words of the pragmatemes found in English, French, and Polish corpora

Based on Figure 18, one can observe that pragmatemes consisting of five and more words were relatively rare across all corpora, particularly in French and Polish (constituting 4.8% of all units in French and 1.8% in Polish, and over 11% in English). Interestingly, while the Polish corpus contains the highest percentage of monolexical pragmatemes (31.1%) among the studied corpora, it is also where the longest pragmateme can be found (*W imię Ojca i Syna, i Ducha Świętego, amen*[154] [Eng. *In the name of the Father, the Son, and the Holy Ghost, amen*], 9 words). Apart from this wordy example, the percentage distribution shows that within the Polish corpus, one- and two-word pragmatemes are the most common. Quite surprisingly, they are more common than in English or French, which seems to challenge a belief that Polish is a language that seems wordy[155]; at least in terms of pragmatemes, the study suggests otherwise.

Another potentially interesting observation arises in terms of the percentage of monolexical pragmatemes in the French corpus. A notable 19.9 percent of the identified French pragmatemes are monolexical. This substantial figure could prompt a reconsideration of Blanco and Mejri's estimate that around five to seven percent of all French pragmatemes are monolexical (Blanco and Mejri 2018). Naturally, it is important to note the size of the corpus used for this study, its type (TV series captions), and the fact that the definition of pragmatemes used here differs slightly from Blanco and Mejri's (see p. 48). Nevertheless, this observation should be regarded as an intriguing point meriting further investigation in future studies.

Figure 19, presenting the mosaic plots for monolexical and polylexical pragmatemes found in the corpora, further displays the importance of monolexical units.

Monolexical pragmatemes are also particularly interesting for one more reason: in terms of the expected number of occurrences per one million words, they are the most frequent in all three languages of the study, with median values of 14 in English[156], 14 in French, and 29 in Polish. Furthermore,

---

154 All examples presented in this section are pragmatemes found in the study's copora.

155 This is a sentiment expressed by many Polish language learners, but it is also an observation made by researchers studying bilinguals. For instance, Dąbrowska (2013: 74) in her study on code-switching among Polish users of Facebook, suggests that Polish people sometimes choose English phrases over their Polish equivalents for language economy, since "[p]erhaps the Polish phrases are too wordy, too heavy chunks."

156 For the purpose of brevity, "English", "French", and "Polish" may be used here to refer to the respective corpus, unless specified otherwise.

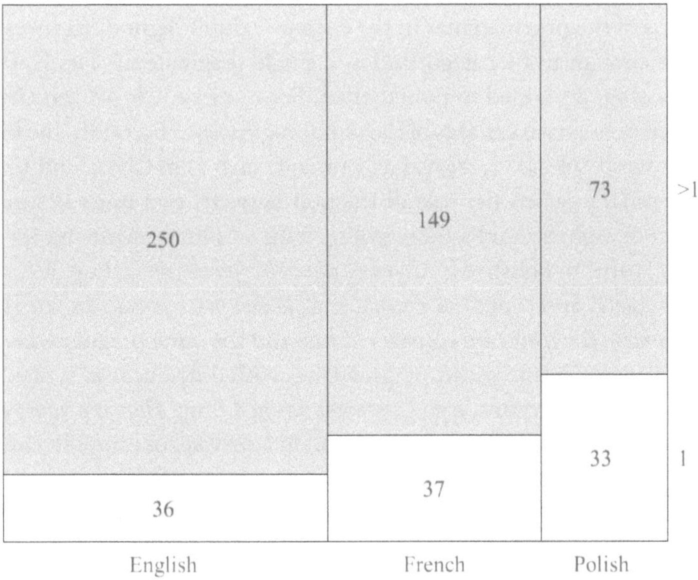

Figure 19. Mosaic plot for monolexical and polylexical pragmatemes found in English, French, and Polish corpora

across all the pragmatemes found in the corpus, median values[157] show that the lower the complexity, the higher the expected number of occurrences per one million words, regardless of the language[158].

---

157 The exact median values of the expected number of occurrences per one million words for pragmatemes of a different complexity are as follows: English: 14 for monolexical pragmatemes, six for two-word, six for three-word, five for four-word, three for five-word, four for six-word, and three for seven-word pragmatemes; French: 14 for monolexical pragmatemes, 14 for two-word, 6 for three-word, five for four-word, three for five-word, three for six-word, and 29 for seven-word pragmatemes (one example only); and Polish: 29 for monolexical pragmatemes, 29 for two-word, 22 for three-word, 22 for four-word, and 14 for both five-word and nine-word pragmatemes (both of which are represented by one example each).

158 Except for a French example of seven words, *Vous êtes sur le répondeur de [PERSON]* (the only pragmateme of this length found in the French corpus), for which the

4.3 Variantivity

Some forms of the pragmatemes in the corpora exhibit slight differences but are similar enough to be categorized as a single pragmateme. Firstly, these differences often pertained to punctuation. For instance, *Cheers!* and *Cheers.* are regarded here as two variants of the same pragmateme. Secondly, the inclusion of the word "please" is treated as a variant, such as in *Check.* and *Check, please*[159]. Similarly, when the sole distinction between two units lies in the direct form of a phrase and a more polite, indirect phrase involving the use of "pan" or "pani" in Polish (e.g., *Co mogę dla ciebie/pana zrobić* [Eng. *What can I do for you, [sir]*]), and "vous" in French (e.g., *Je t'en prie / Je vous en prie* [Eng. *You're welcome*]), the units are considered one and the same pragmateme, but different variants. Furthermore, pragmatemes with differences in syntax can also be regarded as variants, e.g., *Comment vas-tu ?* (Eng. *How are you?*, with inverted syntax) and *Comment tu vas ?* (Eng. *How are you?*, question by intonation, placement of the subject after the object, as in an affirmative sentence). Also, the addition of a vocative after a comma is considered a variant, exemplified by *All set.* and *All set, [NAME].* Lastly, in the case of pragmatemes with slots, the different tokens filling these slots lead to the unit being recognized as a variant, for example, the pragmateme *Have a [POSITIVE ADJECTIVE] night* encompasses variants like *Have a nice night* and *Have a good night*. In most cases, pragmatemes with slots involved the use of a different noun or a person's name. However, they are different from pragmatemes which may involve the use of a vocative (e.g., *All set* and *All set, [PERSON]*), because in pragmatemes with slots, the use of a noun or name is required (e.g., *This is [PERSON] speaking* or *Call me [PERSON]*). The biggest number of pragmatemes with slots was found in the English corpus (43 pragmatemes) and the smallest in the Polish one (4 pragmatemes), while 21 pragmatemes with slots were found in the French corpus. Yet, with the difference in size of these corpora, it cannot be stated that this type is more common in one language or another, given that some pragmatemes with slots seem to be universal (e.g., the equivalent of the English *Have a [POSITIVE ADJECTIVE] day* would be *[POSITIVE ADJECTIVE] dnia* in Polish, which was not found across the Polish corpus). Pragmatemes

median of expected number of occurrences per one million words is 29.

159 In similar cases, that is, when a monolexical pragmateme had polylexical variants, the pragmateme as a unit was still counted as a monolexical one.

with slots refer to specific situations and therefore, should not be confused with pragmatemic patterns (see p. 138). For instance, while *Have a [POSITIVE ADJECTIVE] evening* can be only uttered in reference to a specific time of the day, while *Have a [POSITIVE ADJECTIVE] [TIME]* can be applied in many different situations and be realized with different pragmatemes.

Having discussed what is understood as a variant in this study, it is now possible to analyze their presence in the corpora. Figure 20 presents the percentage distribution of the number of variants of pragmatemes found in corpora.

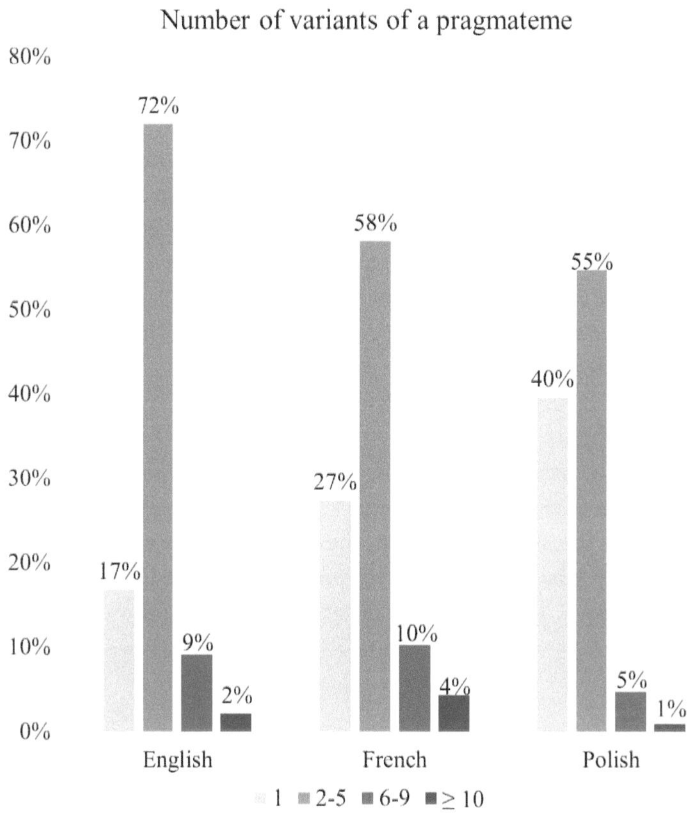

Figure 20. Percentage distribution of pragmatemes found in the corpora on the basis of the number of variants

A noticeable difference in pragmateme forms was the presence of the exclamation mark and the period at the end of a unit, which significantly contributes to pragmatemes of two to five variants constituting the majority in all languages. This observation not only aligns with Banyś's claim (2020) that a detailed study on the prosody of pragmatemes is needed but also underscores the importance of the suggested method of excluding final punctuation marks when searching for pragmatemes in a corpus, so as not to overlook potential instances. Furthermore, it would be particularly interesting to explore this parameter outside of a captions corpus, as one may speculate whether and to what extent aiming at emulating a spoken language influences the use of periods and exclamation marks.

Another observation to be made concerns the significant difference between the percentage of single-variant pragmatemes among the languages studied, especially in English (16.8%) and Polish (39.6%). This discrepancy could be attributed to the number of pragmatemes with slots, which in English (56 pragmatemes, 20.6% of the total in the English corpus), is greater than in French (20 pragmatemes, 10.8%) and even more significant in comparison to Polish (4 pragmatemes, 3.8%). The prominence of pragmatemes with slots in the English corpus may indicate a higher degree of flexibility in English pragmatemes; however, a comprehensive investigation into pragmatemes with slots deserves its own dedicated study.

All of the observations in this subsection can be also visualized with the mosaic plot in Figure 21.

Lastly, the pragmatemes with a different number of variants were analyzed for their number of expected occurrences per one million words. The results indicate that in the studied corpora, the fewer variants of a pragmateme, the smaller the median frequency. This pattern held true for all three of the studied languages[160]. The correlation between frequency and variantivity can

160 The median values of expected number of occurrences per one million words for pragmatemes of different number of variants are as follows: English: median of three for one variant pragmatemes, six for pragmatemes with two to five variants, 34 for six to nine variants, and 204 for ten or more variants, French: median of five for one variant pragmatemes, eight for two to five variants, 59 for six to nine variants, 139 for ten or more variants, and Polish: median of 18 for one variant pragmatemes, 29

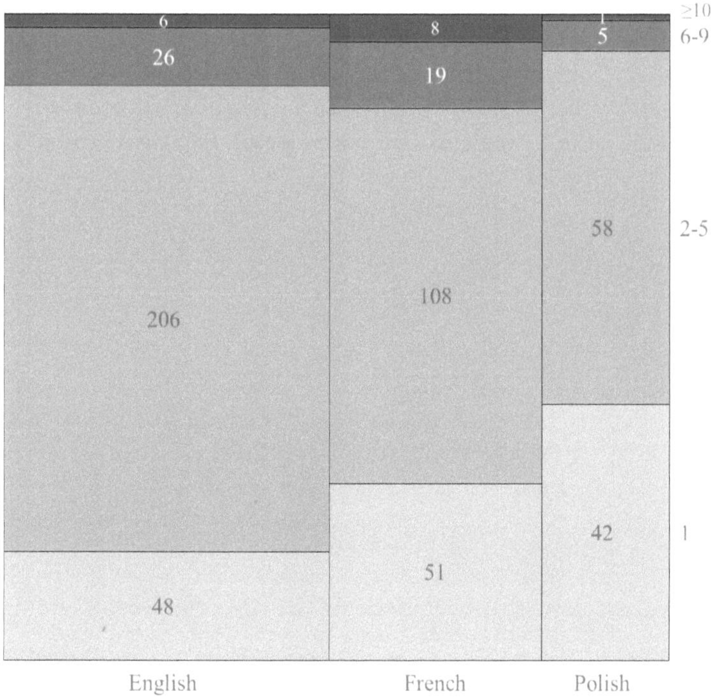

Figure 21. Mosaic plot for pragmatemes found in the corpora on the basis of the number of variants

be explained by the observation that the pragmatemes with a small number of variants are often used in very specific and less frequent situations (e.g., *It's a boy*), whereas pragmatemes with a considerable number of variants are typically greetings (e.g., *See you [DAY], Have a [POSITIVE ADJECTIVE] day, Welcome to [PLACE/EVENT]*), which are more frequently and widely applicable by nature.

for two to five variants, 116 for six to nine variants, and 946 for ten variants (only one unit belonging in that group).

4.4 Imperativeness

Another linguistic trait to be examined is whether pragmatemes found in the corpus are imperative or not, with the imperativeness being a feature that is present either explicitly (e.g., *Call an ambulance*) or implicitly (e.g., *Next in line*). Figure 22 presents that with a percentage distribution across the studied languages.

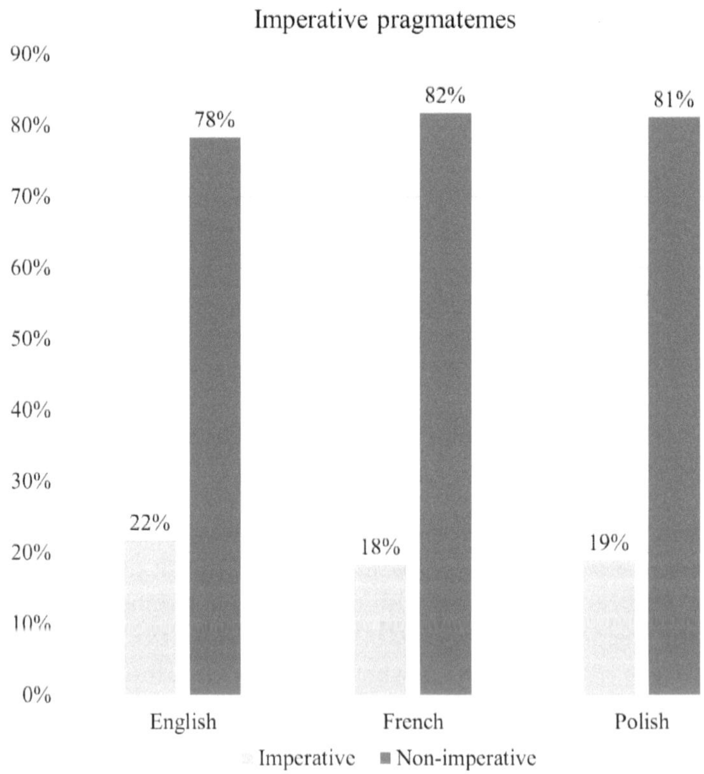

Figure 22. Percentage distribution of imperative and non-imperative pragmatemes found in the corpora

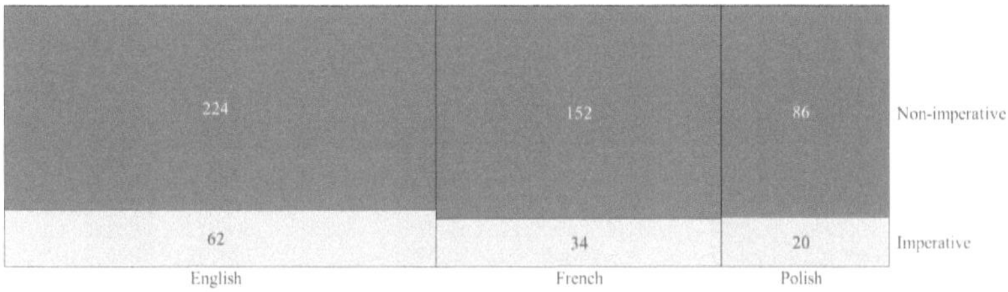

Figure 23. Mosaic plot for imperative and non-imperative pragmatemes found in the corpora

In all three languages, the vast majority of pragmatemes are non-imperative. Additionally, it is worth noting that the differences between the percentage of non-imperative pragmatemes in all three languages are minimal. This may lead to a hypothesis[161] about the general nature of pragmatemes applicable in everyday conversations, i.e., that regardless of the language, the prevailing pattern suggests that the majority of these units are non-imperative, which can be also noted for the analyzed corpora from the mosaic plot in Figure 23.

Furthermore, in terms of the expected number of occurrences per one million words, the median for non-imperative units was higher than for imperative ones in all three of the studied languages[162], meaning that not only were non-imperative pragmatemes more common in the studied corpora than imperative ones, but pragmatemes of the former type also occurred more frequently.

4.5 Presence of verbless forms

When one thinks of common pragmatemes such as *Hello*, *Fresh Paint,* or *Cash or credit?*, one may conclude that a large number of these units may be

161 While this is certainly true for the present study, to make generalizations about pragmatemes as a linguistic phenomenon, a study conducted on bigger corpora would be welcome in order to prove or disprove this hypothesis.

162 The median values of expected number of occurrences per one million words for non-imperative versus imperative pragmatemes in the studied languages are as follows: English: six to five, French: eight to six, Polish: 29 to 22.

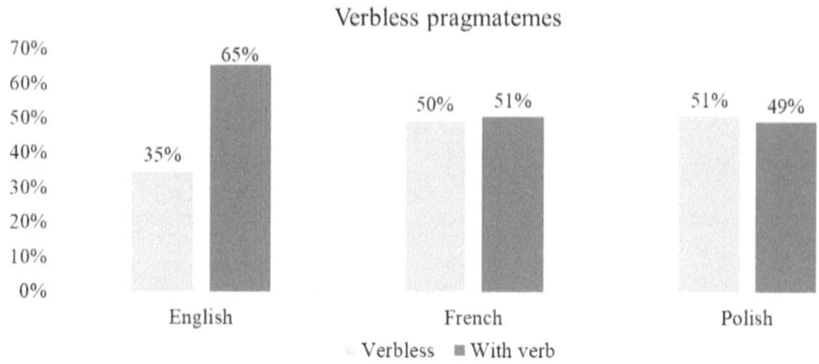

Figure 24. Percentage distribution of verbless and non-verbless pragmatemes found in the corpora

verbless. This presumption was verified for the pragmatemes found in the corpora, with results presented in Figure 24.

In French and Polish, the percentage distribution between verbless pragmatemes and pragmatemes with a verb is nearly equal, divided almost exactly in half. Verbless units are slightly more prevalent in the Polish corpus compared to the French one. A significantly larger disparity is found in the English corpus, where pragmatemes with a verb constitute over 65 percent of the total. The reasons for this difference remain unclear. However, it is worth noting that the English corpus also had the highest percentage of imperative pragmatemes (although the difference was not as pronounced as the one discussed here; see p. 162).

The proportions of verbless and non-verbless pragmatemes according to the language of the analysis are also presented in the form of a mosaic plot in Figure 25.

What is also interesting is that in English, the median number of expected occurrences per one million words for non-verbless pragmatemes is smaller than for the verbless pragmatemes (five to six), while in Polish and French, it is the opposite, i.e., the median is higher for verbless units (29 to 22 in Polish and nine to eight in French). All things considered, it can be concluded that the results observed in the corpora support the hypothesis that a significant

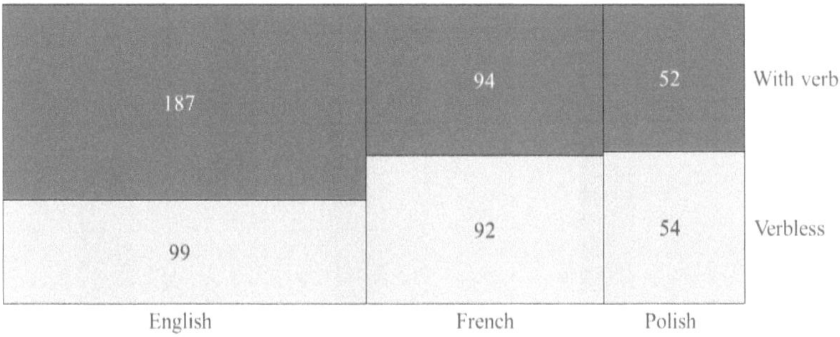

Figure 25. Mosaic plot for verbless and non-verbless pragmatemes found in the corpora

number of conversational pragmatemes are verbless, regardless of whether the language is English, French, or Polish[163].

4.6 Presence of question forms

The next linguistic trait to be investigated among the pragmatemes found in the corpora is the presence of pragmatemes that are questions. This characteristic is examined based on the observation that in the literature review, a considerable number of such units was found, e.g., *How are you?*, *Will you marry me?*, or *Can you hear me?*. Figure 26 presents the percentage distribution of pragmatemes in question form found in the corpora.

---

163 Yet, interesting conclusions can be made when looking at equivalent pragmatemes in the studied languages. For instance, pragmatemes that include specific time tend to be verbless in French and Polish (e.g., the French *À demain* and the Polish *Do jutra*, the French *Bonne journée* and the Polish *Miłego dnia*), while non-verbless in English (e.g., *See you tomorrow* and *Have a nice day*). This observation aligns with the claim made by Chuquet and Paillard (1987: 20) who note that English generally tends to express subordinate temporal relations with the use of verbs rather than nouns, which is a tendency in French.

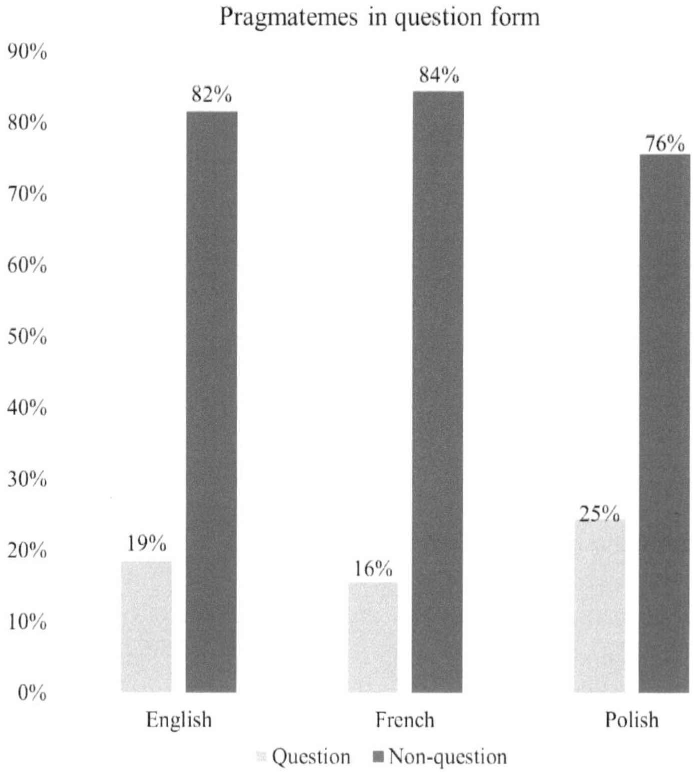

Figure 26. Percentage distribution of question and non-question form of pragmatemes found in the corpora

By a large margin, the question form is not a predominant trait among pragmatemes from the corpora in all three languages; yet, on average one in five pragmatemes is a question. The highest percentage of question-form pragmatemes was found in the Polish corpus, which can be also noted from the distribution presented on the mosaic plot in Figure 27.

Question-form pragmatemes in Polish also had a higher expected number of occurrences per one million words than non-question ones, with

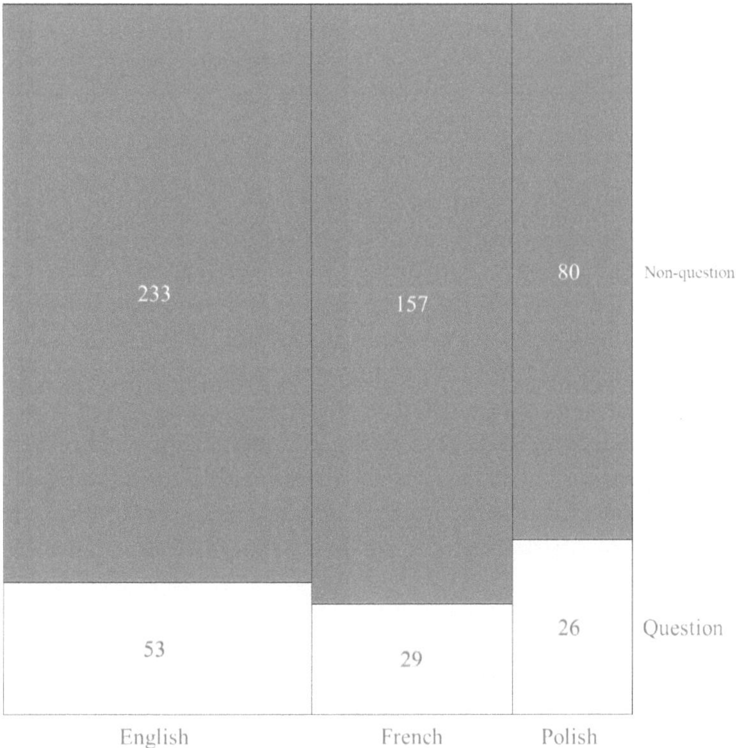

Figure 27. Mosaic plot for question and non-question form of pragmatemes found in the corpora

a median expected frequency of 29 occurrences per one million words for question-form pragmatemes, compared to the median of 22 occurrences for non-question pragmatemes. Likewise, in the English corpus, question form pragmatemes have a higher number of occurrences, with a median expected occurrence of nine instances per million words, compared to five instances for non-question pragmatemes. In the case of French, the expected number of occurrences per one million words was the same for both question and non-question pragmatemes, with a median of eight. Therefore, it can be concluded that in all the studied corpora, despite the fact that the majority of pragmatemes are not questions, question-form pragmatemes occur either equally or more frequently than non-question ones.

4.7 Presence of elliptical forms

Defined by *Longman Dictionary of Language Teaching and Applied Linguistics* as "the leaving out of words or phrases from sentences where they are unnecessary" (Richards and Schmidt 2011: 188), ellipsis has been studied in linguistics from various angles, discussing its purpose and possible typologies (e.g., McCarthy 1991, Aryani 2009, Winkler 2005). In this study, ellipsis represents the omission of linguistic material in a structure and the creation of a fixed unit, often by shortening another fixed unit (e.g., *Nice to meet you* instead of *It's nice to meet you*). However, because the pragmatemes found in the corpus are already subject to many categories of analysis, I decided to investigate whether the units are elliptical or not, without delving further into the possible types of ellipsis. Furthermore, the study does not delve into the etymology of the units. Therefore, only units in which pinpointing the full-length expression was possible without looking into historical sources are considered as elliptical (e.g., *Ça va ?* instead of *Comment ça va ?*)[164].

The ellipsis category was added to the analysis because it is hypothesized that many pragmatemes may be elliptical. This hypothesis is based on White's (2013) study on the VOICE corpus of English as a Lingua Franca that "demonstrated that ellipsis is a strong marker of interaction in oral discourse" (White 2013: 274), and the fact that pragmatemes studied here are an important part of everyday oral interactions. Therefore, Figure 28 presents the percentage of elliptical pragmatemes found in the studied corpora.

---

164 Nonetheless, conducting an etymological study of pragmatemes such as *Dzień dobry* (Polish greeting used to greet someone throughout the day, lit. *Good day*) could be an intriguing topic for future research. Such an investigation might delve into exploring the possibility of these units being elliptical forms derived from longer pragmatemes.

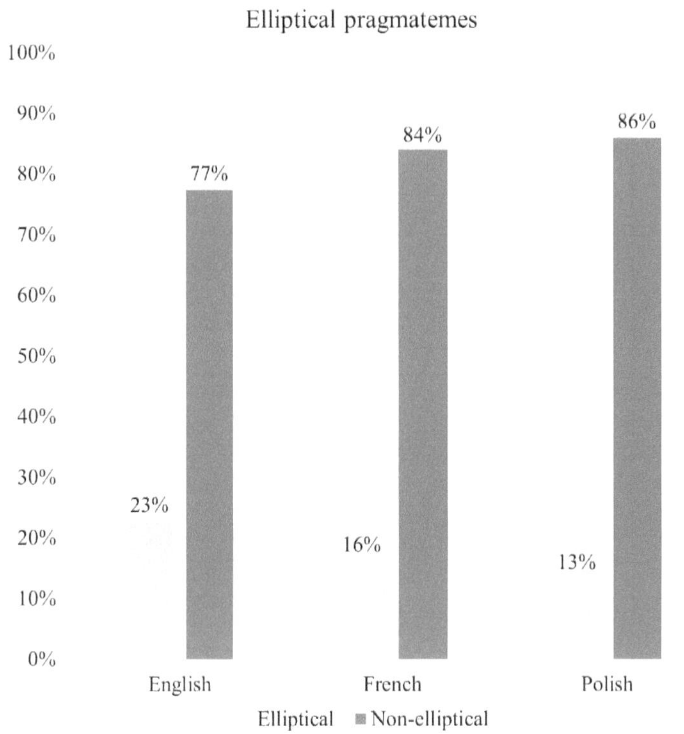

Figure 28. Percentage distribution of the presence of ellipsis in pragmatemes found in the corpora

As shown in Figure 28, the initial hypothesis proved to be false. In all languages, the vast majority of pragmatemes found in the corpora are not elliptical. The biggest percentage of elliptical pragmatemes can be found in the English corpus (22.7%); however, the percentages of elliptical pragmatemes in the French corpus is not significantly different from what was found in the English corpus (16.1%), which is also visible in the mosaic plot in Figure 29.

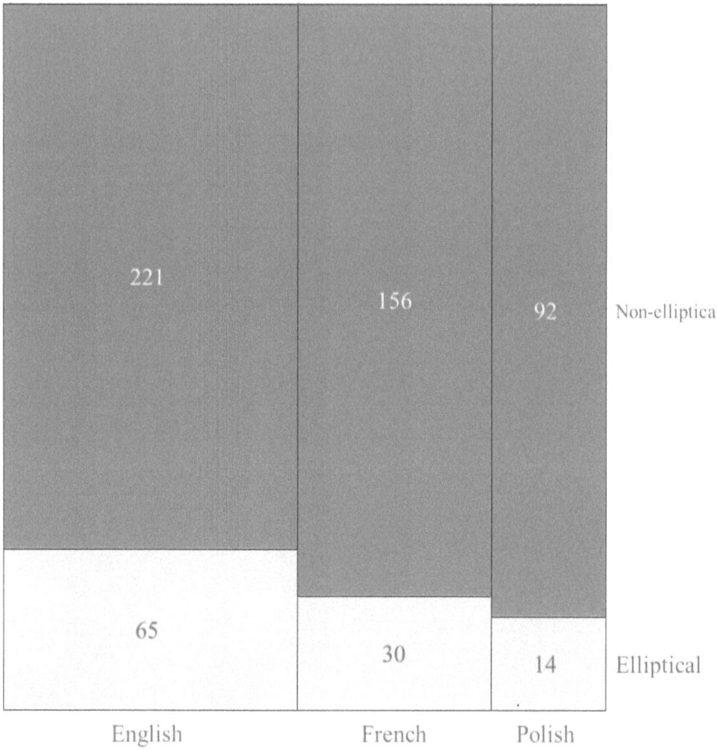

Figure 29. Mosaic plot for elliptical and non-elliptical pragmatemes found in the corpora

In terms of their normalized frequency, in English, non-elliptical pragmatemes are slightly more frequent than elliptical ones, with a median of six expected occurrences per one million words for the former and five for the latter. In French, the median for both is eight, whereas in Polish, the median is higher for elliptical pragmatemes (32) than non-elliptical ones (22). Therefore, while it is clear that most pragmatemes found in the corpora are not elliptical, regardless of the language, an overall statement regarding the frequency of elliptical and non-elliptical pragmatemes cannot be made.

4.8 Presence of deictic expressions

Since the present study discusses the topic of pragmatemes, one of the necessary characteristics in the linguistic analysis is what can be called a *pragmatic universal* (for the discussion on the universality of deixis see, for example, Kryk 1990), something common to all languages[165], i.e., deixis, the linguistic phenomenon of indicating elements "of the situational and/or discourse context, including the speech participants and the time and location of the current speech event" (Diessel 2019: 463).

Bühler (1934: 10) describes the complexity of deixis as follows: "Deictic expressions refer to a deictic field of language whose zero point – the Origo – is fixed by the person who is speaking (the 'I'), the place of the utterance (the 'here'), and the time of the utterances (the 'now')." Hence, three types of deixis can be distinguished: person, place, and time (Lyons 1977). In this study, a fourth category is added and that is discourse deixis, a type of deixis referencing a portion of a discourse in relation to a speaker's given "time" and "place" in the discourse (see for example Guillot 2006, Yang 2011). Based on Kryk's (1990: 49) claim that "[n]ot only are all languages indexical, but so are over 90 percent of the sentences produced by humans", it is hypothesized that the pragmatemes found in the corpora of the three languages of analysis will have a high frequency of deictic expressions (or *deictic markers*, terms used here interchangeably). To examine this issue, the results of the presence of deixis in pragmatemes are presented in Figure 30.

Although the percentage distribution presented in Figure 30 shows the presence of deixis in pragmatemes found in the corpora and not yet the types of deictic expressions, two categories of deixis are already distinguished: explicit and implicit deixis. These categories are created for the purpose of the present study. However, the distinction between explicit and implicit deixis lies not in their function (as both serve the purpose of referring to something within the context), but rather in the sentence structure. Explicit deixis refers to the presence of deictic expressions on the surface of a sentence. The deictic markers found in the analyzed pragmatemes are:

165 Levinson (2004: 97) acknowledges the importance of deixis as a universal characteristics, a one that is probable to have played a crucial role in the evolution of language, and notes that "it is a much more pervasive feature of languages than normally recognized."

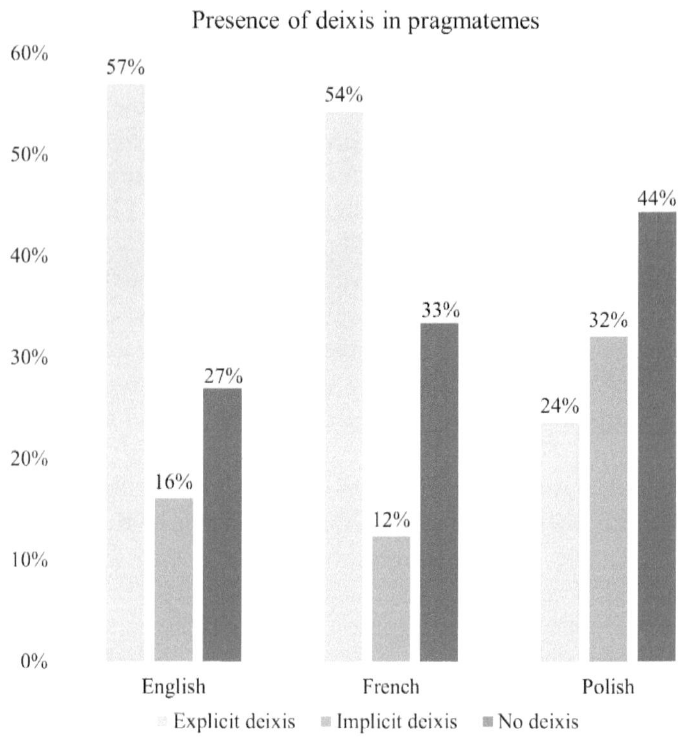

Figure 30. Percentage distribution of the presence of deixis in pragmatemes found in the corpora

- in English: *I*, *we*, *you*, and *ya* (person deixis), *here* and *there* (spatial deixis), *morning*, *afternoon*, *evening*, *night*, and *later* (temporal deixis), and *this* (discourse deixis);
- in French: *je*, *tu*, *il*, *on*, *vous*, *mon*, *mes*, *ton*, *tes*, *votre*, *vos*, *moi*, *toi*, *te*, *and t'* (person deixis), *ici*, *y*, and *là* (spatial deixis), *plus tard*, *plus*, *toute*, *tout de suite*, *la prochaine*, *tout à l'heure*, *vite*, *bientôt*, *demain*, *ce soir*, *soirée*, *soir*, *nuit*, *minute*, and *instant* (temporal deixis), and *c'* (discourse deixis);

- and in Polish: *ci, ciebie, pana, pani, go, mi, moje, mną,* and *siebie* (person deixis), *tam, tu,* and *tędy* (spatial deixis), *chwileczkę, wieczór, na razie, na wieki wieków,* and *na chwilę* (temporal deixis), and *to* (discourse deixis).

For instance, in the pragmateme *I'm sorry I'm late*, there is the deictic marker "I", referring to the speaker themselves twice. Meanwhile, in the Polish equivalent of the same pragmateme, *Przepraszam za spóźnienie*, there are no deictic expressions on the surface of the unit; however, the speaker is referred to in the way the verb is conjugated. Furthermore, the implicit category contains not only pragmatemes with deixis somewhat related to the surface of the sentence, since the reference is made in the conjugated verb that is a part of the sentence, but also elliptical sentences that exclude deictic expressions found in their original counterparts (e.g., *Thanks for coming* instead of *Thank you for coming, Besoin d'aide ?* [Eng. *Need help?*] instead of, for example, *Vous avez besoin d'aide ?* [Eng. *Do you need help?*]). As for non-deictical pragmatemes, examples include units such as *Hi,* or *Peace out*, in which there is no reference towards the context, neither on the surface of the sentence, nor implicitly through ellipsis or the conjugation of the verb.

In order to better visualize the ratio between non-deictical and deictical pragmatemes, without the division into implicit and explicit deixis, the mosaic plot in Figure 31 is presented.

It can be noted from the column chart in Figure 30 and particularly from the mosaic plot in Figure 31, that the results in the three languages of the analysis do not differ greatly. In all three languages, non-deictic pragmatemes constitute between 30 percent and 40 percent of all pragmatemes found in the corpora, with the smallest percentage found in English (27%) and the biggest in Polish (44,3%). In general, the results for the pragmatemes of the corpora are closer to the results presented by Lipińska (2009) in her study on slogans, where 60 percent of studied slogans contained deictic expressions, than to Kryk's (1990) claim that 90 percent of the sentences produced by humans are indexical.

As for the explicit-implicit deixis ratio, the great majority of deixis in both English and French was explicit, while in Polish, implicit deixis was more common. Furthermore, in terms of the expected number of occurrences per one million words, in Polish pragmatemes with implicit deixis were more

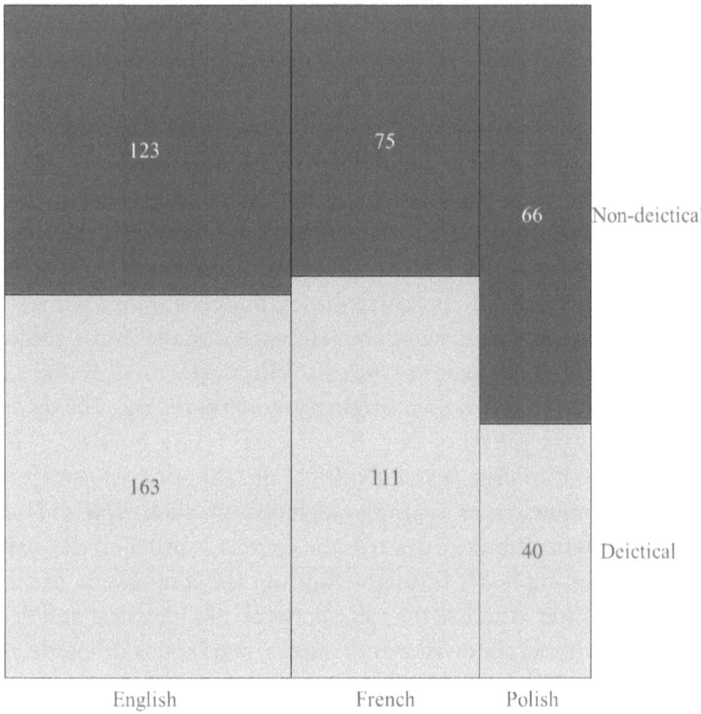

Figure 31. Mosaic plot for deictical and non-deictical pragmatemes found in the corpora

frequent than those with explicit deixis, while in English and French, the contrary was true[166]. The explanation for this is straightforward: the grammatical rules of Polish allow for the omission of the subject in all types of sentences, unlike the grammatical rules of English and French, in which the

166 The exact median values for the expected number of occurrences per one million words are as follows: English: six for pragmatemes with explicit deixis, five for those with implicit deixis, nine for non-deictic pragmatemes, French: eight for explicit deixis, five for implicit, eleven for non-deictic, and Polish: 22 for explicit, 25 for implicit, and 29 for non-deictic.

suppression of the subject is allowed only in the imperative. Therefore, in Polish, the reference to the person is usually made through the conjugated verb, which can be also seen from how prominent "in the verb" implicit deixis is as presented in Figure 32.

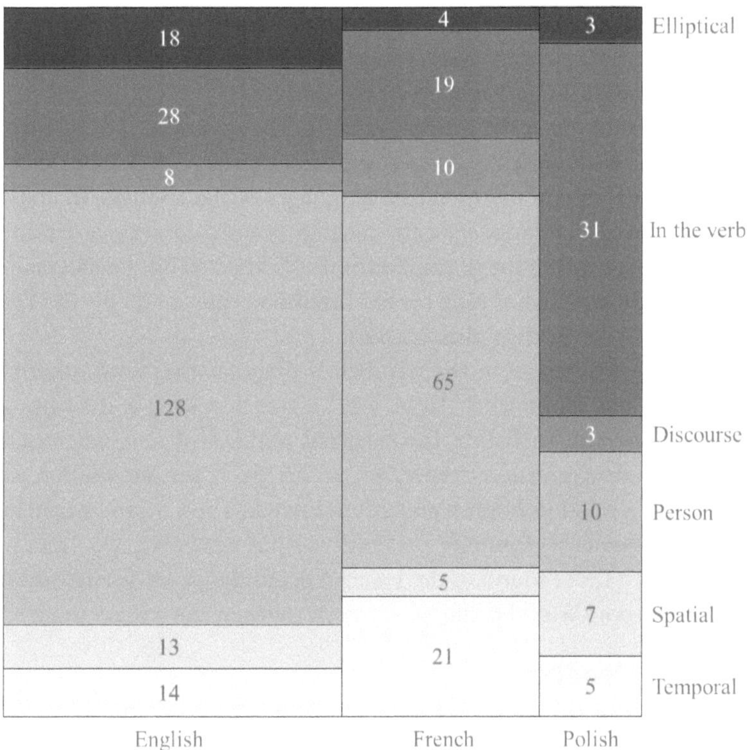

Figure 32. Mosaic plot for different deictic expressions types per one million words in pragmatemes found in the corpora

Figure 32 displays the mosaic plot illustrating types of different deictic expressions found in pragmatemes across the corpora. The mosaic plot was chosen over a column chart for this parameter because it provides a clearer visualization of the raw numerical data. For example, thanks to the proportions of the cells, it can be easily discerned that there was a larger number of deictical pragmatemes to analyze in English than Polish, but, with that in mind, the number of 31 pragmatemes with the "in the verb" deixis is significantly larger than the seemingly close number of 28 pragmatemes with the same type of deixis in English. That is actually what stands out the most in the mosaic plot presented in Figure 32: the proportion of "in the verb" implicit deixis in Polish. Since "in the verb" implicit deixis also refers to a person, it emphasizes the observation that person deixis is the most common type across all the languages of the analysis.

However, looking at the median values of the normalized frequencies of pragmatemes with deictic expressions, pragmatemes with person deixis are not the most frequent in any of the languages of the analysis. In contrast, in all three analyzed languages, the median pointed to pragmatemes with temporal deixis having the greatest number of expected occurrences per one million words (median of nine for the English corpus, of 23 for the French corpus, and of 51 for the Polish corpus).

While the differences in the number of pragmatemes with other types of deixis are not significantly large, what is worth noting is the sum of all deictic expressions. In Polish, the expected number of pragmatemes with different deictic expressions (types, not occurrences) per one million words is 427, while it is 291 in English and 201 in French. Thus, it can be concluded that the pragmatemes found in the Polish corpus were over two times more indexical than those found in the French corpus; however, further research on larger corpora would be necessary to strengthen this observation.

4.9 Speech acts

The role of speech acts in pragmatic phraseologisms was already noted in Kauffer's (2018) study on stereotyped language acts (ALS, see p. 32). Therefore, taking inspiration from that approach, in this study, pragmatemes are also examined from the point of view of speech acts.

Speech act theory, a fundamental framework in the study of language and communication, has been extensively explored and discussed in numerous research papers since its first introduction by Austin (1962) and refinement by Searle (1969, 1979), who laid the foundation for understanding how language is not merely a tool for conveying information but also for performing various actions in human communication. However, since speech act theory is not the main focus of the present thesis, and given its extent, use of that theory will be based on the speech acts[167] taxonomy originally suggested by Searle (1979). The categories in this taxonomy are assertives (here referred to as representatives), directives, expressives, declarations (declaratives) and commissives. Representatives involve making statements or assertions about the world, aiming to represent facts or convey information, e.g., *It's a boy.* Directives, in turn, are concerned with exerting influence over the actions of others, encompassing commands, requests, and suggestions, e.g., *Keep the change.* Expressives center on the speaker's expression of their psychological state or emotions, such as apologizing, congratulating, or commiserating, e.g., *I'm sorry I'm late.* Declarations involve the act of bringing about a change in the external world by the mere utterance itself, e.g., *I now pronounce you husband and wife.* Lastly, commissives pertain to commitments or promises to perform future actions, binding the speaker to a course of action, e.g., *I'll call you back.* All five types can be found throughout the English, French, and Polish corpora used in this study, which is depicted in Figure 33.

As can be observed in Figure 33, in both English and French, the most common speech act performed by pragmatemes in the corpora is the expressive (40.9% in English and 45,2% in French), while the second most common is the directive (38.1% in English and almost the same percentage, 38.2%, in French). In Polish the reverse is the case, with a similar percentage distribution: directive pragmatemes are the most common (41.5%), and expressive are second[168] (37.7%). The fact that in the Polish corpus the most common type is directive may align with research done on cross-cultural directness, in which imperative forms were found to be more common in Polish than in English (e.g., Ogiermann 2009, Zinken and Ogiermann 2013, Wierzbicka 1985).

---

167 To be more precise in terminology, the taxonomy under consideration pertains to illocutionary acts, which is a specific category within the broader field of speech acts. However, for the sake of clarity and consistency, this discussion will employ the term *speech acts* rather than *illocutionary acts*. This choice is based on the fact that the majority of linguistic research revolves around illocutionary acts and commonly labels them as speech acts (Griffiths 2006: 156).

168 However, in terms of the number of occurrences, Polish expressive pragmatemes have a bigger median value of the expected number of occurrences per one million words, i.e., 29, than directive ones (22).

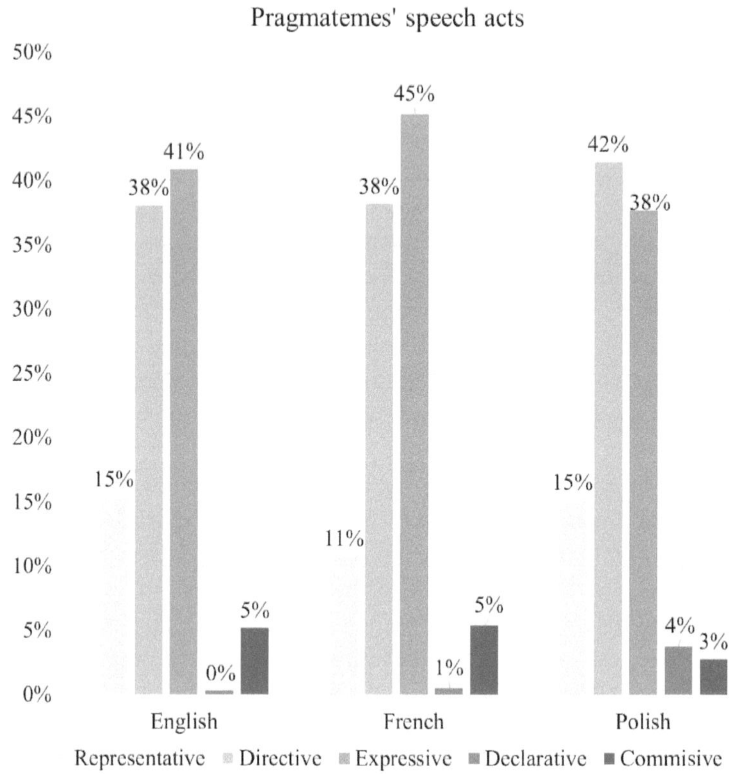

Figure 33. Percentage distribution of speech acts of pragmatemes found in the corpora

Furthermore, the diversity of expressive polite formulas of *Have a [POSITIVE ADJECTIVE]*[169] *[SOMETHING]* type was significantly greater in the English corpus (e.g., *Have a good day, Have a good night, Have a good one, Have a good time*) and the French (e.g., *Bonne nuit, Bonne journée, Bonne route, Bonne soirée*) than in the Polish, where the only pragmateme of this type was *Miłego dnia* (Eng. *Have a nice day*). This diversity in expressive formulas in English and French may help explain why expressive speech acts are more

169 The following adjectives of a positive value were found to be used in this position: "good", "nice", and "great."

prevalent in these corpora compared to directive speech acts, an outcome not found in the Polish corpus, as also visible in the mosaic plot in Figure 34.

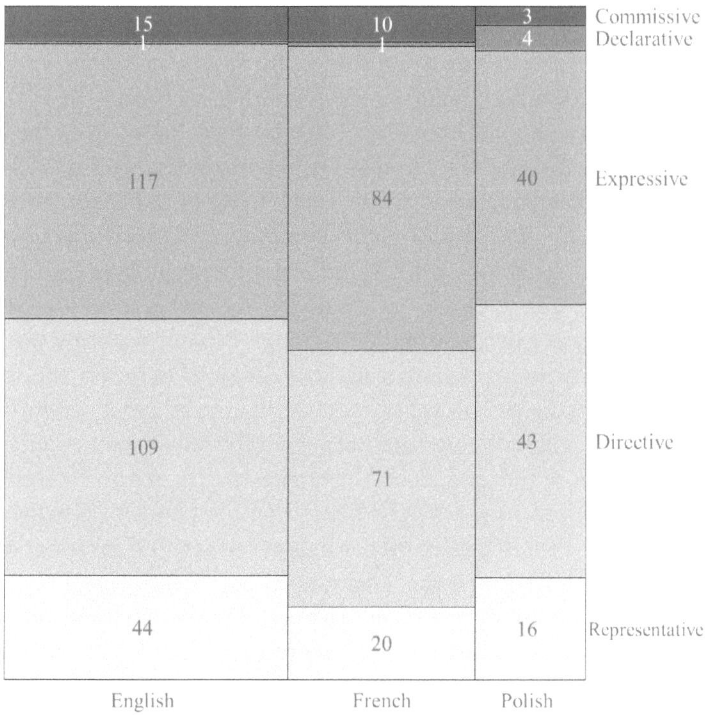

Figure 34. Mosaic plot for speech acts of pragmatemes found in the corpora

As observed both in Figure 33 and in 34, the representative type was found to be the third most common across pragmatemes in all three corpora, but, in terms of the number of occurrences, also across all three corpora, it was characterized by the largest median value of expected number of occurrences per one million words (nine in English, ten in French, and 29 in Polish[170]).

[170] The exact median values of the expected number of occurrences per one million words for the rest of speech acts are as follows: English: six for expressives, five for

Meanwhile, commissive and declarative speech acts were least common among the pragmatemes, which can be explained by the type of the studied corpus, i.e., everyday conversations[171]. In English and French, commissives were more frequent than declaratives (5.2% of commissives to 0.3% of declaratives in English and 5.4% to 0.5% in French), while in Polish, the opposite was true (3.8% of declaratives to 2.8% of commisives). The higher percentage of declarative speech act pragmatemes in Polish can probably be attributed to the presence of pragmatemes used in the Catholic mass within the Polish corpus. However, in the case of religious pragmatemes, one may reflect on whether such a pragmateme is, in fact, declarative or rather representative, such as in the case of *Ciało Chrystusa* (Eng. *Body of Christ*), uttered during the communion ceremony: while some may perceive it as a representative speech act (presentation of the sacramental wafer), believers in the Catholic faith will view it as a declarative one (although it is not explicitly expressed from the linguistic point of view, it signifies the belief in the transformation of the wafer into the real body of Christ during the religious ceremony).

Nonetheless, religious pragmatemes are not the only ones that can be ambiguous in terms of the speech acts they represent, but so too are seemingly phatic constructions such as *Hello?* uttered on the phone or *Good morning* uttered when one enters a place. According to Lyons (1977), phatic constructions have no informative value, and according to Leech (1983), their only purpose is to maintain friendly social relations. With that in mind, one might ask whether phatic constructions can be considered speech acts. However, in Austin's (1962) early taxonomy, greetings belong to the behabitives category of speech acts that constitute a reaction to the behavior of other people and various attitudes towards people. This category was later incorporated into Searle's (1969) one of expressive speech acts. Furthermore, Bach and Harnish (1979) emphasize that greetings are used to express the pleasure of seeing or meeting somebody, while Jibreen (2010) notes that expressive speech acts

directives, five for commissives, and four for declaratives (with only one example of declaratives in the English corpus); French: nine for expressives, five for directives, eight for commissives, and 27 for declaratives (with only one example); and Polish: 29 for expressives and 22 for directives, commissives, and declaratives.

171 It can be hypothesized that in a study on pragmatemes in TV series taking place in court, declarative and commissive units would be more frequent.

establish an interpersonal relation between the interlocutors, which is also key in phatic communication. In terms of studies of phatic communication and not speech act theory per se, Boxer (2002) perceives phatic structures as acts since they convey important information about the wishes and needs of both the speaker and the hearer. Considering all of the above, in this study polite formulas, often of a phatic nature[172], are categorized as expressive speech acts.

4.10 Pragmateme types

Finally, the pragmatemes found in the corpora were also analyzed based on the types of pragmatemes they represent. A detailed discussion of the typology of pragmatemes can be found in the literature review (see p. 42) The typology used for the analysis was the one proposed by myself, as inspired by Kecskés's (2010) work on situation-bound utterances (see p. 35). Figure 35 presents the percentage distribution of different pragmateme types found in the English, French, and Polish corpora.

Plain pragmatemes (i.e., the compositional ones, e.g., *Call an ambulance*) constitute the majority of the units found in all analyzed corpora, comprising 67.1 percent in English, 69.9 percent in French, and 71.7 percent in Polish. The second most common type in both English and French is the loaded one (i.e., non-compositional ones, e.g., *Take your seats*), being 18.2 percent in the former case and 21.5 percent in the latter, while in the Polish corpus, there is a less significant disparity in the percentage distribution between loaded and charged (i.e., the ones whose meaning depend on the context, e.g., *I'm fine, thank you* as either a response to *How are you?* or *Would you like something more to eat?*) pragmatemes, with a slightly higher percentage of charged pragmatemes (15.1%) than loaded ones (13.2%). It is worth noting that the results for the French corpus raise questions about Blanco and Mejri's (2018) definition of a prototypical pragmateme, since they assert that a prototypical pragmateme is compositional, but 30.1 percent pragmatemes found in the present French corpus are either loaded or charged, both of which can be characterized by idiomaticity, not compositionality. While the definition used for this study slightly differs from Blanco and Mejri's (see

172 The use of the word "often" here is intentional, as it is claimed that a unique context should always be examined to determine whether a formula was used in a phatic manner.

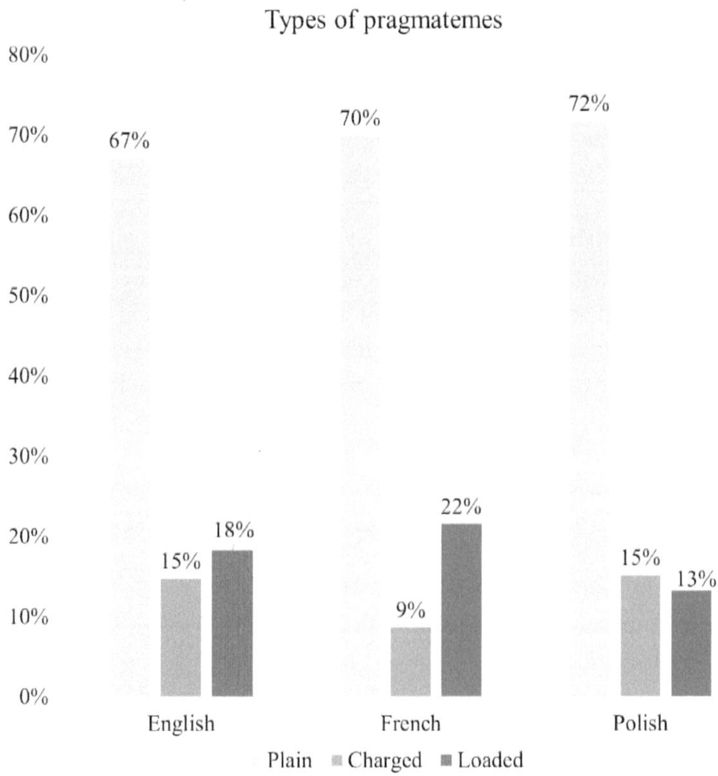

Figure 35. Percentage distribution of pragmateme type of pragmatemes found in the corpora

p. 48), the results found here further suggest that idiomatic pragmatemes do not constitute only a small fraction of all pragmatemes and are worth examination. The relative prominence of idiomatic pragmatemes is also further visualized in Figure 36.

When considering the frequency of pragmatemes of different types, it is notable that in both French and Polish, charged pragmatemes stand out above the others. In French, they have the median value of 14 expected occurrences per one million words (compared to eight for plain and nine for loaded pragmatemes). In Polish, charged pragmatemes have a median

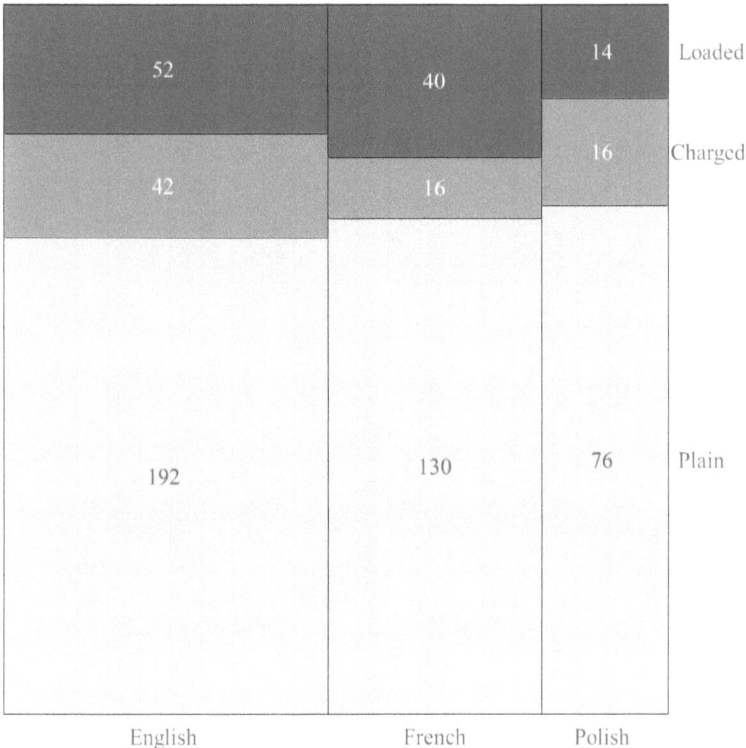

Figure 36. Mosaic plot for pragmateme type of pragmatemes found in the corpora

value of 29 (compared to 22 for both plain and loaded pragmatemes). In English, this phenomenon is not observed, and the median values do not differ significantly. Both plain and charged pragmatemes have a median of six expected occurrences per one million words, while loaded ones have a median of four.

Next, the three types of pragmatemes were compared, taking into account the characteristics discussed in the preceding subsections. The percentage distribution of these characteristics, categorized by the given pragmateme type, is presented in Table 7.

Table 7. Percentage distribution of different characteristics used throughout the analysis according to the pragmateme type

	Plain ENG	Plain FR	Plain PL	Charged ENG	Charged FR	Charged PL	Loaded ENG	Loaded FR	Loaded PL
Frequency									
Average	16.02	**25.36**[173]	13.95	**39.1**	21.19	5.81	8.4	**28.35**	3.36
Median	**5**	**5**	3	4.5	**9**	4	3	**6**	3
2-9	70.8%	70.8%	**75%**	69%	50%	**87.5%**	84.6%	67.5%	**100%**
10-19	**15.1%**	8.5%	11.8%	9.5%	**31.3%**	6.3%	3.8%	**12.5%**	0%
20-29	**5.2%**	2.3%	2.6%	2.4%	**12.5%**	6.3%	3.8%	**7.5%**	0%
30-50	3.6%	**10%**	5.3%	**11.9%**	0%	0%	3.8%	**7.5%**	0%
51-99	2.1%	**3.1%**	1.3%	**4.8%**	0%	0%	3.8%	0%	0%
> 100	3.1%	**5.4%**	3.9%	2.4%	**6.3%**	0%	0%	**5%**	0%
Expected number of occurrences per million words									
Average	21	38	**101**	**51**	32	42	11	**43**	24
Median	6	8	**22**	6	14	**29**	4	9	**22**
2-9	**63%**	61.5%	0%	**64.3%**	43.8%	0%	**76.9%**	52.5%	0%
10-19	21.4%	11.5%	**32.9%**	11.9%	18.8%	**25%**	11.5%	20%	**42.9%**
20-29	2.6%	6.2%	**30.3%**	2.4%	18.8%	**37.5%**	1.9%	7.5%	**42.9%**
30-50	5.2%	3.1%	**6.6%**	7.1%	**12.5%**	6.3%	3.8%	**10%**	0%
51-99	4.7%	**11.5%**	7.9%	11.9%	0%	**25%**	3.8%	5%	**14.3%**
> 100	3.1%	6.2%	**22.4%**	2.4%	**6.3%**	**6.3%**	1.9%	**5%**	0%
Number of words									

(Continued)

173 The highest number linearly in the given language set is put in bold.

Table 7. (Continued)

	Plain ENG	Plain FR	Plain PL	Charged ENG	Charged FR	Charged PL	Loaded ENG	Loaded FR	Loaded PL
Average	**3.1**	2.75	2.14	**2.29**	2.06	1.81	**2.85**	2.58	2.5
Median	**3**	**3**	2	2	2	2	**3**	2.5	2
Exactly:									
1	11.5%	23.1%	**30.3%**	23.8%	25%	**43.8%**	7.7%	7.5%	**21.4%**
2	25.5%	20%	**35.5%**	35.7%	**50%**	37.5%	36.5%	42.5%	**57.1%**
3	**27.1%**	26.2%	25%	**33.3%**	18.8%	12.5%	30.8%	**35%**	7.1%
4	20.8%	**23.8%**	7.9%	4.8%	**6.3%**	**6.3%**	**17.3%**	15%	7.1%
5	**8.9%**	3.8%	1.3%	0%	0%	0%	5.8%	0%	0%
6	**5.2%**	2.3%	0%	**2.4%**	0%	0%	0%	0%	0%
7	**1%**	0.8%	0%	0%	0%	0%	**1.9%**	0%	0%
9	0%	0%	0%	0%	0%	0%	0%	0%	**7.1%**
Number of variants									
Average	3.31	**3.51**	2.36	2.6	**3.5**	1.63	2.67	**2.68**	1.71
Median	**3**	2	2	2	**3**	2	**2**	**2**	1
Exactly:									
1	16.7%	26.2%	**35.5%**	21.4%	18.8%	**43.8%**	13.5%	35%	**57.1%**
2-5	**69.3%**	58.5%	56.6%	**76.2%**	62.5%	56.3%	**78.8%**	55%	21.4%
6-9	**11.5%**	10%	6.6%	0%	**12.5%**	0%	7.7%	10%	**14.3%**
≥ 10	2.6%	**5.4%**	1.3%	2.4%	**6.3%**	0%	0%	0%	**7.1%**
Imperative									
Yes	**22.4%**	20%	19.7%	**21.4%**	6.3%	12.5%	19.2%	0%	**21.4%**
No	77.6%	80%	**80.3%**	78.6%	**93.8%**	87.5%	80.8%	**100%**	78.6%
Verbless									
Yes	31.3%	45.4%	**47.4%**	42.9%	**68.8%**	50%	40.4%	55%	**78.6%**
No	**68.8%**	54.6%	52.6%	**57.1%**	31.3%	50%	**59.6%**	45%	21.4%

(Continued)

Table 7. (Continued)

	Plain ENG	Plain FR	Plain PL	Charged ENG	Charged FR	Charged PL	Loaded ENG	Loaded FR	Loaded PL
					Question				
Yes	19.3%	10%	**22.4%**	11.9%	18.8%	**43.7%**	21.2%	**32.5%**	14.3%
No	80.7%	**90%**	77.6%	88.1%	**81.3%**	56.3%	78.8%	67.5%	**85.7%**
					Ellipsis				
Yes	**20.8%**	8.5%	10.5%	23.8%	**43.7%**	25%	28.8%	**30%**	14.3%
No	79.2%	**91.5%**	89.5%	**76.2%**	56.3%	75%	71.2%	70%	**85.7%**
					Deixis				
Yes explicit	58.9%	**60.8%**	23.7%	**54.8%**	43.8%	25%	**51.9%**	37.5%	21.4%
Yes implicit	16.1%	15.4%	**32.9%**	14.3%	12.5%	**43.8%**	**17.3%**	2.5%	14.3%
No	25%	23.8%	**43.4%**	31%	**43.8%**	31.3%	30.8%	60%	**64.3%**
					Deixis type				
Temporal	12.5%	**17.2%**	4.7%	6.9%	**22.2%**	9.1%	2.8%	18.8%	**40%**
Spatial	7.6%	6.1%	**14%**	**13.8%**	0%	0%	13.9%	6.3%	**20%**
Person	**61.8%**	49.5%	20.9%	**58.6%**	55.6%	9.1%	61.1%	**68.8%**	0%
Discourse	4.2%	**15.2%**	2.3%	10.3%	11.1%	**18.2%**	**2.8%**	0%	0%
In the verb	14.6%	18.2%	**53.5%**	6.9%	11.1%	**54.5%**	13.9%	0%	**40%**
Elliptical	**6.9%**	2%	4.7%	**13.8%**	11.1%	9.1%	**11.1%**	6.3%	0%
					Speech act				
Representative	12.5%	10%	**15.8%**	**26.2%**	18.8%	18.8%	**17.3%**	10%	0%
Directive	40.6%	40%	**43.4%**	28.6%	**37.5%**	**37.5%**	**36.5%**	32.5%	35.7%
Expressive	40.6%	**42.3%**	38.2%	38.1%	**43.8%**	31.3%	44.2%	**55%**	42.9%
Declarative	0%	**0.8%**	0%	2.4%	0%	**6.3%**	0%	0%	**21.4%**
Commisive	6.3%	**6.9%**	2.6%	4.8%	0%	**6.3%**	1.9%	**2.5%**	0%

Several key observations can be derived from Table 7. These points are presented below in the order of the present analysis up to this point:

1) **Frequency.**

What can be deduced from Figure 37 is that in both the English and the French corpora, the predominant category consists of pragmatemes with expected frequencies ranging from two to nine occurrences per one million words, regardless of the type of pragmateme. However, it is worth noting that in the French corpus, such pragmatemes constitute 43.8 percent of charged units, a percentage smaller compared to the ones in French plain and loaded units, as well as all types of English units, where pragmatemes with two to nine expected occurrences collectively account for more than half of all pragmatemes. In contrast, the Polish corpus exhibits greater diversity among pragmateme types. In the plain category, pragmatemes

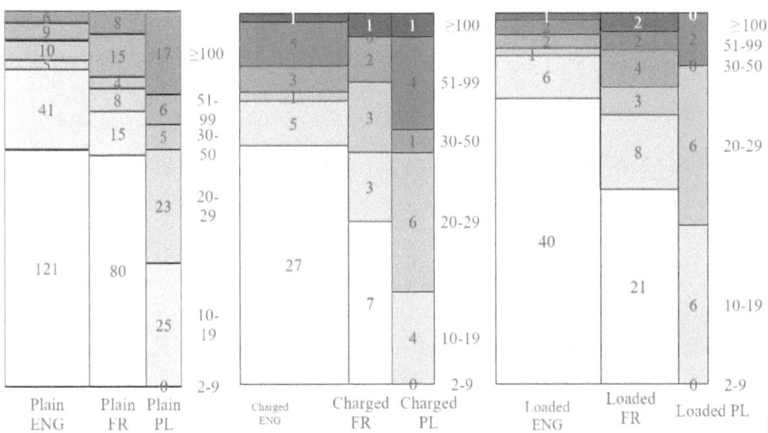

Figure 37. Mosaic plots for the estimated number of occurrences per one million words according to the language of the analysis and the pragmateme type (plain, charged, and loaded)

with ten to 19 expected occurrences are the most prevalent (32.9% of Polish plain pragmatemes), whereas in the charged category, pragmatemes with expected occurrences ranging from 20 to 29 are the most common (37.5% of Polish charged pragmatemes), and in the loaded category, both of these frequency ranges were equally common (42.9% in both cases of Polish loaded pragmatemes).

2) **Complexity.**

Mosaic plots in Figure 38 highlight the prevalence of polylexical pragmatemes across all pragmateme types and all languages under study. More precisely, across all languages and pragmateme types, the median values pertaining to the number of words constituting a pragmateme indicate that two- and three- word pragmatemes are the most common. The lack of a bigger difference in those characteristics across the studied languages is especially pronounced in the case of charged pragmatemes, the median

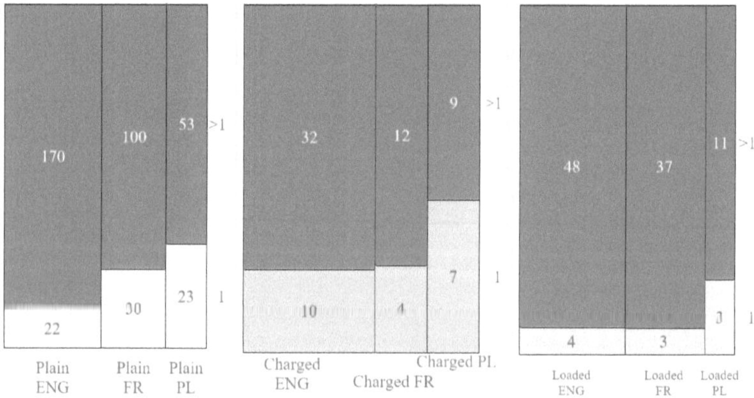

Figure 38. Mosaic plots for monolexical and polylexical pragmatemes according to the language of the analysis and the pragmateme type (plain, charged, and loaded)

for which is two in all languages. The observation of pragmatemes most commonly consisting of two and three words contrasts slightly with the general analysis of complexity for the Polish language, as the majority of pragmatemes found in the Polish corpus are either monolexical or two-word units (see p. 154).

3) **Variantivity.**

As can be seen in Figure 39, median values of the found pragmatemes of nearly all types across all languages indicate that pragmatemes of two and three variants are the most common, with the exception of Polish loaded units, for which median value of variants is one. While the number of Polish loaded pragmatemes (i.e., five units in the Polish corpus) may preclude making broad generalizations, this observation may inspire further research aimed at investigating whether Polish idiomatic pragmatemes are more fixed (as they appear in fewer variants in the present study) than English and French.

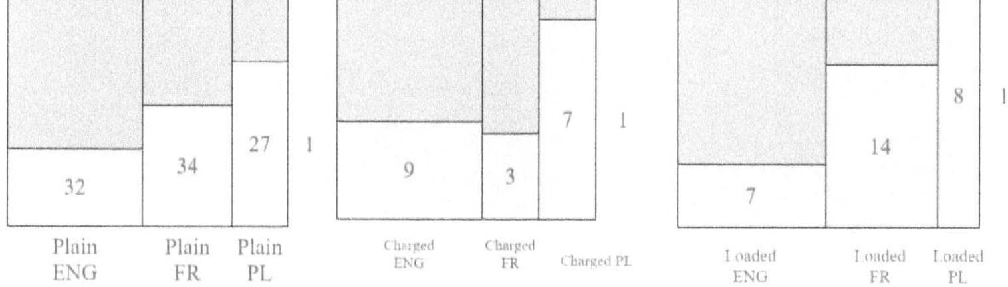

Figure 39. Mosaic plots for pragmatemes of different number of variants according to the language of the analysis and the pragmateme type (plain, charged, and loaded)

4) **Imperativeness.**

What is particularly noteworthy in the examination of this characteristic in relation to the pragmateme type, is the absence of loaded pragmatemes in the imperative form within the French corpus. Furthermore, the percentage of charged imperative pragmatemes was also notably smaller in the French corpus than in the English and Polish corpora. Even though the number of imperative loaded and charged units in Polish is not high either (three units in the first type, two units in the latter), it has to be stressed that their estimated numbers of occurrences per one million words is significant, with the loaded units being estimated to occur 14 and 29 times per one million words and the charged ones 22 and 58 times. As the absence of imperative loaded pragmatemes and the small number of charged ones were not striking in the general analysis (see p. 162), further investigation into a potential relationship between imperativeness and

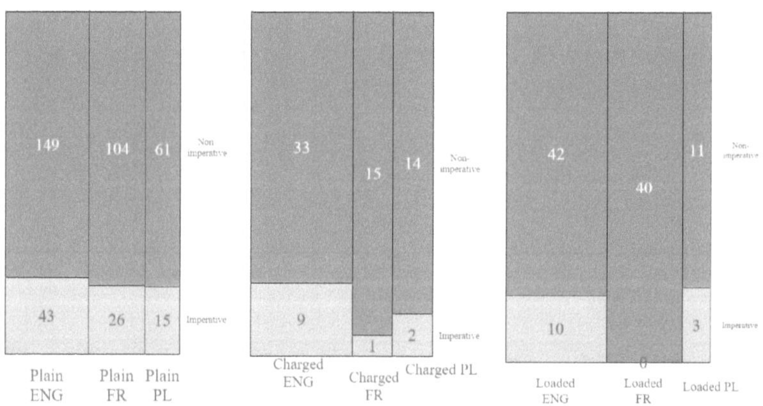

Figure 40. Mosaic plots for imperative and non-imperative pragmatemes according to the language of the analysis and the pragmateme type (plain, charged, and loaded)

idiomaticity, especially in French and Polish, could be an intriguing topic for future studies.

5) **Presence of verbless forms.**

As can be observed in Figure 41, in the English corpus, pragmatemes with verbs are the most common across all types. This observation aligns with the general analysis and elucidates why the English corpus stood out as that in which the highest percentage of pragmatemes with verbs was found (see p. 163). In contrast, in the French corpus, the majority of charged and loaded pragmatemes are verbless, potentially indicating a connection between idiomaticity and the absence of verbs in these units in the French language. Similarly, in the Polish corpus, the majority of loaded pragmatemes are verbless, and in terms of charged units, the percentage distribution is even.

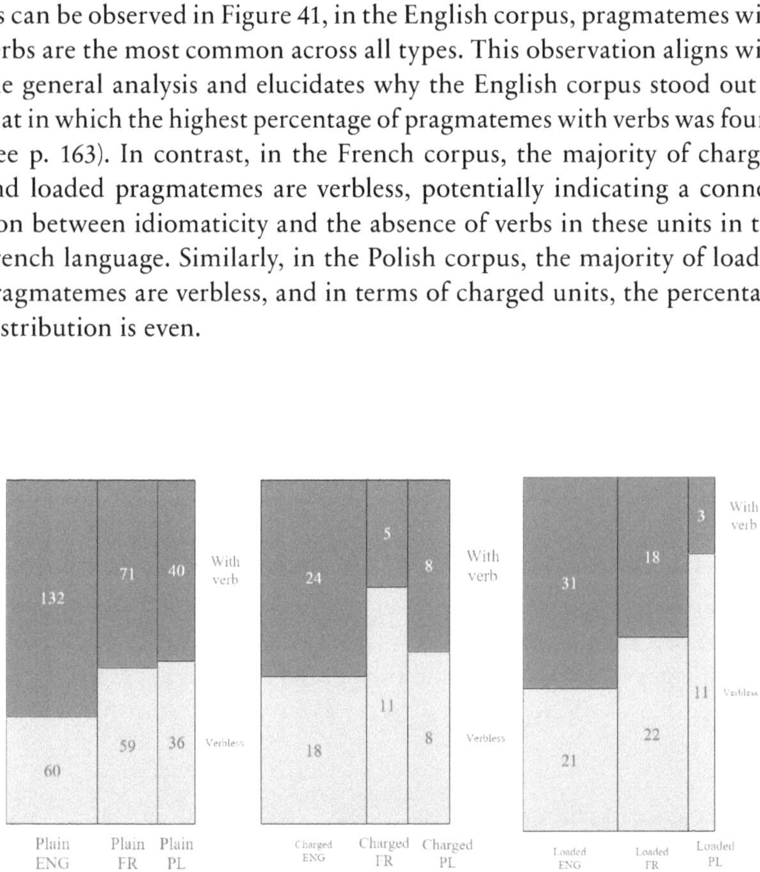

Figure 41. Mosaic plots for verbless and non-verbless pragmatemes according to the language of the analysis and the pragmateme type (plain, charged, and loaded)

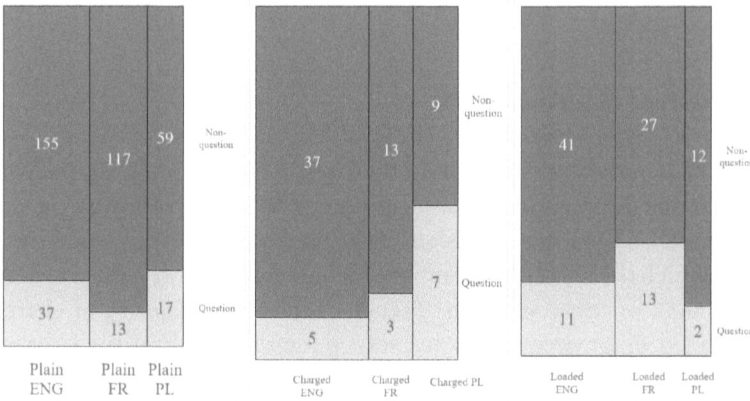

Figure 42. Mosaic plots for question and non-question form of pragmatemes according to the language of the analysis and the pragmateme type (plain, charged, and loaded)

6) **Presence of question forms.**

Across all languages and pragmateme types, as presented in Figure 42, the majority of the pragmatemes found are not questions, which is consistent with the general analysis (see p. 166). However, it is worth noting that the percentage difference is smallest in the case of Polish charged pragmatemes (56.3% of non-question pragmatemes vs. 43.7% of question types). This discrepancy may serve as a potential starting point for further research.

7) **Presence of elliptical forms.**

Regarding elliptical forms, the most pronounced disparity that can be noted when considering pragmateme types is found in French. Notably, in the case of French plain pragmatemes a substantial majority (91.5%) are not elliptical, while within charged pragmatemes the difference is not so evident,

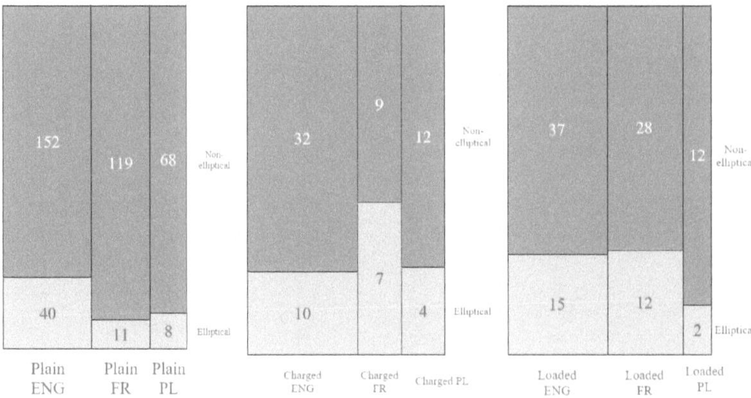

Figure 43. Mosaic plots for elliptical and non-elliptical pragmatemes according to the language of the analysis and the pragmateme type (plain, charged, and loaded)

with non-elliptical pragmatemes also constituting the majority, but not so large (56.3%) as in the case of the plain ones, as depicted in Figure 43. While more studies are needed to draw more general conclusions, the fact that 91.5 percent of the plain pragmatemes that were found were non-elliptical suggests an interesting characteristic of the French language which may be worth investigating.

8) **Presence of deictic expressions.**

While the general results for this characteristic suggest that the majority of the pragmatemes found contain deictic markers (see p. 171), a closer investigation, as depicted in Figure 44, proves this to be untrue for French and Polish loaded units, in which non-deictic pragmatemes prevail (60% of French units and 64.3% of Polish). Therefore, this observation prompts a similar question to the one raised concerning the verbless characteristic, namely whether there is a connection between idiomaticity and deictic expressions in these languages.

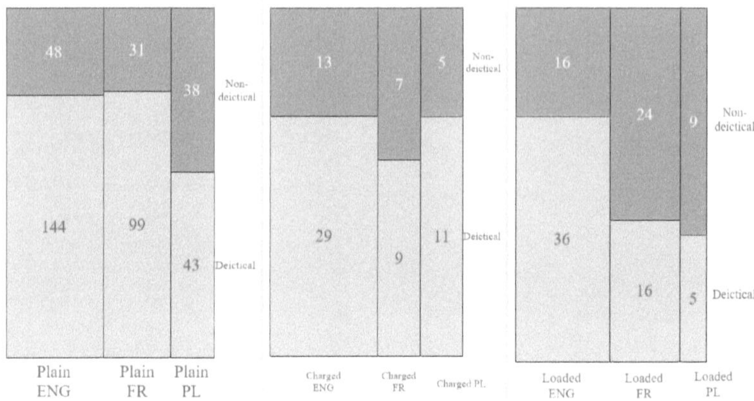

Figure 44. Mosaic plots for deictical and non-deictical pragmatemes according to the language of the analysis and the pragmateme type (plain, charged, and loaded)

From Figure 45, which illustrates different deictic expressions across the pragmateme types and languages under study, it is possible to conclude that these findings align with the general ones, as person deictic markers are most common in English and French, while the "in the verb" deixis is the most common in Polish[174].

9) **Speech acts.**

As depicted in Figure 46 and contrary to the general results (see p. 176), in English plain pragmatemes no difference was found between the percentage distribution of directive and expressive units (78 units, i.e., 40.6% in both cases). Furthermore, in Polish loaded pragmatemes, expressive speech acts are slightly more prevalent than the directive ones (42.9% vs. 35.7%). Despite the apparent insufficiency of data, as the number of Polish loaded pragmatemes is

174 The observation concerning the results in Polish is true for all types but loaded, in which person deixis is the most common; however, since there are only five Polish loaded pragmatemes in the corpus, this observation does not seem reliable enough to challenge the general results.

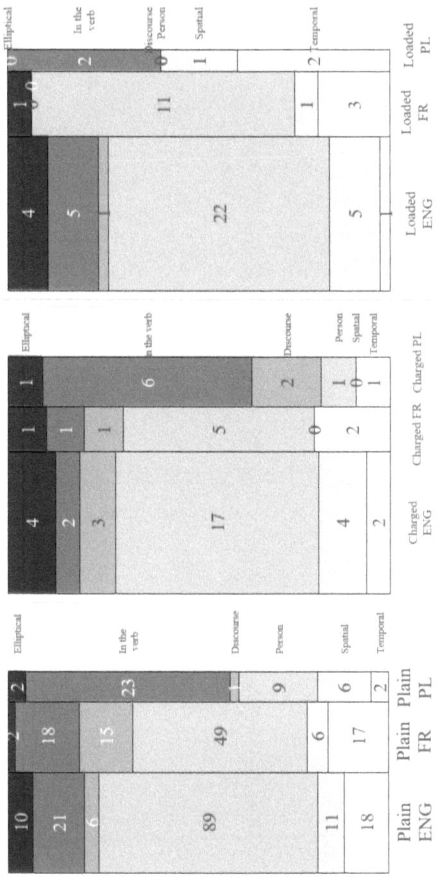

Figure 45. Mosaic plots for different types of deictical expressions in pragmatemes according to the language of the analysis and the pragmateme type (plain, charged, and loaded)

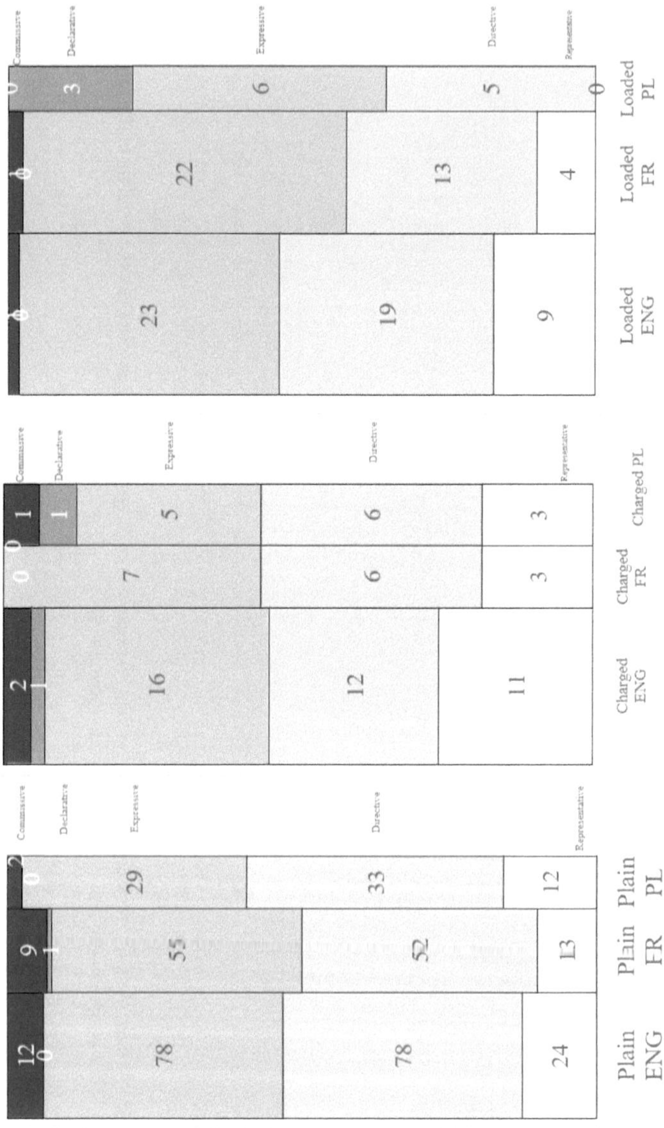

Figure 46. Mosaic plots for speech acts of pragmatemes according to the language of the analysis and the pragmateme type (plain, charged, and loaded)

not large, the results discussed in this subsection support the significance of conducting analyses not only from a general perspective, but also according to different pragmateme types separately.

This subsection explored the differences in various linguistic parameters applied in the analysis of pragmatemes within the English, French, and Polish corpora, particularly focusing on percentage distribution of the identified characteristics. The next subsection will further discuss the findings, using associated probabilities for the same characteristics.

4.11 Probability ratio

The statistical analysis conducted to reach a finding to complement the observations made in the preceding subsection is the probability ratio. According to Brezina (2018: 115), probability ratio (PR, relative risk, or risk ratio) is "a ratio of two probabilities from the cross-tab table comparing the probability of a particular linguistic outcome (...) occurring in one context type relative to the same outcome occurring in the other context type." Since the ratio in question is calculated based on two values, each linguistic category in this study was paired based on the specific investigative focus (e.g., representative speech acts in English and French, English and Polish, and French and Polish, the same for all other speech acts, etc). To calculate the probability ratio, the probabilities of all values were first calculated by dividing the values of the observed frequency by the row totals. Then, the equation suggested in Brezina (ibid) was used:

probability ratio = probability of outcome of interest in
context 1 / probability of outcome of interest in context 2

The probability ratios for the analyzed linguistic characteristics of pragmatemes both confirm, and provide additional insights into, what was observed in the previous subsection. They offer a deeper understanding of the likelihood of a characteristic occurring more or less frequently in one corpus than in another. The PRs will now be discussed in the same order as the characteristics discussed throughout this section. Only selected examples will be presented in each category, while the comprehensive results of the probability ratios are made available online: https://drive.google.com/file/d/1bvBHgKdAcUoMoGhRycfi5QX7aEIxe1OB/view?usp=sharing

1) **Frequency.** In terms of the expected number of occurrences per one million words in a given language, in English and French, pragmatemes of two to nine occurrences were the most likely to occur, showing the highest PRs compared to other types of occurrences (for instance, English pragmatemes of two to nine expected occurrences per one million words were over 26 times more likely to occur than the pragmatemes of 20-28 occurrences, over 12 times more likely than the pragmatemes of 30-50 occurrences, and over 23 times more likely than pragmatemes of 100 and more occurrences). Meanwhile, due to the absence of pragmatemes expected to occur between two and nine times per one million words in the Polish corpus, the pragmatemes with the frequency of 10-19 and 20-29 exhibited the largest PRs (e.g., pragmatemes with the frequency of both 10-19 and 20-29 occurrences per one million words were almost 6 times more likely to occur than the pragmatemes of 30-50 occurrences). In a comparison of different languages, no difference was observed in the probability of pragmatemes of 30-50 occurrences across all languages under study, as the PRs in all possible combinations were around one. The largest PR was found when examining the likelihood of pragmatemes of 20-29 occurrences per one million words in Polish compared to English, pragmatemes of this frequency being over 13 times more likely to occur in Polish than English.
2) **Complexity.** Due to numerous possible combinations of number of words possible in a pragmateme, PRs for this category were calculated only for monolexical and polylexical units. Across all languages, polylexical units were more likely to occur than monolexical ones, with the smallest PR observed in Polish, where polylexical pragmatemes were just slightly more than two times likely to occur than monolexical ones. In contrast, in English, the PR was nearly seven. Monolexical pragmatemes were one and a half times more likely to occur in Polish than in French and over two times more likely than in English.

3) **Variantivity.** For the same reason as in the characteristic above, the PRs for variantivity were calculated only for two categories: pragmatemes of one variant and pragmatemes of more than one variant. Pragmatemes with more variants were more likely to occur than pragmatemes of one variant across all three languages, but the highest PR for this factor was found in English, with a PR of almost five. However, while units of more than one variant were also more likely to occur than units with one variant in Polish, the probability of one variant pragmatemes in Polish was greater than in French (PR of almost one and a half) and English (PR of over two).
4) **Imperativeness.** While non-imperative units were more likely to occur in all languages, with similar PRs (almost four in English and over four in French and Polish), when the comparison was of imperative and non-imperative pragmatemes in language pairs, the PRs revealed no difference between the two.
5) **Presence of verbless forms.** With almost all PRs calculated in this category being close to one, i.e., not indicating any difference between two studied contexts, the only larger PRs were found in relation to English. Non-verbless pragmatemes were 1.8 times more likely than verbless ones in English; the non-verbless units were also slightly more likely to occur in English than in Polish and French, with PRs of 1,3 for both.
6) **Presence of question forms.** In all languages, non-question pragmatemes were more likely to occur than question ones, with the most substantial PR found in French, where the non-question units were over five times more likely to occur than the question ones (compared to four times in English and three times in Polish).
7) **Presence of elliptical forms.** Non-elliptical forms were more likely to occur than elliptical ones in all three languages. The highest PR in this pair was found in Polish, where non-elliptical units were over six and a half times more likely to occur than elliptical ones, compared to over five times in French and over three times in English. When comparing the units across languages, elliptical

pragmatemes were relatively more likely to occur in English than in French (PR of 1.4) and Polish (PR of 1.7).

8) **Presence of deictic expressions.** Pragmatemes with deictical expressions were more likely to occur than those without them in English and French, but not in Polish; however, the PRs do not point to as large of a difference as the ones found, for instance, in the presence of question forms, with the PR for deictical units over non-deictical ones being 1.3 in English and 1.5 in French, and, conversely, the PR for non-deictical over deictical units being 1.7 in Polish. Furthermore, non-deictical units are also more likely to occur in Polish than in English and French (PRs of 1.5 for both).
9) **Speech acts.** Given the numerous combinations examined in this category, various observations can be made in terms of the likelihood of one type over another in a given language. Unsurprisingly, the largest PRs can be found in the analysis of the infrequent speech acts, such as declarative and commissive pragmatemes (e.g., expressive pragmatemes are 117 times more likely to occur in English than declarative ones). However, when comparing the likelihood of a particular speech act in one language versus another, in the majority, PRs do not point to any large differences between the two languages, with PRs of around 1 in most cases but a few. First, for representatives, pragmatemes of this speech act are 1.4 times more likely to occur in Polish than in French and also 1.4 times more likely in French than in English. Then, in terms of the commissive speech act, these units are 1.9 more likely to occur in Polish than in French and English (PRs of 1.9 in both cases). Finally, the most substantial PR can be found in the analysis of the likelihood of declarative pragmatemes in one language compared to another: declaratives are nearly eleven times more likely to occur in Polish than in English and seven times more likely than in French. Furthermore, declarative pragmatemes are also more likely to occur in French than in English, with a PR of 1.5.
10) **Pragmateme types.** In terms of the likelihood of one type over another in a given language, noticeable differences were observed in different languages. In French, PRs for all type combinations indicated

> no differences, with PRs equal to one in all cases. Meanwhile, both in English and Polish, PRs revealed differences in terms of plain pragmatemes being more likely to occur than charged and loaded ones (almost five times more than charged and almost four times more than both loaded in English, and around five times more likely than charged and loaded in Polish), but not in terms of charged versus loaded pragmatemes. Then, when comparing the likelihood of a pragmateme type in two languages, no difference was found in plain pragmatemes across all combinations. Yet significant differences were observed in other types. For instance, charged pragmatemes were nearly five times more likely to occur in French than in English and Polish. Furthermore, loaded pragmatemes were also more likely to occur in French, specifically, over five times more likely than in Polish and almost four times than in English.

While the previous subsections primarily focused on individual linguistic parameters in the analysis of pragmatemes found in the corpora, the next subsection will delve into a more advanced statistical method of analysis: multiple correspondence analysis.

4.12 Multiple correspondence analysis

According to Greenacre and Blasius (2006: 4), correspondence analysis (CA) is "an exploratory multivariate technique for the graphical and numerical analysis of almost any data matric with nonnegative entries." Greenacre (2010: 613) adds that the data visualization possible with the CA method is particularly well-suited for cross-tabular data, as in the case of the present study, which involves counts of different linguistic characteristics of pragmatemes. Since simple CA is applicable for 2x2 contingency tables, the method used for this study is the multiple correspondence analysis (MCA). MCA extends the examination to the correlations among a set of more than two variables and assesses the strength of these relationships (Greenacre 2007). MCA is typically performed on homogeneous variables, i.e., revolving around the same issue (ibid). Through MCA, co-occurring patterns of categorical variables can be explored, and underlying dimensions explaining the relationships between them can be identified.

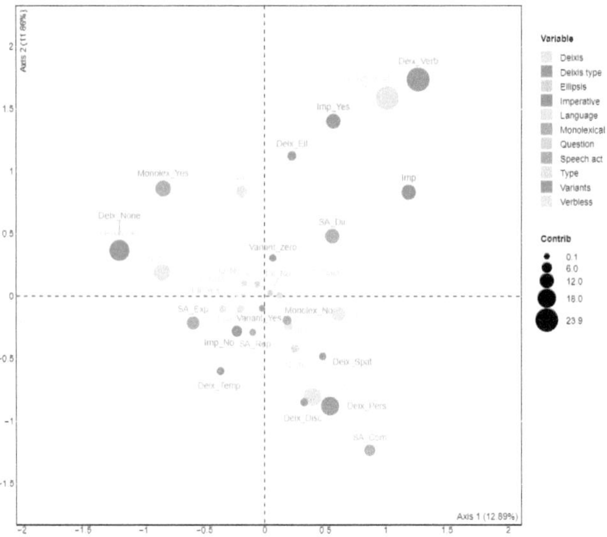

Figure 47. Multiple correspondence analysis of the linguistic characteristics of pragmatemes found in all studied corpora

In the present study, MCA was conducted with the use of R, a software for statistical computing and graphics, and, more precisely, the FactoMineR package available for R[175]. Firstly, MCA was conducted for the linguistic parameters of pragmatemes in all languages[176] under study as a collective analysis, the result of which is presented in Figure 47.

The description of the labels in the MCA charts presented in this subsection is as follows:

175 The exact R script used for every MCA in this thesis is available online, along with MCA graphs in color in .svg format: https://drive.google.com/file/d/1cakrVCK9m7N34IUAMLeoE3idfonqidjM/view?usp=sharing

176 The decision to conduct MCA on all three typologically different languages simultaneously may be regarded as controversial. Therefore, separate MCAs are also performed for each language to more effectively illustrate the similarities and differences between them.

- Deixis: "Deixis_Yes" for pragmatemes with explicit deictic expressions, "Deixis_Yes_impl" for pragmatemes with implicit deixis, and "Deixis_No" for pragmatemes without deixis;
- Deixis.type: "Deix_None" for pragmatemes without deixis, "Deix_Temp" for pragmatemes with temporal deictic expressions, "Deix_Spat" for pragmatemes with spatial deictic expressions, "Deix_Disc" for pragmatemes with discourse deictic expressions, "Deix_Pers" for pragmatemes with person deictic expressions, "Deix_Ell" for pragmatemes with elliptical deixis, and "Deix_Verb" for pragmatemes with the "in the verb" type of deixis;
- Ellipsis: "Ell_Yes" for pragmatemes with elliptical structures and "Ell_No" for pragmatemes without elliptical structures;
- Imperative: "Imp_Yes" for pragmatemes with imperative structures and "Imp_No" for pragmatemes without imperative structures
- Language (applied only in Figure 47): "ENG" for English, "FR" for French, and "PL" for Polish
- Monolexical: "Monolex_Yes" for monolexical pragmatemes and "Monolex_No" for polylexical pragmatemes (for better clarity and visual representation, pragmatemes consisting of multiple words were collectively presented under "Monolex_No", without specifying the exact number of words as a separate category);
- Question: "Q_Yes" for pragmatemes in a question form and "Q_No" for non-question pragmatemes
- Speech.act: "SA_Dir" for directive pragmatemes, "SA_Com" for commissive pragmatemes, "SA_Exp" for expressive pragmatemes, and "SA_Rep" for representative pragmatemes;
- Type: "T_Plain" for pragmatemes of the plain type, "T_Char" for pragmatemes of the charged type, and "T_Load" for pragmatemes of the loaded type;
- Variants: "Variant_zero" for pragmatemes that were noted only in one form and "Variant_Yes" for pragmatemes appearing in different variants;
- Verbless: "Vless_Yes" for verbless pragmatemes and "Vless_No" for non-verbless pragmatemes

Before interpreting the data in Figure 47, it is important to note that, for the sake of a clearer visualization, all parameters with fewer than ten occurrences were excluded from the analysis. In the case of the analysis encompassing all languages, only the declarative speech act was excluded, due to its total count of eight units.

Several key observations emerge from the MCA of all languages depicted in Figure 47. In the left upper part, characteristics such as monolexicality, verblessness, the absence of deixis, and the Polish language are prominent. Furthermore, charged type and non-question form are also situated in this part; however, as these parameters are close to the center and their sizes indicates a small contribution, they are not taken into consideration. Therefore, from the interpretation of the data in the discussed part, it can be concluded that monolexical pragmatemes tend to[177] be verbless and lack deictic markers, which is particularly noticeable in Polish. Then, in the upper right part, parameters such as elliptical deixis, imperativeness, implicit deixis, "in the verb" deixis, and directive speech act are indicated as contributing to the whole. Since implicit deixis encompasses both elliptical and in the verb deixis, it can be concluded that implicit deixis (across all languages) is strongly associated with the imperative structure and the directive speech act. Moving to the lower part of the MCA chart, in the left part, a lot of parameters are found next to each other, but also near the center, which, along with their modest contributions, do not point to prominent correlations. However, one tendency that can be noted is that representative, expressive, and loaded pragmatemes are not likely to be associated with the imperative form. Finally, in the lower right part, the proximity and the size of the "Deixis_Yes" and "Deix_Pers" confirm the prevalence of the person deixis in deictical pragmatemes across the studied languages. Furthermore, there is an association indicating that polylexical pragmatemes tend to be non-verbless, and that there is a relationship between non-verbless pragmatemes and the English language, which confirms the observations made in one of the previous subsections, where English showed a slightly higher likelihood of containing non-verbless pragmatemes compared to the other two languages (see p. 163).

After presentation of results of the MCA for all three languages collectively, the results of the MCA conducted separately for English, French, and Polish will be now presented. Figure 48 shows the MCA for the linguistic parameters of pragmatemes in English:

177 It is important to emphasize that MCA points to observable tendancies, which, nevertheless, may not hold true in every individual case.

178 In the case of English pragmatemes, units of the declarative speech act (one pragmateme) and discourse deixis (eight pragmatemes) were excluded from the analysis.

In addition to the findings observed in the collective MCA, such as the tendency for monolexical units to be verbless and non-deictic (upper left part of Figure 48), the association of units with implicit deixis with imperativeness and the directive speech act (upper right part of Figure 48), and the significance of person deixis in deictical units (lower center of Figure 48), other relationships between categories in English can be observed. For instance, the size and the proximity question-form pragmatemes to the presence and type of deixis in the lower center of Figure 48 suggest that question pragmatemes tend to include person deictic markers. Furthermore, the data in the lower left part of the chart indicates that expressive pragmatemes tend not to be imperative, while the data in the lower right part suggests that plain pragmatemes tend to be polylexical with more than one variant, and not verbless. However, it has to be remembered that the data near the center, with small contributions, may not indicate as strong connections as data further from the center with larger contributions.

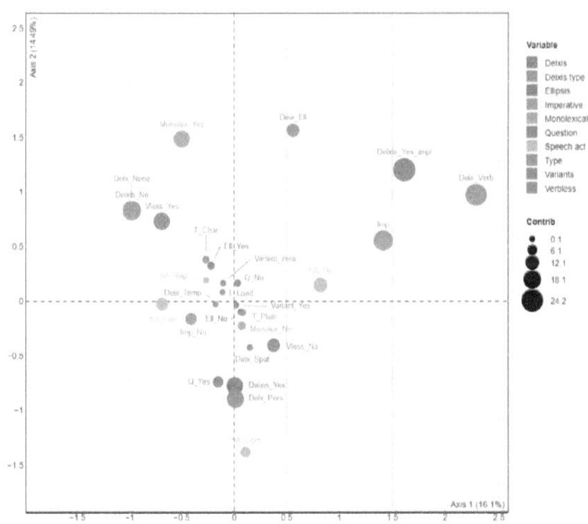

Figure 48. Multiple correspondence analysis of the linguistic characteristics of pragmatemes found in the English corpus[178]

Then, the results of the MCA analysis for the linguistic parameters of French pragmatemes are shown in Figure 49:

Figure 49 not only confirms the characteristics already discussed in the collective MCA and the English MCA, such as monolexical units tending to be verbless and non-deictical (upper left part of Figure 49), and units with

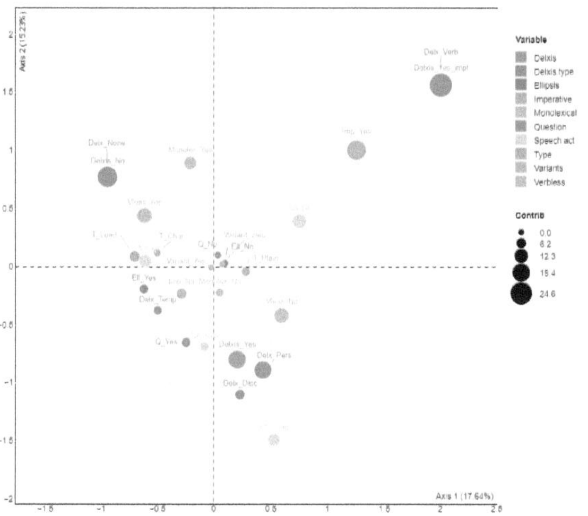

Figure 49. Multiple correspondence analysis of the linguistic characteristics of pragmatemes found in the French corpus[179]

implicit deixis tending to be imperative and directive (upper right part of Figure 49), but it also reveals a few features specific to the French MCA. For example, the data in the upper right part of the chart suggests a relationship between pragmatemes of one variant and the absence of elliptical structures and question forms. Furthermore, the data in the lower right part shows, similarly to the English MCA (see p. 205), that plain pragmatemes tend to be

179 In the case of French, declarative units (one pragmateme), units with spatial deixis (five pragmatemes), and elliptical deixis (four pragmatemes) were not taken into account in the MCA.

polylexical. It also aligns with the collective MCA (see p. 202) in emphasizing the prevalence of person deixis, especially in commissive pragmatemes, which, additionally, tend to be non-verbless.

Finally, Figure 50 presents the result of the MCA of linguistic parameters of pragmatemes found in the Polish corpus:

While some observations from the interpretation of the MCA of lin-

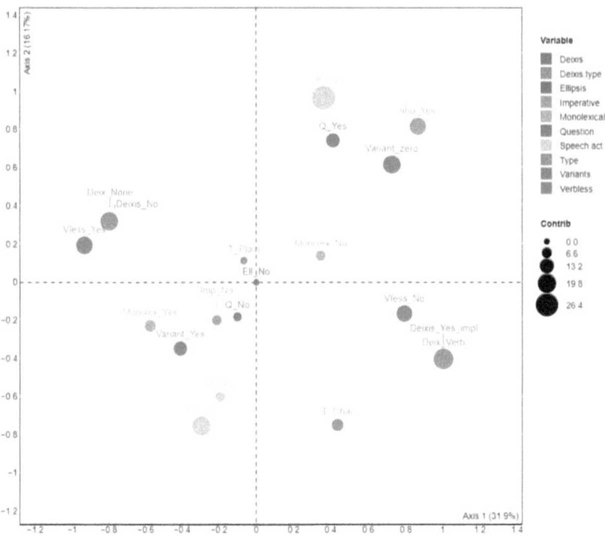

Figure 50. Multiple correspondence analysis of the linguistic characteristics of pragmatemes found in the Polish corpus[180]

guistic parameters of Polish pragmatemes align with the collective results (see p. 202), they are not as convergent with them as the English and the French MCA were. For instance, the data in the upper right part of Figure 50 may suggest, as did the collective MCA, that directive units tend to be imperatives. However, this does not hold true for the majority of directive pragmatemes in the Polish corpus. Therefore, it appears that the data in this part of the Figure 50 should be interpreted differently, rather horizontally, suggesting that, instead, polylexical directive pragmatemes tend to appear in question form, while imperative pragmatemes tend to exist in one variant.

Furthermore, similarly to both the collective MCA and the MCA of the English and French pragmatemes, the MCA of Polish pragmatemes points to relationships between deixis (or lack thereof) and verblessness. The data in the upper left part of Figure 50 indicates the tendency of non-deictical pragmatemes to be verbless, while the data in the lower right part illustrates that pragmatemes with the "in the verb" deixis tend to be non-verbless, which is a seemingly evident correlation, but one that was not to be noted in the previously discussed MCAs. Finally, the data with lower contributions near the center suggests a relationship between plain and non-elliptical pragmatemes, whereas the data of higher contribution present in the lower left part of Figure 50 suggests that monolexical pragmatemes tend to have more than one variant and that both expressive and representative pragmatemes show a tendency to be in a non-imperative and non-question form, with more than one variant.

After a thorough linguistic examination of the phenomenon of pragmatemes in English, French, and Polish, the next section will be devoted to its analysis from a translational perspective, with the focus on the charged type.

---

180 For MCA of the parameters of pragmatemes from the Polish corpus, the exclusion of infrequent units was carried out in two stages. First, commissive and declarative pragmatemes (three and four units, respectively) were excluded, along with units containing discourse deixis (three counts), elliptical deixis (three), spatial deixis (seven), and time deixis (five). Then, as due to the first stage of exclusion other categories were affected, for the purpose of an enhanced visualization of the data, more units were removed from the analysis: pragmatemes with elliptical structures (seven units), with deictical expressions (eight units), namely person deixis (eight units), and loaded pragmatemes (nine units). Consequently, none of these categories appear in Figure 50. Furthermore, the second stage of exclusion also resulted in a scarcity of representative and charged pragmatemes (eight units each). However, it was decided that the two-stage exclusion process was sufficient for achieving clear data visualization.

CHAPTER 5

Translational Analysis of Charged Pragmatemes

While the previous section focuses on the linguistic analysis of pragmatemes of all types found in English, French, and Polish corpora from a linguistic point of view, in this section, translations will constitute the focal point. Due to time and spatial constraints of the doctoral research, only translations from English as the SL to French and Polish as TLs will be analyzed (the corpus used for this stage of the research is the same English corpus that is discussed in the "Methods" section, see p. 123). For the same reasons, the analysis will be devoted solely to charged pragmatemes. This type was chosen as it is hypothesized that due to the ambiguous nature of charged pragmatemes (i.e., the fact that they can have different meanings depending on context), they are most likely to pose problems in translation. For instance, *Here you go* may be used to cheer on somebody doing something well or as a statement uttered when giving someone what they requested.

In the English corpus, there are 42 charged pragmatemes that occur more than once. Initially, the list of charged pragmatemes found in the corpus was more extensive, but upon the investigation of their contexts, four pragmatemes had to be deleted from the list as their occurrences in the context were not pragmatemic. Such was the case of *That's all*, which was used in its non-pragmatemic meaning as an ending to one's statement (which is considered to be not specific enough to be a pragmateme) instead of its pragmatemic usage, which would be to state that there is nothing more one wants to buy, and of *The usual* which occurred as a non-pragmatemic comment describing somebody's behavior and not in the pragmatemic usage of asking for the habitual thing in a bar or a restaurant. Furthermore, the pragmatemes *Relax* and *You hear me* were deleted from the list for they only appeared once in their pragmatemic usage (which is during a massage, not when somebody is in an emotional state, in the first case, and the literal meaning, not used as a harsh way to say "Do you understand", in the latter). Also, some occurrences of certain pragmatemes were deleted as not all of them were specific enough to be considered pragmatemic (such was the case in the following units: *Bingo*,

Check, and *Here* [one occurrence deleted], *I'm fine*, *One moment*, *How much*, *To [SOMETHING/PERSON]*, *Love you*, *Slow down*, *That's it*, and *You're up* [two occurrences deleted], *Here we are*, *Here you go*, *I'll take it*, and *Stop right there* [three occurrences deleted.]) Of the 42 pragmatemes, 41 will be analyzed here from the point of view of translation techniques as described in Subchapter 2.5 (see p. 114). The 41 pragmatemes occur together 511 times in the corpus. The one pragmateme missing from the analysis is *Hey*, whose occurrence is so frequent (1,133 throughout the corpus) that it seems fit to be subject to an analysis on its own, to which a separate article may be devoted in the future.

This section aims to examine whether already proposed technique typologies can be applied to pragmatemes and, if not, to offer a typology suited for the translation of units that depend so heavily on context as charged pragmatemes. The three typologies used here to analyze the units are: Molina and Hurtado Albir's (2002) dynamic and functionalist approach to translation techniques, Hejwowski's (2015) model for translating idioms, and Díaz-Cintas and Remael's (2007) model for rendering cultural elements in subtitling. While the differences between these approaches may appear striking, charged pragmatemes are applicable to all of them. Consequently, the analysis starts with the most general approach, i.e., the one proposed by Molina and Hurtado Albir (2002), which does not refer to any specific language units or translation problems. The analysis is then followed by Hejwowski's (2015) approach, which delves into a more specific linguistic perspective, focusing on idiomaticity. Lastly, Díaz-Cintas and Remael's (2007) typology is applied as the most specific among the three, as it not only addresses one type of units (cultural elements), but also refers to a narrow translation type, i.e., subtitling. Through the application of various translation techniques, ranging from the broadest to the most specific, a more comprehensive overview of the issue can be presented, so that the new typology, to be introduced after the analysis, can take multiple viewpoints into consideration.

5.1 Dynamic and functionalist translation techniques: Molina and Hurtado Albir's (2002) model

The typology of techniques in translation proposed by Molina and Hurtado Albir (2002) is the most comprehensive one out of those analyzed here in terms of the number of suggested techniques. It covers eighteen techniques and encompasses both a linguistic point of view (with techniques that focus strictly on the translated lexeme, such as transposition or modulation, among others) and a textual one (with techniques that affect a bigger text chunk, such as compensation or amplification).

Nonetheless, despite the taxonomy being seemingly exhaustive, a few methodological problems appeared during its application. Firstly, according to Molina and Hurtado Albir (2002: 510), in the established equivalent[181] technique, the SL term is translated with "a term or expression recognized (by dictionaries or language in use) as an equivalent in the TL", and while the presence of a term in dictionaries can be easily verified in the case of most lexemes (however, not in the case of all formulaic units such as pragmatemes), the addition of "language in use" may pose methodological questions. That is why, due to the lack of specification on the part of the authors of this taxonomy, I decided to rely on my language intuition, which appears to be a rather controversial solution and therefore, will be resolved in Subsection 5.4 (see p. 234). Another issue that was found during the analysis was that often it was possible to match one translation with a number of techniques. For instance, the French translation of the English *Here*, with the account of the context, can be *Tiens*[182] (lit. *Hold it*), which can be considered an established equivalent as it functions in the same way in the language, but it is also a particularization as *Tiens* on its own refers to a particular context, while *Here* may evoke a few different ones. Because the original typology (Molina and Hurtado Albir 2002) does not take this kind of situation into account, additional parameters were added to the analysis to ensure its clarity, because labeling translations with multiple techniques could add a certain degree of chaos to the analysis as a whole, since with other analyzed typologies (see p. 223 and p. 228), each translation is matched with one technique. Therefore, if a translation was considered an established equivalent but also had the characteristics of another technique, the

---

181 While equivalence is "a central concept in translation theory" (Kenny, 2001a: 77), in this thesis, the concept of an *equivalent* is approached from a unit-based perspective and not a text-based one, making various approaches to equivalence less directly relevant to the discussion of an equivalent as a translation technique. For further discussion on the different perspectives regarding equivalence, see, for example, Kenny (2001a).

182 E.g., *The Baby-Sitters Club*, S01E05 (i.e., season one, episode five), time: 15:09.

latter was considered the main one and regarded as such in the categorization, as it was held to be more specific. Hence, in the example above, *Tiens* is categorized as particularization and not established equivalent. Furthermore, techniques that have an impact on the text as a whole (on its length, as in the case of linguistic amplification or compression, or on its structure, as in the case of compensation) are always put above others that may also be observed in a translation. For example, while the French equivalent of the elliptic pragmateme *You're up* can be both *À toi*[183] and *C'est à toi*[184], the technique for the first one is considered here an established equivalent as it is also elliptic, while the latter is considered a linguistic amplification since the full phrase is given, even though the elliptic equivalent is possible[185].

Borrowing

In the corpus, translations performed with the technique of borrowing resulted in TL words fully incorporated from the SL (without any changes to their spelling). In the French translations, pragmatemes translated with borrowing were *Bingo*[186] and *Yo*[187] (22 occurrences altogether, or 4% of all units), while in Polish, only two occurrences of *Bingo*[188] (0,4%) were translated with the use of this technique.

Literal translation

In Molina and Hurtado Albir's (ibid) taxonomy, literal translation is translation word for word, but when the form coincides with the meaning. Three examples of this technique found in both French and Polish translations are presented in Table 8.

183 E.g., *Ginny and Georgia*, S01E03, time: 30:50.

184 Source: *Dash and Lily*, S01E06, time: 20:37.

185 However, one can argue that modulation can also be considered a technique used in both cases (especially in the latter one, since the first one is elliptic and lacks the subject) as there is a point of view shift in the sentence: in English, "you" is the subject, while in French, "you" is the object. This example further demonstrates that to use Molina and Hurtado Albir's (2002) typology in a coherent way, one needs to add more parameters to the analysis.

186 E.g., *You*, S01E05, time: 19:54.

187 E.g., *Never Have I Ever*, S02E03, time: 18:59.

188 Sources: *You*, S01E05, time: 19:54; *Never Have I Ever*, S02E09, time: 4:11.

Table 8. Examples of the use of the literal translation technique

Source	Context	English (SL)	French (TL)	Polish (TL)
Dead to Me, S02E04, time: 13:14	raising a toast	*To Steve.*	*À Steve.*	*Za Steve'a.*
Sweet Magnolias S01E04, time: 24:51	finishing a conversation	*Anything else?*	*Autre chose ?*	*Coś jeszcze?*

With 70 pragmatemes translated with the use of literal translation (which constitutes 14% of all analyzed pragmatemes), it is the second most common technique among Polish translations and the fourth most common among French translations (51 pragmatemes, i.e., 10%).

Established equivalent

Despite the categorization of some instances of established equivalents as being other techniques (which is discussed at the beginning of this subsection, see p. 211), that technique still proved to be the most frequent one in both translations. A few examples of the use of the established equivalent technique for both French and Polish translation of charged pragmatemes found in the corpus are presented in Table 9 below.

Table 9. Examples of the use of the established equivalent technique

Source	Context	English (SL)	French (TL)	Polish (TL)
Atypical S04E01, time: 16:18	finishing a conversation	*Is that all?*	*C'est tout ?*	*To wszystko?*
You S02E01, time: 3:07	shouted by the director on set to stop filming	*Cut!*	*Coupez !*	*Cięcie!*

In the French translation, the established equivalent technique was found 196 times (38% of all translations of charged pragmatemes in the corpus) and 205 times in Polish (40%).

Discursive creation

According to Molina and Hurtado Albir (ibid: 510), discursive creation is a technique in which the translator creates the equivalence of a SL unit, but this equivalence is not predictable outside of the given context. However, even though instances of "total unpredictability" may be conceivable, there are certainly situations where the predictability relies on the speaker's language intuition, given the absence of a precise explanation from the authors of this taxonomy. In the corpus, translations created with this technique are often related to both the conversational and visual contexts (for more on the topic of context-related techniques, see Subsection 5.4, p. 234). For instance, the translation of the English *Yes, I'm fine* to the Polish *Też*[189] (lit. *[Me] too*) is an example of discursive creation that is based on the context of the whole conversation[190], while *Here* translated to French as *Regarde* and to Polish as *Patrz*[191] (both lit. *Look)* represents discursive creation based on the visual context, as the viewer sees on the screen the main character showing another a picture, as presented in Figure 51.

Figure 51. A screenshot presenting an example of the discursive creation technique based on the visual context[192]

Discursive creation proved to be a slightly more frequent technique among Polish translations (24 units, i.e., 5%) than among French (15 units, 3%).

---

[189] Source: *Atypical* S01E03, time: 24:23.

[190] The conversation goes as follows:
Miss Jablonski: *Is everything okay?* Sam: *Yes. Thank you. Is everything okay with you?* Miss Jablonski: *Yes, I'm fine.*

[191] Source: *Ginny and Georgia*, S01E07, time: 49:34.

[192] Source: *Ginny and Georgia*, S01E07, time: 49:34. Director: Aleysa Young, producers: Claire Welland, Todd Aronauer.

Generalization

With only three examples among French translations (0.6%) and two among Polish (0.4%), one can speculate that the TLs used for the analysis do not favor generalization, especially given the much greater frequency of the contrasting technique, i.e., particularization (see the following paragraph). In French, all of the examples of this technique are found in translations of one pragmateme: *Check*, which was translated three times as *C'est bon*[193] (lit. *It's good*), which can be used in a number of different situations (e.g., to express one's opinion on a delicious meal). Interestingly, *C'est bon* was chosen over *C'est coché*, which would evoke the same mental image one has when hearing *Check*, that is, checking off the boxes on a checklist. In Polish, all the generalization examples are found in translations of *It's a date*, which are *Jesteśmy umówieni*[194] (lit. *We're all set*, meaning that "we have an appointment"), a more general phrase that does not imply a romantic meeting.

Particularization

In comparison to generalization, particularization proved to be a much more frequent technique, especially among French translations, where it was the second most frequent one, with 94 units (18%). In Polish, it was the fifth most favored technique, with 42 units (8%). Many examples of particularization were found in translations of *Enjoy*, which is an expression that does not have in either language an equally versatile equivalent, and therefore has to be translated with a more precise unit, depending on context, e.g., as *Bon appétit*[195] in French or *Smacznego*[196] in Polish (both meaning "enjoy your meal"). However, particularization was used not only when there was no other option in the TL, but also when an established equivalent was possible, as in the case of *Hello?* uttered at the beginning of a video call, which was translated to French as *Bonjour*[197] (lit. *Good morning*) and not *Allô ?*.

---

[193] Sources: *Good Girls*, S04E13, time: 24:13 and 24:15, *Sweet Magnolias*, S01E05, time: 1:33.

[194] Sources: *Sweet Magnolias*, S01E09, time: 39:02, *Ginny and Georgia*, S01E01, time: 39:31.

[195] E.g., *Sweet Magnolias*, S01E04, time: 34:14.

[196] E.g., *Good Girls*, S01E07, time: 7:13.

[197] Source: *You*, S02E09, time: 5:28.

Description

Description is one of the least frequently used techniques out of Molina and Hurtado Albir's (ibid) typology found during the analysis of charged pragmatemes, with seven units in French (1%) and none in Polish. In French, while one translation seems to result from the lack of an equivalent (the English *Clear!* translated to *La voie est libre !*[198] [lit. *The way is free!*]), the other ones, all being translations of *Hello?* in the context of "is anyone there", "are you there", can be explained by the fact that *Allô ?*, the most common equivalent of *Hello?*, is mostly associated with conversations on the phone, and that is why a description technique seems to have been chosen over the equivalent (examples of translations here are: *Il y a quelqu'un ?*[199] [lit. *Is anyone there?*], *Qui est là ?*[200] [lit. *Who is there?*]).

Linguistic amplification

Linguistic amplification was found only five times (1% of all units) in the French translation and was absent from the Polish translation. However, the low frequency of this technique should not come as a surprise as it is a technique rather uncommon in subtitling, which is an AVT type that aims at being concise due to time and space constraints (for more on this see p. 93), while linguistic amplification consists of adding linguistic elements in translation. An example of the use of this technique can be found in the eighth episode of the first season of the TV series *Atypical* (time: 21:56), where the English *Here you go* is translated to French as *Voilà vos casques* (lit. *Here are your headphones*). The element added in the translation is visible on the screen, and there seems to be no clear reason why the translator did not use an all-encompassing *Tenez*, which would be equivalent to *Here you are* in this case and also suitable for subtitling[201].

---

198 Source: *Good Girls*, S01E10, time: 19:43.

199 E.g., *Emily in Paris*, S01E07, time: 9:01.

200 Source: *You*, S01E06, time: 21:54.

201 This example, along with other cases of linguistic amplification present in the French translation, is further discussed in the next subsection (see "idiosyncratic addition", p. 251)

Linguistic compression

According to Molina and Hurtado Albir (ibid), linguistic compression is a technique common for subtitling. Therefore, one might expect it to be frequently used in the analyzed examples; however, while linguistic compression was noticeable, its frequency was not striking, especially in the French translation, where it constituted only 3 percent of all units (16). In comparison, linguistic compression was used 45 times (9%) in the Polish translation. In the analysis, several methods of synthesizing linguistic elements were observed. Firstly, the compression could be contextual, as in the translation of *Love you too*[202] to the French *Moi aussi* (lit. *Me too*) and the Polish *Ja ciebie też* (lit. *I you too*). Seconly, the compression could be purely linguistic, either by the omission of elements present in the ST, as in *Je prends* (lit. *I take*), the French translation of *I'll take it*[203], where apart from the tense change (from future[204] in English to present in French), the object is omitted, or by using an elliptic alternative of a TT unit, for instance when *Cheers.*[205] is translated to Polish as *Zdrowie.* instead of *Na zdrowie.*

Reduction

While Molina and Hurtado Albir (ibid) understand reduction in the same way as Díaz-Cintas and Remael (2007) and Hejwowski (2015) understand omission, i.e., as the full suppression of an ST element in the TT, due to the presence of the substitution technique in this typology (see the next paragraph), the overall number of units assigned to the reduction technique is smaller than the number of omitted units assigned in the application of the two other typologies (see p. 223 and p. 228). In the French translation, 58 pragmatemes were suppressed (11%), and in the Polish, 69 pragmatemes (13.5%).

202 Source: *Never Have I Ever*, S01E06, time: 2:32.
203 E.g., *Good Girls*, S01E06, time: 38:09.
204 Although not used to convey the future in this example, grammatically, it is the Future Simple that appears in this pragmateme.
205 E.g., *Firefly Lane*, S01E03, time: 40:52.

Substitution

In the typology developed by Molina and Hurtado Albir (2002), substitution occurs when a linguistic element is changed to a paralinguistic one, e.g., by intonation or gestures. For the purpose of this analysis, substitution is held to be used when the translator decides to omit the ST element in translation, and this decision seems to be based on the fact that the verbal layer can be understood by the non-verbal communication visible on the screen. For instance, in both French and Polish translations, the most common occurrence of substitution is found in translations of *Here* uttered when something is handed over to somebody, an action which is usually visible on the screen. Furthermore, often the next sentence is uttered very quickly after the exchange, which makes the decision to omit the pragmateme even more reasonable, as in the third episode of season one of *The Baby-Sitters Club*, when the person speaking says *Here. Take this paper.* when handing over a roll of paper, an action shown on the screen at the same time. To avoid redundancy of the visual and verbal channels and for space reasons, both the French and the Polish translators decided to omit the pragmateme in translation, which is presented in Figure 52.

Figure 52. A screenshot presenting an example of substitution in French and Polish translations[206]

[206] Source: *The Baby-Sitters Club*, S01E03, time: 2:54. Director: Andrew DeYoung, producers: Meg Schave, Ann M. Martin, Lyle Friedman, Ashley Glazier, Matthew Chipera.

The presence of substitution throughout the analyzed examples is noticeable, with an occurrence of two percent both in French (nine examples) and Polish (10 examples).

Compensation

This technique is one of the least frequently employed and is used only for the Polish translation of *Yo.* in the eighth episode of the second season of *Good Girls* (time: 8:24). The pragmateme is here followed by *Chill,* which indicates that the pragmateme functions as an informal exclamative used to draw attention rather than as a greeting. In the Polish translation, *Yo* itself is omitted, but the informality it gives to the text is conveyed by the addition of the informal vocative *mordo* (which could be translated to "pal" or "dude"). Both sentences are then combined, and the Polish viewer sees the subtitle *Spokojnie, mordo.* (in the first part, the verb is changed into an adjective, so a literal translation might be: *Easy, pal*).

Modulation

Modulation, i.e., the change of the point of view in translation, was found nine times in the French translations (2% of all units) and more than twice as often in the Polish translations, with 21 units translated this way (4%). An example of modulation in the French translation is the pragmateme *I'm fine* translated to *Tout va bien*[207] (*Everything is fine*), which, although it does not convey any cognitive change, is linguistically less personal due to the lack of a personal pronoun, while in the Polish translation, it is the pragmateme *Hey, you stop right there!* translated as *Nie ruszajcie się!*[208] (lit. *Don't move*!), which changes the focus from the act of stopping a movement to not making any further movements.

Transposition

A change of grammatical category, that is, the transposition technique, was found to be rather infrequent on its own, with nine units being translated this way in the French translation (2%) and four in the Polish translation (0.8%). The reason for this technique appearing rarely in the analyzed translations

[207] Source: *Ginny and Georgia*, S01E06, time: 43:40.
[208] Source: *Ginny and Georgia*, S01E06, time: 22:08.

may be explained by the fact that it is associated rather with compositional units, the number of which is not frequent in charged pragmatemes in the analyzed corpora. This is visible in the examples, which are as follows: *Slow down!*, containing a phrasal verb in imperative, translated to Polish as *Wolniej!*[209] (lit. *More slowly!*), an elliptical phrase containing nothing but an adverb in the comparative, and *Let me in!* translated to French as *Laisse-moi entrer !* (lit. *Let me come in!*), where the preposition is changed to an infinitive verb in translation.

Variation

The change of language variation was found 17 times in the French translation (3% of all units) and 13 times in the Polish translation (2.5%). However, the changes do not seem significant to the overall understanding of the texts, and a large number of them were found in translations of a very informal greeting *Yo*, which was sometimes translated as *Salut*[210] (French equivalent of *Hi*) and to Polish as *Cześć*[211] (Polish equivalent of *Hi*) or *Hej*[212] (Polish equivalent of *Hey*).

Despite the fact that the majority of the techniques proposed by Molina and Hurtado Albir (ibid) were found in the analysis of the translations of charged pragmatemes, there are three that were absent. The first of these is adaptation, for which there appeared to be no need, as no pragmatemes were so specific to the source culture that they would need to be replaced with a target culture element. The second is amplification, which is different from linguistic amplification and is centered around adding information in order to explain the ST element, which was not needed in the case of the analyzed pragmatemes. The third and final one is calque, i.e., the technique of translating literally every element of the ST unit. In the typology, calque, being perceived as artificial in a language, is separate from literal translation, in which the form has to coincide with meaning and function (ibid: 509).

In comparing the use of Molina and Hurtado Albir's (ibid) techniques in the two TLs, French and Polish, the differences are not striking in most cases. Figure 53 portrays the comparison in detail.

---

209 Source: *Good Girls*, S04E11, time: 30:00.

210 E.g., *Good Girls*, S03E05, time: 43s.

211 Source: *Never Have I Ever*, S02E04, time: 4:24.

212 E.g., *Dash and Lily*, S01E03, time: 20:33.

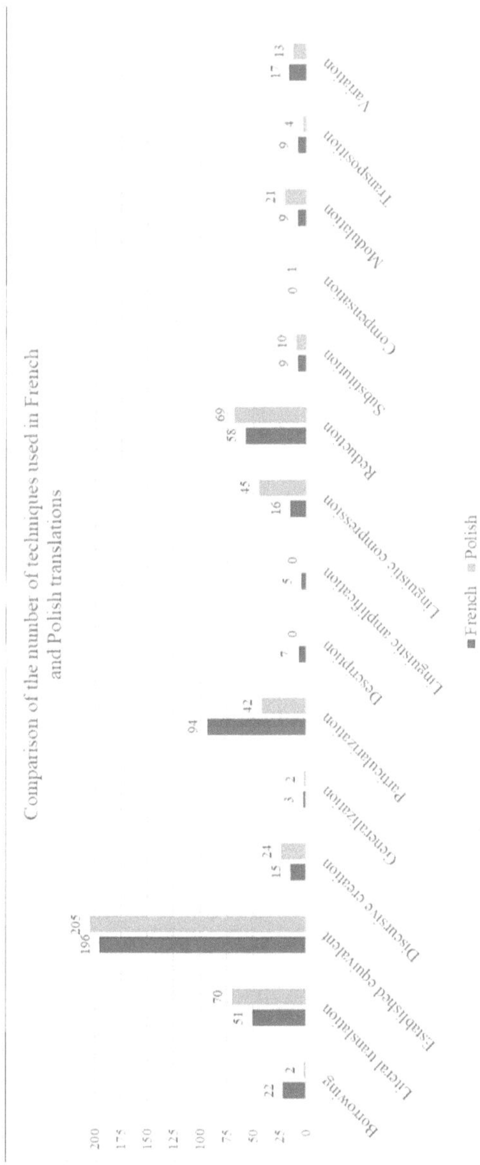

Figure 53. Comparison of the number of pragmatemes translated to French and Polish with the use of the techniques according to Molina and Hurtado Albir's (2002) technique typology

The same technique was used by French and Polish translators in 209 cases, which constitutes 41 percent of all translations and is the smallest number when compared to the results of the analysis of Hejwowski's (2015) and Díaz-Cintas and Remael's (2007) typologies (see p. 223 and p. 228). The reason for that difference may be the fact that the typology of Molina and Hurtado Albir (2002) consisted of the greatest number of techniques, which may therefore suggest that using a more comprehensive typology will show more discrepancies between translations. Furthermore, Molina and Hurtado Albir's (ibid) classification focuses on purely linguistic characteristics in a number of techniques (e.g., transposition), which gives the researcher the ability to further differentiate between techniques used in French and Polish, which linguistically are two very different languages as they belong to different language families.

The most significant divergence is found in the use of borrowing, where Polish translations constitute only eight percent of all occurrences of this technique, which is surprising considering the fact that out of the two, French is said to be the one that is more likely to reject foreign elements in the language (the same observation is made in the analysis of the loanword technique according to Díaz-Cintas and Remael's [2007] technique typology, see p. 228). Noticeable differences are also visible in the linguistic compression technique, which was observed much more often in Polish, and particularization, which was more frequent in French. However, here the reason is not as straightforward, especially given that other scholars may argue for the superiority of the established equivalent technique over linguistic compression, for example when the English *Cheers* is translated into Polish as *Zdrówko* and not *Na zdrowie*. Therefore, the question already raised at the beginning of this subsection regarding the multiplicity of techniques that can be associated with a given translation (see p. 210) may have a considerable impact on the percentage distribution of particular techniques in French and Polish translations.

To sum up, the analysis with the use of Molina and Hurtado Albir's (2002) technique typology proved to be a good start for further investigation of pragmatemes in subtitling, since this typology did not fully fit the researched phenomenon. Therefore, the next subsection focuses on the topic from a different perspective, which is Hejwowski's (2005) typology of techniques used for the translation of idioms.

5.2 Translation of idioms: Hejwowski's (2015) model

Hejwowski's (2015) typology of techniques used for the translation of idioms is used for the present analysis as it may suit well the topic of pragmatemes, which, like idioms, are formulaic sequences[213]. Furthermore, charged pragmatemes may also be idiomatic (e.g., *Help yourself*). However, to fully adjust Hejwowski's typology for the translation of pragmatemes, wherever the term *idiom* appeared in the name of a technique, it was changed to *pragmateme* (similarly, *idiomatic* was changed to *pragmatemic*, etc.).

During the analysis, one methodological problem appeared that has to be addressed. In the discussion of the suggested technique types, Hejwowski (ibid) does not specify how the decision on whether the translation is an idiom should be made (whether it should be based on its presence in dictionaries, frequency in corpora, native speakers' intuition, etc.), similarly to the lack of an explanation on the part of Molina and Hurtado Albir (2002) in terms of the established equivalents, as discussed in the previous subsection (see p. 210). Furthermore, Hejwowski (2015) notes that idioms are difficult to define since many researchers have different opinions on the topic[214] and that often, there are no clear lines between what can and cannot be considered an idiom (ibid: 247-249). Without any clear guidelines from Hejwowski, in this analysis, the decision on which unit is a pragmateme was based on my own intuition, which, as is further discussed in Subsection 5.4 (see p. 234), is not an ideal solution and should be further investigated.

Use of a pragmateme that has a similar form and meaning

This technique was found to be the most frequently used for the translation of pragmatemes in the corpus, with 178 units being translated this way in the French translation (35% of all pragmatemes) and 156 in

---

[213] Hejwowski himself (2015: 250) noted that this typology can also be used for other types of formulaic sequences, such as proverbs and sayings, and that is one of the reasons why I decided to investigate whether it can be extended even further to examine pragmatemes.

[214] Hejwowski (2015: 248) asserts that all definitions of idioms have their weak points.

the Polish translation (31%). What needs further explanation is what is here understood by *a similar form*. The pragmatemes counted here are not necessarily literal translations (although they may be, e.g., *It's a date* translated to French as *C'est un rencard*[215]), but they also include units that follow the same grammatical pattern in accordance with the rules of the TL (e.g., *Are you there?*[216], a pragmateme consisting of a verb, 2nd person singular, and a deictic marker, is translated to French as *Tu es là ?*, which consists of the same elements, but in a slightly different order, and to Polish as *Jesteś tam?*, which consists of an equivalent deictic marker and a verb that is conjugated to denote the 2nd person singular) and loans (e.g., *Bingo* translated to both French and Polish as *Bingo*[217]), none of which seem artificial in the TL (contrary to translations that are a result of using the syntagmatic translation technique).

Use of a pragmateme that has a similar meaning but a different form

Translations that contain a pragmateme of similar meaning but a different form represent the second most frequent technique (163 units in French, i.e., 32%, and 107 units in Polish, i.e., 21%). In this group, there are TT pragmatemes of the exact same meaning as the ST ones (which may lose their context dependence in translation, such as in the French translation of *Clear!* which is the explicit *La voie est libre !*[218] [lit. *The way is free*]), but also those that are a result of adjusting the unit to the context (e.g., the translation of a more general *Enjoy* to the French *Bon séjour*[219] [lit. *Enjoy the stay*] or the Polish *Miłego wieczoru*[220] [lit. *Have a good evening.*]) The latter resemble the explicitation technique proposed by Díaz-Cintas and Remael (2007; see p. 230), but here the aspect of being a pragmateme is also taken into account.

215 E.g., *Sweet Magnolias*, S01E09, time: 39:02.
216 E.g, *You*, S02E04, time: 31:25.
217 E.g., *You*, S01E05, time: 19:54.
218 Source: *Good Girls*, S01E10, time: 19:43
219 Source: *You*, S02E07, time: 16:13.
220 Source: *Emily in Paris*, S01E06, time: 21:58.

Use of a non-pragmatemic expression

The use of a non-pragmatemic expression turned out to be a quite frequent technique, especially in the Polish translations, where it was the second most frequently used, with 123 pragmatemes being translated this way (24% of all units). In French, it was not infrequent either, with 73 pragmatemes being translated with the use of a non-pragmatemic expression (14%). The translations found here were either paraphrases or more general lexemes based on the context (e.g., *Yes, I'm fine* translated to French as *Très bien, oui* [lit. *Very well, yes*] when it was the answer to *Is everything okay with you?*[221], or *Check* translated to Polish as *Tak* [lit. *Yes*] when it was the answer to *You got the ammo?*[222]), or direct translations that are much less specific than the pragmateme used in the ST (e.g., *Here you go*[223] translated as *Voilà* in French and *Proszę* in Polish, both of which can be used in many more situations than the source unit).

Syntagmatic translation

This group is the second smallest one, with 25 pragmatemes being translated this way in French translations (5%) and 27 in Polish (5%). This technique may resemble Hejwowski's (ibid) first one, as some examples of the "Use of a pragmateme that has a similar form and meaning" also happen to have the exact same syntagmatic form as the ST. Nonetheless, in this category, the translations are not units fixed in the language. Additionally, for the purposes of this study, translations that may be considered equivalent to the units used in the ST (both in form and in meaning) but are not used correctly in the particular context, are also counted in this category and constitute its majority. The most striking example in this category is the syntagmatic translation of *Love you*[224], which is translated as *Je t'aime* in French and *Kocham cię* in Polish, even though the context suggests not a romantic exchange but an ordinary goodbye[225].

---

221 Source: *Atypical*, S01E03, time: 24:23.
222 Source: *Firefly Lane*, S01E03, time: 27:39.
223 E.g., *Sweet Magnolias*, S01E10, time: 35:07.
224 E.g., *Firefly Lane*, S01E10, time: 15:18.
225 This example will be further elaborated on in Subsection 5.4 (see p. 245).

Creation of a new pragmateme

According to Hejwowski (2015: 272), the term *new idiom* "jest oksymoronem: idiom z definicji jest utrwaloną jednostką frazeologiczną języka" [is in itself an oxymoron since idioms are, by definition, a language's fixed phraseological units], but translators do sometimes invent phraseologisms that "sound" like an idiom. Similarly, there are a few examples found in the translations of the corpus that resemble pragmatemes, either existing ones (which is the case for all French translations where this technique was found, such as the English *I'll take it.* translated to *Je prends.*[226], where the object is omitted, instead of *Je le prends.*) or by taking somewhat of inspiration from the ST (for instance, one occurrence of the English *Enjoy!*, which can be understood in many ways if taken out context, was translated to Polish as *Baw się!*[227], which does not sound natural in the given context but rather seems to aim at the larger meaning of the ST unit). However, in this study, this technique was the least frequently found out of Hejwowski's (ibid) typology, with only five units found among French translations (1%) and 14 among Polish translations (3%).

Omission

Omission, i.e., a deletion of the entire pragmateme in translation, was present 67 times in the French translation (13%) and 82 times in the Polish translation (16%). While the author does not divide this technique type further, upon observation of the corpus, several reasons for the omissions can be enumerated, such as guidelines regarding repetition, time constraints (lines uttered quickly one after another), or relevance reasons (all of which are further discussed in Subsection 4.4).

Contrary to Molina and Hurtado Albir's (2002) technique typology discussed in the previous subsection (see p. 210), Hejwowski's (2015) classification proved to apply to the translations of all the charged pragmatemes found in the English corpus. Furthermore, examples of all the techniques proposed by Hejwowski (ibid) were found among the translations. However, the methodology behind assigning particular techniques could be much more

[226] Source: *Ginny and Georgia*, S01E03, time: 42:48.
[227] Source: *Sweet Magnolias*, S01E10, time: 42:51.

detailed to avoid personal judgments on formulaicity, especially when used for formulaic sequences other than idioms which are often missing from various dictionaries. This typology also does not take into account some procedures that translators may take, such as compensation, and factors such as context. That is why, overall, while the focus on formulaicity provides a new point of view, the results of the analysis with the use of Hejwowski's (ibid) classification seem rather vague.

Figure 54 presents the comparison of the techniques used in the French and Polish translations. In the case of both languages, the use of a pragmateme of a similar form and meaning (to save space, labelled "Pragmateme +form" in Figure 54) was the most frequent. The second most frequent technique differs depending on the language: in French, it is the use of a pragmateme with a different form, but similar meaning ('Pragmateme'), while in Polish it is the use of a non-pragmatemic expression, which was much less frequent in French. Translators in both languages did not favour the creation of a new

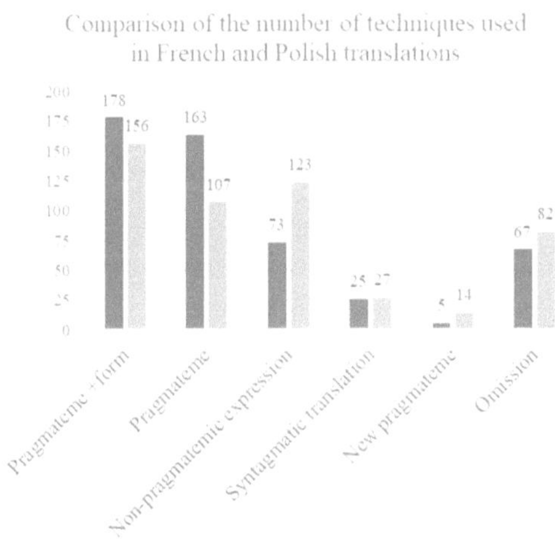

Figure 54. Comparison of the number of pragmatemes translated to French and Polish with the use of the techniques according to Hejwowski's (2015) technique typology

pragmateme, a possible reason for which may be simply that they did not need to do so in order to convey the message. Meanwhile, the technique not favored by Hejwowski (ibid), who views omission as a sign of the translator's indolence, was quite frequent in both translations, as one might expect it to be in subtitling.

While the frequency of the use of particular techniques differs visibly in a few cases, the same technique was used in both translations for 263 pragmatemes, which constitutes slightly more than half of all examples (51.5%). It can be therefore observed that their decisions differed less than when analyzed with the use of Molina and Hurtado Albir's (2002) technique typology: in that case, the same technique was observed in 41 percent of pragmatemes (see p. 222).

To conclude, the analysis of techniques according to Hejwowski's (2015) classification showed a few translation techniques useful from the point of view of formulaicity, but still, in order to investigate the phenomenon thoroughly, a typology that would take the type of translation into account seems to be needed. For that reason, the following subsection covers the analysis of the translation of pragmatemes with the use of Díaz-Cintas and Remael's (2007) typology.

5.3 Translation of cultural elements in subtitling: Díaz-Cintas and Remael's (2007) model

Díaz-Cintas and Remael's (2007) technique typology refers to translation techniques used for the translation of cultural elements in subtitling (for a more complex description of this typology, see p. 121). Since pragmatemes can be considered cultural elements and the researched corpus consists of subtitles, it was initially hypothesized that this typology would be highly applicable for the purposes of this research. However, in the process of analysis, it turned out that certain categories need to be adjusted to fit pragmatemes, primarily due to the fact that the cultures researched here are not that distant from one another, although some excluding differences can be found (e.g., the payment methods in France and Poland). The following subsections exemplify how the categories were adjusted for the purpose of the present analysis and how often they were used in translation.

Loan

In Díaz-Cintas and Remael's (ibid) typology, loan is a technique consisting of a full incorporation of the source unit (without changes to its form) used when no other translation exists in the TL. For the purposes of this analysis, all translations of the same form as in the ST are considered loans, even if another translation was possible. For instance, the English *Yo* was translated to French as *Yo* 19 times (out of 50 total occurrences), even though the translator could have used *Salut*, which is closer to the English *Hi*, or *Wesh*, which has a similar level of informality (both of these translations are also found in other occurrences of the English *Yo*[228]). Altogether, loan was not a common technique and was used for the translation of 21 instances of pragmatemes in French (4.1%) and only 2 in Polish (0.4%). The discrepancy between the number of units in the French translation compared to the Polish one is interesting since it is French rather than Polish that is known for its reluctance to absorb English influences.

Calque

To avoid etymological investigations on an expression's language origin, calque, or literal translation (both terms used by Díaz-Cintas and Remael, ibid), is understood here as the equivalence of words used in the expression in the ST and TT, even when their syntactic order is not exactly the same (e.g., *Is that all?* translated to *C'est tout ?* in French [which literally puts the components in a different order: *That is all ?*] and *To wszystko?*[229] in Polish [which lacks a verb but has an equivalent deictic marker and the equivalent of the word "all"]). Together with omission, it is the second most frequent technique found in French translations (67 occurrences, 13%) and the third most frequent in Polish translations (52 occurrences, 10%). A canonical example of a calque is found in translations of the pragmateme used for raising a toast *To [SOMETHING/PERSON]*, whose almost all occurrences are

[228] E.g., *Yo* is translated to *Salut* in the fifth episode of the third season of *Good Girls* (time of the utterance: 43 second) and to *Wesh* in the eighth episode of the first season of the same series (time: 24:00).

[229] E.g., (for both French and Polish translations), *Babysitters*, S01E02, time: 20:52.

translated as *À [SOMETHING/PERSON]* in French and *Za [SOMETHING/PERSON]*[230] in Polish.

Explicitation

Since Díaz-Cintas and Remael (ibid) focus on single lexemes rather than whole expressions, in their typology, explicitation refers to the use of a hyponym or a hypernym (with a subordinate also being possible). In order to adjust this category to pragmatemes, most of which contain more than one word, explicitation will be used when the translation conveys a message that is semantically either broader or narrower, that is, reveals more or less information in comparison to the ST. Interestingly, while according to Díaz-Cintas and Remael (ibid), generalization is a more frequent type of explicitation, in this study a large number of translations that specify the original message was found. For instance, in many episodes of different TV series analyzed in the study (namely *Good Girls*[231] and *Emily in Paris*[232]), the charged pragmateme *Hello?* uttered by a character who wants to know if someone else is in the room, was translated into French as *Il y a quelqu'un ?* (lit. *Is anyone there?*) which is a plain pragmateme as it evokes its meaning even without the context. Explicitation was the most frequent technique found in the corpus out of Díaz-Cintas and Remael's (ibid) classification, with 161 translations in French (31.5% of the total) and 137 in Polish (27%), which further attests to the importance of context in the translation of charged pragmatemes and suggests that charged pragmatemes may often lose their ambiguity in translation.

Substitution

Díaz-Cintas and Remael's (ibid) use of the term substitution refers to the use of a hypernym or hyponym despite the existence of an equivalent for spatial reasons (for the discussion on constraints in subtitling, see p. 93). For lack of examples that would fit this exact definition, in this study, the technique used by the translator was labeled *substitution* when the chosen translation

[230] E.g., (for both French and Polish translations), *Dead to Me*, S02E04, time: 20:04.
[231] All examples were found in season four, episodes: four, five, and fourteen (respective times: 22:01, 19:16, 14:19).
[232] S01E07, time: 9:01.

could be considered a short option from among possible translations. Some substitutions were shortened versions of literal translations, such as the translation of the English *Anything else you need right now?* to the French *Autre chose ?*[233] (lit. *Anything else?*; instead of, e.g., *Vous avez besoin de quelque chose d'autre maintenant ?*), while others were based on the context, for instance, the translation of the English *I'm fine*, as a response to *How are you*, to the French *Oui*. and the Polish *Tak.*[234] (both lit. *Yes*). Substitution was found to be a less frequent technique, with a slightly higher frequency in Polish (36 units, i.e., 7%) than in French translations (18 units, i.e., 3.5%).

Compensation

Because Díaz-Cintas and Remael (ibid) view compensation similarly to Molina and Hurtado Albir (2002), the same example from the Polish translation is found in the corpus, and it has been already discussed in Subsection 5.1, see p. 219.

Omission

In French translations, omission, i.e., deletion of the entire pragmateme in translation, was noted 67 times (13%), which corresponds to the number of omitted pragmatemes found in the analysis with the use of Hejwowski's (2015) technique typology (see p. 226). However, due to the absence in Hejwowski's (ibid) scheme of a technique equivalent to Díaz-Cintas and Remael's (2007) compensation (which appeared once in the Polish translation, see p. 217), the number of omitted units in Polish is smaller by one pragmateme according to Díaz-Cintas and Remael's typology: 81 pragmatemes (16%). Omission is the second most frequent technique of the Díaz-Cintas and Remael's (ibid) typology found in the corpus.

Addition

Addition, a technique rather infrequent in subtitling, does not figure largely in the translation of pragmatemes in this corpus. However, some occur: 8 in the French translation (1.6%) and 6 in the Polish (1.2%). While

[233] Source: *Sweet Magnolias*, S01E02, time: 25:28.
[234] E.g., (for both French and Polish translations), *Dead to Me*, S02E10, time: 26:30.

Díaz-Cintas and Remael (ibid) note that there has to be a valid reason for the use of addition, for example to overcome possible problems with understanding, the observation of the examples in the corpus leads to the conclusion that this principle is not followed. On the contrary, the examples seem rather arbitrary, as if they depended solely on the stylistic preference of the translator. For instance, in the series *Atypical*, S01E08 (time: 21:56), characters line up to get headphones for a silent disco. The person handing out the headphones says: *Here you go,* and the French translation is: *Voilà vos casques* (lit. *Here are your headphones*), while the equivalent *Tenez* would serve just as well. In general, the examples of addition found in the corpus seem to go against the notion that subtitles aim to be as short as possible.

Although most techniques proposed by Díaz-Cintas and Remael (ibid) were found in both French and Polish translations, two techniques were found to have been used in neither translation. These were transposition and lexical recreation. The absence of the first may result from the fact that the SL pragmatemes did not convey any particular meanings that could be replaced by TL units only referring to the target culture, while the absence of the latter suggests that there was no need to create a neologism, especially in that the analyzed pragmatemes were not neologisms to begin with. Furthermore, for a large number of translations, it was impossible to categorize them under any of Díaz-Cintas and Remael's (ibid) proposed techniques. That was the case for 169 French translations (33% of all units) and 188 Polish translations (37% of all units). In those cases, the SL pragmatemes were translated into units of very similar meaning, neither broader nor more narrow, units which could be considered equivalents by some. However, no type of equivalence is proposed by Díaz-Cintas and Remael (ibid); therefore, in those cases, this typology is simply not applicable. For instance, the frequent pragmateme *Cheers*, which appears in the corpus only as a saying used to raise a toast, is usually translated by the French *Santé* and the Polish *Na zdrowie*[235], both of which can be considered direct equivalents of the SL unit and do not fit any of the categories proposed by Díaz-Cintas and Remael (ibid).

[235] E.g., *You*, S02E04, time: 35:10, *Firefly Lane*, S01E04, time: 33:07.

The comparison of techniques used in the French and Polish translations revealed minimal significant differences. This can be observed in Figure 55, which illustrates the frequency of particular techniques in both translations.

Translators decided to use the same technique in both French and Polish translations 284 times, which constitutes the majority of all instances (56%). It also signifies that among the three typologies used in the analysis, the application of Díaz-Cintas and Remael's (ibid) model resulted in the highest level agreement between the French and Polish translators (56% of units translated with the use of the same technique according to Díaz-Cintas and Remael's [ibid] model, 51.5% according to Hejwowski [2015], and 41% according to Molina and Hurtado Albir's [2002] model). The most noticeable difference in the usage of Díaz-Cintas and Remael's (2007) techniques between French and Polish translations can be found in the use of the loan technique, which was used 21 times in French, but only two times in Polish, which, as already mentioned, is noteworthy because French, more than Polish, is associated with avoiding loanwords.

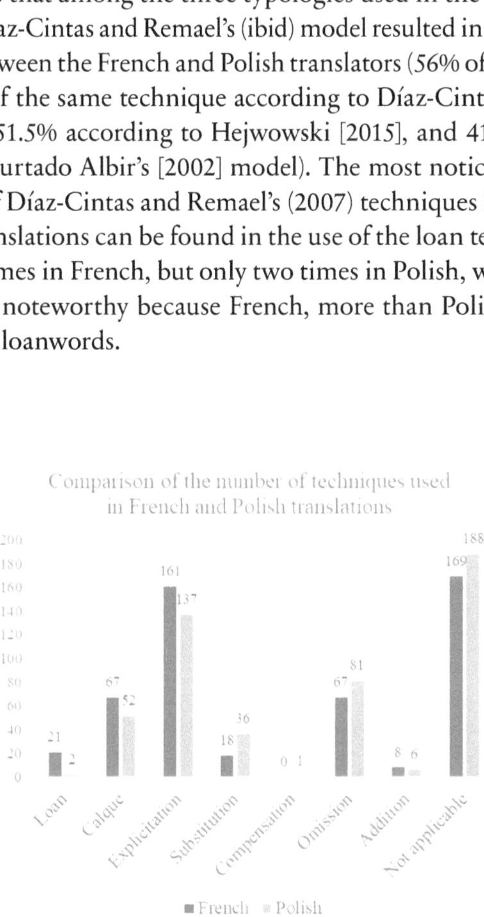

Figure 55. Comparison of the number of pragmatemes translated to French and Polish with the use of the techniques according to Díaz-Cintas and Remael's (2007) technique typology

After the analysis of the translations of charged pragmatemes from the corpus from the point of view of three different technique typologies proposed by different researchers, it is clear that all of them have their strong and weak points. With all of what has been noted in this chapter so far, I have decided to propose a typology on my own, which is the topic of the next subsection.

5.4 A new typology of translation techniques in subtitling: context-based approach

The analysis of charged pragmatemes using three sets of techniques proposed by researchers representing varying perspectives led to many observations discussed in the previous subsections. Yet, the main and reoccurring observation is that one element was consistently absent from the proposed models, and that was the context. The techniques presented in previous subsections allow researchers to look at nothing but examples in isolation. Meanwhile, context is key to human communication, both in terms of linguistic context, i.e., the linguistic elements (words, phrases) surrounding a given part of discourse, and extralinguistic context, i.e., the social setting regarding the speakers and spatio-temporal elements of the situation of communication, and as such it ought not to be disregarded in such analyses.

The striking lack of the concept of context in the typologies of translation techniques discussed above is the driving force behind proposing my own set of techniques: a set of ten translation techniques that take context into account. These techniques are:

1) deletion (context-based, technical constraints-based, repetition-based, and visual-based),
2) ostensibly redundant rendition,
3) compression (syntactic and contextual),
4) erroneous equivalent,
5) consistency equivalent,
6) contextual interpretation,
7) idiosyncratic addition,

8) creative rendition,
9) ostensible idiomatic equivalence,
10) equivalent.

Below, each of these techniques is examined and exemplified by drawing from the corpus, aiming to demonstrate the practical application of the suggested typology.

Deletion

Deletion, as proposed here, is to be understood as the technique of fully suppressing of the ST element in the TT. The reasons why similar terms used previously by different researchers, such as *omission* or *reduction*, are avoided here, are rather subjective and could be subject to discussion; however, it seems that in the TS field, the associations with the term *omission* are often negative, as if the translator were unable to think of a better solution, while the term *reduction* points to something that is reduced, not fully suppressed. Therefore, the term *deletion* is suggested here to point to a conscious decision of a translator and to avoid any negative associations. Furthermore, it must be stressed that deletion may result from many factors, which are often out of the translator's control, and that is why one should not analyze every case of deletion in the same way. For this reason, this technique is further classified into four subcategories: context-based, technical constraints-based, repetition-based, and visual-based deletion, all of which will be further discussed below.

1) **Context-based deletion**

In the introduction to this section (see p. 234), two types of context were enumerated, namely linguistic and extralinguistic context. However, for spatial limitations, every time the term "context" is mentioned in relation to context-based deletion, it refers to the linguistic one.

Context-based deletion is a technique in which the translator decides to suppress a ST element in translation either due to relevancy or for redundancy reasons. In some cases, translating the ST element may seem unnecessary as the element uttered by the characters on the screen is very similar, if not

Figure 56. A screenshot presenting an example of context-based deletion in French and Polish translations[236]

the same, in the TL. Such is the case in one of the episodes of *Good Girls*, presented in Figure 56.

Here, the character utters *Hey, hey* not as a greeting but rather as an expression of interest and consolation. In Polish, in the same situation, one could use expressions such as *No, no* or *No nie*, but also words such as *hej* or *ej*, both of which sound similar to the English form. Meanwhile, in the French translation, the deletion of *Hey, hey* seems to be made purely out of relevancy reasons, as this element does not bring any new nor relevant information to the communication.

Another frequent example of context-based deletion can be found in translations of *Yeah, I'm fine* which is a phrase that appears several times throughout the corpus[237] as an answer to *Are you okay?* and which is translated as *Oui* in French and *Tak* in Polish (both of which are more formal equivalents of "yeah"). Because it is the context of the entire conversation that allows for this translation, it is categorized here as an example of the use of context-based deletion; however, one can argue that it is also an example of technical constraints-based deletion because the TT is much shorter than

[236] Source: *Good Girls*, S02E03, time: 28:28. Director: Dylan K. Massin, producers: Minnesota Logging Company, Universal Television.

[237] E.g., *Dead to Me*, S02E02, time: 1:08, *Ginny & Georgia*, S01E05, time: 34:20, and others.

what was originally said. And while aiming at short subtitles is definitely a technicality of this AVT type (for the characteristics of subtitling see p. 93), it is the context that is the main factor for such a translation to be possible, hence its categorization in this technique type.

2) **Technical constraints-based deletion**

Technical constraints-based deletion refers to the removal of the ST element in the TT due to technical constraints related to subtitling (for more on these constraints, see p. 95-98). The spatio-temporal constraints of subtitling sometimes force the translators to fully remove the element that is of the least importance when it is uttered between two other utterances. For instance, in *Firefly Lane*, S01E05, time: 42 s, there are many characters talking one after the other, and the sentences are short but uttered in quick succession, which may have led the French translator to delete the pragmateme *I'm talking to you* in the translation (interestingly, the Polish translator decided to translate the pragmateme with a Polish equivalent despite the rapid conversation and quick shot changes). Similarly, in *Atypical*, S01E04, time: 18:38, the pragmateme *Help yourself* is deleted in the Polish translation as it is quickly uttered between what seems to be two parts of one sentence spoken by the same character: *We have cheese. Help yourself. And figs.* (again, interestingly, this pragmateme is preserved with an equivalent in the French translation). While technical constraints may also refer to guidelines regarding repetition in subtitling, to separate this latter issue from the spatio-temporal constraints it will be classified as a separate subtype and discussed below.

3) **Repetition-based deletion**

According to Netflix's Timed Text Style Guide both for French[238] and Polish[239], translators are required not to "translate words or phrases repeated more than once by the same speaker" and to "time subtitle to the audio but translate only once, [i]f the repeated word or phrase is said twice in a row." Furthermore,

[238] Source: https://partnerhelp.netflixstudios.com/hc/en-us/articles/217351577-French-Timed-Text-Style-Guide, accessed on the July 25, 2022.

[239] Source: https://partnerhelp.netflixstudios.com/hc/en-us/articles/216787928-Polish-Timed-Text-Style-Guide, accessed on the July 25, 2022.

in the French guidelines, the following requirement is added: "When two characters repeat the same thing simultaneously, time the subtitle to the audio, and just translate the term/phrase once without a hyphen." While sometimes these guidelines are not followed (which is further discussed in ostensibly redundant rendition technique type, see p. 241), this subtype of deletion is used many times throughout the corpus. The most striking example is represented in Figure 57 below:

Figure 57. A screenshot presenting an example of repetition-based deletion in French and Polish translations[240]

In this scene, a woman calls one of the main characters on the phone, and the call is also answered in that character's car (which is linked to the character's iPhone) in the form of a speakerphone. The woman then continues to repeat *Hello?* a few times as she tries to contact the character, who is in such shock that she does not speak. The pragmateme is repeated throughout the conversation:

Annie (the main character): **Hello?**
The woman (calling on the phone): **Hello? Hello? Hello?** *Did I lose you?* **Hello?**
Annie: **Hello?**

Interestingly, in the Polish translation, only the initial *Hello?* is translated, while in the French translation, only the two middle repetitions uttered by the woman are suppressed. Although it cannot be argued that the French translator did not follow the guidelines, since the elements retained in the TT are separated by *Did I lose you?*, because the time between the repeated pragmateme is very short, the translation may nonetheless seem redundant for the viewer.

4) Visual-based deletion

Visual-based deletion is the decision of a translator based on the argumentation that viewers can understand what is said from what is visible on the screen at a given moment. An example of such a situation is presented in Figure 58.

Figure 58. A screenshot presenting an example of visual-based deletion in French translation[241]

In the situation depicted in Figure 58, the character picks up the phone and says *Hello?*, which is a standard pragmateme used in such a situation. Since it is not characteristic solely of the ST culture, it can be assumed that the viewer will understand this utterance even without any subtitles. Such must have been the reasoning of the French translator, who decided to suppress this pragmateme in translation. However, making this kind of assumption is not standard practice, especially when subtitles' timing and placement allow

240 Source: *Good Girls*, S01E03, time: 26:44. Director: Kenneth Fink, producers: Minnesota Logging Company, Universal Television.

for translating the unit (as the translation would not be too long, nor would it be visible on the screen for too little time), which is visible in the Polish translation, in which the pragmateme *Hello?* was preserved and translated with the equivalent *Halo?*.

Other examples of visual-based deletion are multiple suppressions of the pragmateme *Here* used to pass something over (shortly discussed in the analysis of Molina and Hurtado Albir's [2002] substitution technique, see p. 218). Figure 59 depicts one of them.

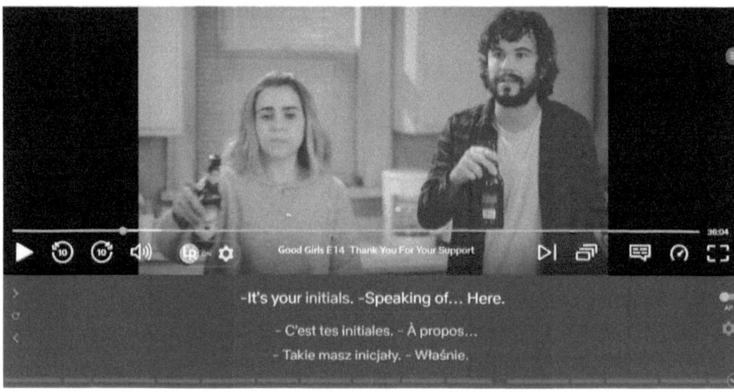

Figure 59. A screenshot presenting an example of visual deletion in French and Polish translations[242]

In Figure 59, the character speaking points to an object that she wants to hand over. Because the utterances right before (*Speaking of...*) and right after are separated only by this short pragmateme and the sequence as a whole is rather quick, translating *Here* would not be ergonomic from the point of view of the standard reading speed (for more on this topic see p. 95). Therefore, both the French and the Polish translators decided to fully suppress it, given the fact that what the character refers to is visible on the screen (and that difference is why these examples are categorized here, not in the technical constraints-based

241 Source: *Atypical*, S01E05, time: 23:34. Director: Michael Patrick Jann, excutive producers: Robia Rashid, Seth Gordon, and Mary Rohlich.

deletion). There are more instances of the translation of *Here* being suppressed in the exact same situation, namely five in French and nine in Polish.

As a whole, the deletion technique was the second most frequent for the translation of English pragmatemes to French (71 units, 14%), and the third most frequent for Polish translations (83 units, 16%). However, looking at deletion as a whole does not necessarily provide answers as to why it was so frequent in both languages. That is why it is necessary to examine which type of deletion appeared the most frequently, which is represented in Figure 60.

In both cases, the context-based deletion was the most frequent, with 37 pragmatemes being suppressed for this reason in the French translation and 40 in Polish. This points to the importance of the surrounding linguistic context, which makes it easier to understand the situation, which results in the possibility of suppressing the pragmateme. The second most frequent types of deletion in French were both repetition-based and visual-based types, with 15 units being suppressed for each these reasons. In contrast, in the Polish translation, there is a visible difference between the number of pragmatemes suppressed on the repetition (14) and visual (23) basis, which may suggest that Polish translators were more eager to take into consideration the visual factor than their French counterparts. The least frequent type of deletion was the technical constraints-based deletion in both TLs, with only two examples in each TL. However, that can be explained by the distinction made between constraints regarding repetition, visual-based redundancy and spatio-temporal constraints, all of which represented a different type of deletion technique.

Ostensibly redundant rendition

Ostensibly redundant rendition is a technique used when the translator, despite the company's guidelines (see p. 107), decides to translate a repeated sequence. Figure 61 presents an example of this technique in a situation when the crowd repeats the words of a toast made by a family friend. While

[242] Source: *Good Girls*, S04E14, time: 6:55. Directors: Ken Whittingham and Michael Weaver, producers: Minnesota Logging Company, Universal Television.

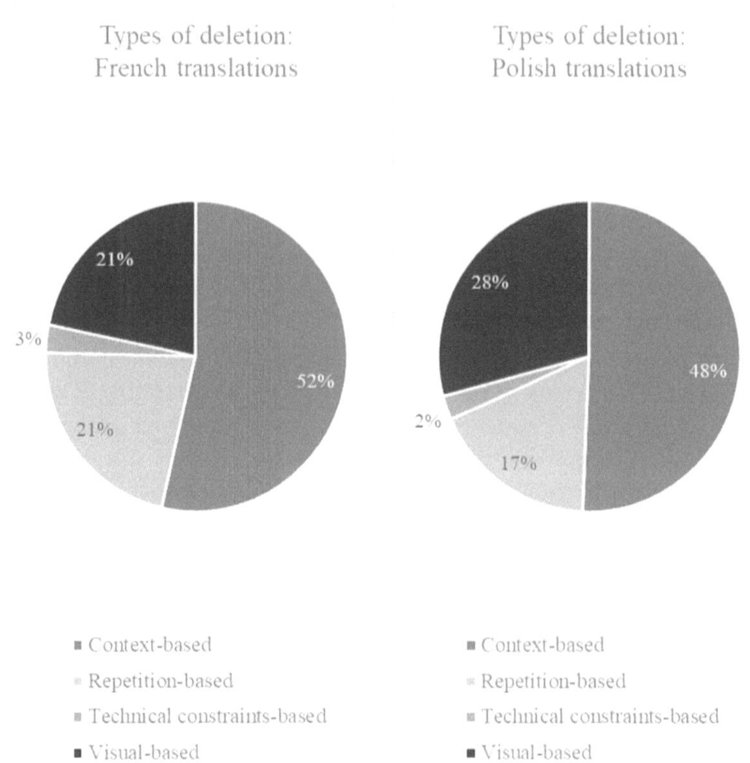

Figure 60. Comparison of the frequency of different types of deletion in French and Polish translations of English pragmatemes

the French translator decided to follow the guidelines, the Polish translator rendered the repetitions in translation.[243]

Ostensibly redundant rendition should be considered a translation mistake not simply because it is against the guidelines but, as implied by the

[243] Source: *Firefly Lane*, S01E08, time: 31:49. Director: Fred Gerber, producers: Aaron Au, Arielle Boisvert.

Figure 61. A screenshot presenting an example of ostensibly redundant rendition in Polish translation[243]

technique's name, because of its obvious redundancy; the application of this technique may unnecessarily distract the viewer's attention from what is happening on the screen. Thankfully, while it was indeed present in the corpus, the ostensibly redundant rendition was not frequent, with only three occurrences (0.6%) in the translation into French and four (0.8%) into Polish.

Compression

Compression is a technique that can be further divided into two types: syntactic compression and contextual compression, both of which will be now discussed.

1) Syntactic compression

Syntactic compression occurs when the translator decides to use a shortened version of an equivalent utterance. It can be the result of a need for a shorter subtitle line when its display time is short, or it can be an arbitrary decision based on the translator's preference, not a necessity. For example, in *Good Girls*, S01E03, time: 24:58, the pragmateme *Check, please.* is translated into French as *L'addition !* (lit. *Check!*) instead of *L'addition, s'il vous plaît*, and in *Good Girls*, S03E09 nine, time: 21:33, the pragmateme *Let me in* is translated into Polish as *Wpuść* (lit. *Let in*) instead of *Wpuść mnie*.

2) Contextual compression

Contextual compression is a technique used for space-saving reasons, and it refers to replacing the equivalent TL unit with a completely different utterance that fits the context. In the corpus, a common occurrence of this technique is found in translations of *I'm fine*, when this is a response to a question about one's well-being. In French translations, it is often translated as *Oui*[244], and in Polish, as *Tak*[245] (both meaning *Yes*).[246]

While the compression technique was not the most frequent one in either among French or Polish translations, it was still noticeable in the corpus, with 24 units being translated with it in French (5%) and 30 units in Polish translations (6%). Figure 62 presents the percentage distribution of different compression types' frequency in French and Polish translations.

In French, the use of syntactic compression was much more frequent than that of contextual compression (19 units to five), which may suggest that French translators were not as willing to replace the ST elements with completely different ones based on the context as the Polish translators were, as in the Polish translations of charged pragmatemes, the number of occurrences of both compression types is the same (15). However, since the study only examines compression in terms of pragmatemes, it would be interesting to see whether this might be a more common phenomenon differentiating French and Polish translators' approaches or preferences in subtitling.

Erroneous equivalent

While the definition of an erroneous equivalent is quite self-explanatory, one could argue that it should not be placed among translation techniques as no translator makes a conscious decision to provide an erroneous translation.

---

[244] E.g., *Atypical*, S02E05, time: 13:51, *Emily in Paris*, S01E08, time: 6:35, *Dead to Me*, S02E10, time: 26:30.

[245] E.g., *Good Girls*, S04E11, time: 40:52, *Atypical*, S02E05, time: 13:51, *Never Have I Ever*, S01E06, time: 15:31.

[246] While this example may point to the resemblance of contextual compression to Díaz-Cintas and Remael's (2007) substitution, it may, but does not have to, overlap, as not all contextual compressions are necessarily hypernyms or hyponyms.

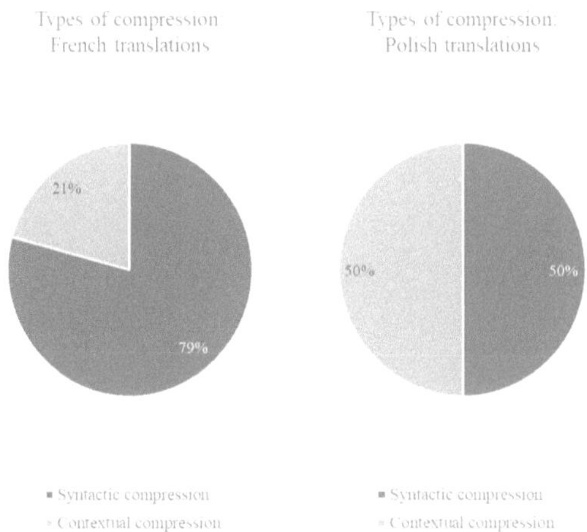

Figure 62. Comparison of the frequency of different types of compression in French and Polish translations of English pragmatemes

However, this phenomenon is categorized as a translation technique for the purposes of the analysis in order to acknowledge the issue and separate it from other translation mistakes that could appear in subtitling, e.g., from the ostensibly redundant rendition discussed on p. 241.

In translating pragmatemes, erroneous equivalents may result from misunderstanding the context or not taking into account cultural differences. The latter case is visible in both French and Polish translations of the pragmatemes *Love you*, *Love ya*, and *Love you too* used as a form of goodbye among family members and friends. In the majority of occurrences, this pragmateme is translated literally as *Je t'aime* in French and *Kocham cię* in Polish, even though in both cultures, this is not a common way to say goodbye, and both of these phrases are reserved for more intimate situations. A more suitable equivalent of *Love you* that conveys both the goodbye meaning and the friendly and/or loving relationship is *Bisou* (e.g., used by the translator of *Sweet Magnolias* in S01E07, time: 10:55) or *Bisous* (e.g., *Good Girls*, S03E08, time: 12:59) in French, and *Buziaki* (e.g., *Good Girls*, S02E08, time: 23:01) or *Buziaczki* (e.g., *Good*

Girls, S03E01, time: 03:07) in Polish. Figure 63 below presents an example of an erroneous equivalent used for this pragmateme:

Figure 63. A screenshot presenting an example of erroneous equivalent in French and Polish translations[247]

In Figure 63, the character presented on the screen is simply leaving and not being particularly affectionate; therefore, the translations may seem unnatural to French and Polish viewers.

Erroneous equivalents of the abovementioned pragmatemes constitute all examples of this phenomenon in the Polish translations of English pragmatemes and almost all in the French translations (in both cases, 27 occurrences, i.e., 5%). However, the presence of erroneous equivalents in translation sometimes cannot be explained by context ambiguity or its misunderstanding, and an example of this is presented in Figure 64.

In the shot presented above, the woman is asking the bartender for a check with a *please*; in the French translation, however, instead of a standard pragmateme *L'addition, s'il vous plaît*, the word *please* is replaced with a *thank you* (*merci*). The phrase *L'addition, merci* is not a standard pragmateme and can only be used in more particular situations, for instance, ironically, when one is dissatisfied with the service or when the waiter

[247] Source: *You*, S01E09, time: 9:35. Director: Martha Mitchell, producers: Ryan Lindbum, Adria Lang, Jason Sokoloff, Jennifer Lence, Wayne Carmona, Hillary Benefiel, Carl Ogawa, Penn Badgley, Stephanie Johnson.

Figure 64. A screenshot presenting an example of erroneous equivalent in the French translation[248]

brings something when the customer is asking for the check at the same time. Nonetheless, in the example shown in Figure 64, no such occurrence is taking place, the situation of asking for the check is standard, so it is rather difficult to explain the translator's reason for not using the equivalent pragmateme.

The examples discussed in this part are errors on the translator's part, but sometimes, what may seem like an erroneous equivalent at first glance, is rather a conscious decision of the translator made for the sake of consistency, which is the focus of the next technique.

Consistency equivalent

Consistency equivalent is the technique used for units that reappear throughout a movie or TV series in similar contexts. In this technique, the translator decides not to translate the unit with its equivalent but rather creates their own and continues to use it each time the unit occurs. For this technique to

[248] Source: *Dead to Me,* S01E05, time: 14:09. Director: Minkie Spiro, producers: Joe Hardesty, Linda Cardellini, Peter Chomsky, Buddy Enright, Denise Pleune, Carrie A. Tyson, Emma Rathbone, Kelly Hutchinson.

be used, a particular context has to be present. In the corpus, one such unit is observed, and that is the pragmateme *Love you* used throughout the TV series *Ginny and Georgia*[249] as a part of a fixed goodbye sequence between a group of teenage friends. The whole sequence is as follows:

Friend A: Love you. Mean it.
Friend B: Hate you. Kidding.

Although it was observed above that translating *Love you* into the Polish *Kocham cię* may be considered an erroneous equivalent (see p. 244), in this case, it is a consistency equivalent as the translation is consistent each time this pragmateme occurs in that exact context. Nonetheless, it seems that the French translator rendered the sociolect character of this pragmateme better, translating it as *J'vous kiffe*, which is equivalently colloquial to the original and similarly characteristic of young people's language.

Contextual interpretation

Contextual interpretation is a technique used for the translation of context-sensitive units such as charged pragmatemes. The term *context* is understood here widely, with no restriction to exclusively linguistic or extralinguistic context. In this study, this technique was found to be the third most frequent among the French translations with 68 units (13%) and second most frequent among the Polish with 96 units (19%).

In some instances, the interpretation might be an arbitrary decision on translator's part. For instance, in *Good Girls*, S02E12, time: 2:45, the pragmateme *Are you there?* is translated to French as *Vous m'entendez ?* (lit. *You hear me?*). The situation of the utterance is that of when one is talking on the phone with somebody but does not hear a response for a while, so both the translation suggested by the translator, as well as the literal translation *Êtes-vous là ?* (or, rather, without the inversion to keep the resemblance of oral speech: *Vous êtes là ?*) are possible, but the translator decided to use

[249] The pragmateme appears in this form and context three times in the first season of the series: in episodes two (time: 27:06), five (08:07), and eight (16:21).

a TL unit that is less ambiguous without the context, hence the classification as this technique type.

In other instances, contextual interpretation might be inevitable due to the lack of a similarly context-sensitive equivalent in the TL. In that case, the translator is obliged to find a narrower equivalent that suits the given context. Sometimes, they will be able to determine the context from the linguistic layer, for example, when *We're fine*[250] is an answer to *What can I get you guys to drink?* (the French translation is then *Ça ira* [lit. *It'll go*] and the Polish is *Nie trzeba* [lit. *No need*], both of which are examples of contextual interpretation). Other times, they will have to reach for the visual layer to determine the context, such as in the situation depicted in Figure 65.

Figure 65. A screenshot presenting an example of contextual interpretation in French and Polish translations[251]

[250] Source: *Good Girls*, S01E07, time: 20:49.

[251] Source: *Atypical*, S02E02, time: 16:22. Director: Ryan Case, producer: Jennifer Jason Leigh.

The situation depicted in Figure 65 is that of a waiter handing the customer their meal in a school cafeteria, and it happens right after the shot change, so the linguistic context is not related to what has been said before. Therefore, the translator has to rely on the visual image for a proper translation of the charged pragmateme *Enjoy* and deduce on that basis that it refers to serving food, not wishing somebody that they enjoy their night at a party, for example. Both the French and the Polish translators understood the context correctly, as the translation to French is *Bon appétit* and the Polish is *Smacznego* (both meaning *Enjoy your meal*).[252]

An interesting occurrence is when both linguistic and extralinguistic contexts may be taken into account in translation. In *Good Girls,* season two, episode ten, time: 18:27, a woman says *Enjoy* when handing a juice box to a little girl. The utterance is preceded by a short conversation between the two characters in which it is visible that the woman is not pleased with the little girl talking to her:

Little girl: Can I get a juice box?
Woman: I don't know. Can you? [scoffs]

In the French translation, the translator decided to follow up on the woman's attitude and translated the charged pragmateme as *Éclate-toi*, which can be translated as *Have a blast*, which sounds sarcastic in the context. Meanwhile, the Polish translator decided to rely on the visual image of the woman handing the girl the juice and translated the pragmateme as *Smacznego*, which could be translated here as *Enjoy your drink*, which, while it still could be understood sarcastically, is a more neutral equivalent than the one chosen by the French translator. That is the one example that showcases how contextual

[252] While the examples evoked here may suggest that the contextual interpretation technique resembles Molina and Hurtado Albir's (2002) particularization technique, it does not have to be so; contextual interpretation may also involve generalizations or units of a similar semantic meaning.

interpretation is a technique in which the translator is presented with a number of choices from which they choose one to fit the context best, according to their own understanding.

Idiosyncratic addition

In translation, addition is sometimes inevitable due to cultural and/or linguistic differences and the need to convey the message and the overall style of the ST despite them. However, some additions may seem less necessary than others, and those are the cases to which the term *idiosyncratic addition* is applied. In subtitling, idiosyncratic addition can be related to conveying in the TT not only the message of the ST but also what is visible on the screen. Such is the situation in French translations depicted in Figures 66, 67, and 68.

Figure 66. A screenshot presenting an example of idiosyncratic addition in the French translation[253]

[253] Source: *Ginny and Georgia*, S01E06, time: 03:48. Director: Sudz Sutherland, producers: Claire Welland, Todd Aronauer.

Figure 67. A screenshot presenting an example of idiosyncratic addition in the French translation[254]

Figure 68. A screenshot presenting an example of idiosyncratic addition in the French translation[255]

In Figure 68, the character points at some wine bottles. The pragmateme uttered here is *Help yourself* which does not necessarily imply serving oneself with alcohol, but still, in the French translation, the pragmateme is translated as *sers-toi un verre* (lit. *help yourself to a glass*). The addition of the word "un verre" is not necessary (the basic equivalent *sers-toi* would be appropriate) but is related to the context. However, this addition holds the value of explicitation of future events as the wine bottles are shown on the screen after the shot visible in Figure 66, so the French TT viewer is informed about them before the ST viewer, which is not standard practice, especially if it is not necessary. Other examples of visual-based idiosyncratic addition, while holding a value of linguistic explicitation, do not refer to what happens after the shot but express what is shown on the screen at the given moment (see Figures 67 and 68).

Both in Figure 67 and Figure 68, the element added in the French translation (*casques* [headphones] in Figure 67 and *verre* [*glass*] in Figure 68) is visible on the screen at the moment the subtitle is displayed, which, unlike in the situation presented in Figure 66, does not make the TT viewer privileged to know what comes next, but still makes the translation redundant. Furthermore, it goes against the standard subtitling practice of making the subtitle short when possible, and in both situations, the equivalent *Tenez* would be as suitable.

Nonetheless, idiosyncratic addition in subtitling does not appear only in visual-based contexts.[255] For instance, it may be the result of the translator's stylistic preference, as when the toast *To Mindy!* is translated to *À la santé de Mindy !*[256] instead of the equivalent *À Mindy !* It may also be the result of a translator's apparent indecisiveness in wanting to convey both possible equivalents, making the translation redundant on the linguistic level. Such is the case when the pragmateme *That's it.* is translated to *Voilà, c'est fini.*[257]

---

254 Source: *Atypical*, S01E08, time: 21:56. Director: Michael Patrick Jann, producer: Jennifer Jason Leigh.

255 Source: *Never Have I Ever*, S01E10, time: 07:59. Director: Tristram Shapeero, producers: Kaling International, Original Langster, 3 Arts Entertainment, Universal Television.

256 Source: *Emily in Paris*, S01E08, time: 18:57.

257 Source: *Ginny and Georgia*, S01E05, time: 34:45.

instead of either *Voilà* or *C'est fini*. Both of these examples may point to translators' choosing their own preference over the subtitling practice of translating with the shortest equivalent.

Interestingly, idiosyncratic addition is found only among French translations of English pragmatemes from the corpus; no such occurrences are found in the Polish translations. This may indicate that Polish translators truly avoid any unnecessary additions as Polish is already a language that tends to be longer than English, and for that matter, longer than compared to French as the TT, but because only five occurrences of idiosyncratic addition are found in this study, more research on this topic would be needed to reliably support such a conclusion.

That said, addition in translation does not have to be always idiosyncratic; it may also be a part of the translator's creative rendition, which is further discussed in the discussion of the next technique.

Creative rendition

In some instances, translators are obliged to use their creativity more than usual. The most commonly known examples of when translator's creativity is especially needed are wordplays and puns. However, an example found in the Polish translation shows that creative rendition can also be useful in situations that seemingly do not pose an unsolvable translation problem. In *Good Girls*, season two, episode eight, time: 8:24, two young men are talking to a middle-aged car salesman, and one of them answers the agitated car salesman with *Yo. [Chill.]*[258] In the Polish translation, the pragmateme *Yo.* is not translated, but the colloquial character it holds is rendered by the addition of a colloquial nickname in a vocative form: *Spokojnie, mordo*[259], even though there exists an equivalent of "yo" in Polish (and that is either "hej" or "ej"). In this case, the translation through creative rendition was possible because the pragmateme used in the ST was a phatic one, i.e., was used purely

[258] Square brackets added to give more context to the pragmateme *Yo.*

[259] The same example is discussed for Díaz-Cintas and Remael's (2007) compensation technique. However, according to Díaz-Cintas and Remael's (2007) original suggestion, compensation should be done in a form of overtranslation or addition in another place in translation, while in terms of creative rendition, the placement of the technique is not relevant.

to attract attention, not to convey any detailed meaning and only providing the information about the character of the conversation.

Ostensible idiomatic equivalence

Ostensible idiomatic equivalence occurs when the ST idiomatic unit is translated with a TT idiomatic unit but one that does not fit the context. One example of this technique[260] is found in the Polish translation of *Good Girls*, season two, episode seven, time: 6:53, where the character, a woman in her early 40s, utters the pragmateme *I'll take it*, as a response to a compliment. The translation contains the idiomatic sequence *W to mi graj*, which, in fact, expresses the feeling of liking something, finding it pleasant, but does not fit the context of a daily, friendly conversation, as it may seem anachronistic, and more suitable nowadays for literary language.

Equivalent

Throughout the literature, the term *equivalent* is usually used to refer to a TL unit that is used in similar contexts, conveys a similar meaning as the SL unit, and is generally recognized in the TL. What may seem to be a simple definition in theory becomes problematic when one is to use it in practice: then, questions arise of what being "generally recognized" may exactly mean. For some, native speakers' intuition is enough (which poses methodological problems on its own); for others, a unit has to be present in dictionaries or be frequent in the corpora. Though the latter is more methodologically convincing, it does not apply to all language units, for instance, pragmatemes. As already noted in Chapter 3 (see p. 123), so far, there are no dictionaries of pragmatemes. Furthermore, many pragmatemes belong to everyday spoken language, which makes it difficult to find them in the available corpora, which are most often corpora of written texts. Therefore, for the analysis of equivalents of these particular formulaic language units, another method is needed. In this study, DeepL, a neural machine translation system (for more on DeepL, see, for example, Rushton 2022), is proposed to be used in order to determine whether the translation is an equivalent or not. To do so, the

[260] Again, it can be argued that because this is not a well perceived nor recommended practice, the term *technique* is not the best label here, but it is so named for the purposes of the analysis.

TL unit (translated by the human translation) is translated to the SL with DeepL and then compared with the original SL utterance. The same can also be done in another direction, i.e., starting with the SL unit and then comparing it with the proposed human translation, but the first method is more advisable here as it is better for units that are ambiguous without the context in the SL (for instance, the pragmateme *Help yourself* is translated in DeepL to French literally as *Aidez-vous vous-même*, but when one starts with its situational equivalent, *Sers-toi*, and translates it in DeepL to English, the result is *Help yourself*). Table 10 depicts this process.[261]

Table 10. The process of confirming the equivalence of a unit with DeepL

TT	DeepL translation to SL	ST	DeepL translation to TL
French: *Autre chose ?* Polish: *Coś jeszcze?*	*Anything else?*	*Anything else?*[261]	French: *Autre chose ?* Polish: *Coś jeszcze?*

In this study, the use of equivalent was the most commonly found technique, with 307 occurrences of 29 pragmatemes in the French translation (60%) and 264 occurrences of 30 pragmatemes in Polish (52%). One of the possible explanations for such large numbers is the fact that this technique was often found among pragmatemes of high frequency.

While the equivalent technique is rather self-explanatory from the translation point of view, to combine the two analytical chapters, a closer look at the linguistic features of the equivalents found will now be taken in comparison to the results presented in Chapter 4.

The 29 charged pragmatemes translated into French were translated with the use of 42 different equivalents, indicating variability in the translation of certain pragmatemes. For instance, the pragmateme *I'm fine* was translated either as *Ça va* or *Je vais bien*. Within these 42 equivalents, nine corresponded to the pragmatemes listed initially for the corpus search (see p. 134). Additionally, four equivalents resembled the pragmatemes found in the list, differing only in the usage of articles or grammatical person (e.g., the list included the pragmateme *Minute*, but not the equivalent *Une minute*, *C'est à vous*, but not *C'est à toi*). Notably, the majority, 29 equivalents,

[261] Source: *Sweet Magnolias*, S01E04, time: 24:51.

were absent from the initial list of pragmatemes. This discrepancy may be attributed to various reasons. It could suggest, as previously argued (see p. 134) that the sources used for compiling the list were flawed. Another explanation points to some of the equivalents being seemingly too broad to be considered pragmatemes in the TL (e.g., *Hé* or *Voilà*). Meanwhile, the translation of the 30 pragmatemes into Polish involved 41 equivalents. Similarly to French, an example of a pragmateme translated with different equivalents also includes *I'm fine*; in Polish, it was translated either as *Wszystko gra*, *Wszystko w porządku*, or *Nic mi nie jest*. 17 equivalents corresponded to the initial pragmatemes list, a higher number compared to the French equivalents, suggesting potentially better quality sources for the Polish language. However, 24 units were not found in the list, implying that the sources used may not have been sufficient nonetheless. Yet, among the Polish equivalents, there were also a few units that seemed too broad to be considered pragmatemes, such as *Proszę*.

Furthermore, an assessment was conducted to determine whether the units that appeared in translation were as ambiguous without the context as the SL charged pragmatemes. In the French translation, the ambiguity was observed in 50 percent of cases, whereas in the Polish translation, in 43.9 percent of the cases. Then, in French as the TL, 35.7 percent of the studied units were identified as idiomatic (loaded), while only 14.3 percent as compositional (plain). Conversely, in Polish as the TL, the opposite was true, with the majority, specifically, 46.3 percent of units, being compositional and only 9.8 percent idiomatic.

Table 11 depicts the comparison of linguistic features of French and Polish equivalents extracted from the translations of English charged pragmatemes (indicated as "French_TL" and "Polish_TL" in the table) and charged pragmatemes retrieved from the French and Polish corpora (marked as "French_SL" and "Polish_SL").

Before analyzing the data in Table 11, it is important to note that the count of French charged pragmatemes in "French_SL" and Polish charged pragmatemes in "Polish_SL" stood at 16 each, while the number of equivalents amounted to 42 in the French translation ("French_TL") and 41 in the Polish translation ("Polish_TL"), meaning that the SL units were fewer than the TL equivalents. Yet, several noteworthy observations can be made from the data.

Table 11. Comparison of linguistic fseatures in equivalents found in the French and Polish translations and charged pragmatemes found in the French and Polish corpora

	French_TL	French_SL	Polish_TL	Polish_SL
		Number of words		
Median	2	2	2	2
1	**38.1%**[262]	25%	**46.3%**	43.8%
2	33.3%	**50%**	36.6%	**37.5%**
3	**26.2%**	18.8%	**14.6%**	12.5%
4	2.4%	**6.3%**	2.4%	**6.3%**
		Imperative		
Yes	**16.7%**	6.3%	**19.5%**	12.5%
No	83.3%	**93.8%**	80.5%	**87.5%**
Verbless				
Yes	52.4%	**68.8%**	**61%**	50%
No	**47.6%**	31.3%	39%	**50%**
		Question		
Yes	16.7%	**18.8%**	12.2%	**43.8%**
No	**83.3%**	81.3%	**87.8%**	56.3%
Ellipsis				
Yes	21.4%	**43.8%**	**31.7%**	25%
No	**78.6%**	56.3%	68.3%	**75%**
		Deixis		
Yes	**69%**	56.3%	53.7%	**68.8%**
No	31%	**43.8%**	**46.3%**	31.3%
		Deixis type		
Temporal	13.8%	**22.2%**	4.5%	**9.1%**
Spatial	**3.4%**	0%	**4.5%**	0%
Personal	41.4%	**55.6%**	**22.7%**	9.1%
Discourse	**17.2%**	11.1%	9.1%	**18.2%**
In the verb	**13.8%**	11.1%	50%	**54.5%**
Elliptical	10.3%	**11.1%**	9.1%	9.1%
		Speech act		
Representative	**23.8%**	18.8%	**26.8%**	18.8%
Directive	**38.1%**	37.5%	31.7%	**37.5%**
Expressive	33.3%	**43.8%**	**36.6%**	31.3%
Declarative	**2.4%**	0%	2.4%	**6.3%**
Commissive	**2.4%**	0%	2.4%	**6.3%**

[262] The highest percentage linearly of the SL-TL pair is put in bold.

First of all, the median word count was 2 words across all cases, which may attest to the nature of charged pragmatemes. Then, for Polish, the discrepancies between Polish_SL and Polish_TL were generally within a 10 percent range for most cases. The most significant differences were noted in terms of the presence of verbless forms, question forms, and deictic markers, while the most notable similarities were found in features such as the number of words, speech acts, presence of imperative forms, and "in the verb" deixis.

In terms of French, however, the discrepancies were more pronounced, and substantial similarities between the studied characteristics were observed solely in speech acts and the presence of question forms. Yet, it has to be stressed that the majority ratio was the same in nearly all cases, both for Polish and French. The only discrepancies in majority ratios were as follows: the most common speech act (directive in Polish as SL and expressive in Polish as TL, whereas the opposite in French: expressive in French as SL and directive in French as TL[263]), the presence of verbless forms in Polish (50% of units being verbless in Polish as SL and 61% in Polish as TL), and the word count in French (two-word pragmatemes constituted the majority at 50% for French as SL, while monolexical units were predominant at 38.1% for French as TL). Finally, it was investigated how many units were translated using equivalents of the same linguistic characteristics as the SL pragmatemes. Ten pragmatemes were translated with units with exactly the same linguistic features in French and only five in Polish. More commonly, pragmatemes were translated using units sharing the same linguistic features except for one; this occurred in 12 instances in French and 14 in Polish. Translations with the use of units with similar linguistic features but differing in two characteristics were the most prevalent in French, with 14 pragmatemes translated with such equivalents, and as common as the previous group in Polish, with 14 pragmatemes. The least common group for French involved the presence of translations differing in linguistic features in three or more characteristics, with six units translated with such equivalents, and eight for Polish, which was the second least common. While it may be tempting to

[263] The discrepancy in Polish may have been explained by the fact that in the SL, i.e., English, expressive pragmatemes were dominant over directive units; however, that would not explain the fact why the opposite was true for the French translation.

assume that the reason for French TL units being more commonly closer in their linguistic features to the English SL pragmatemes than the Polish TL units is due to French being generally linguistically closer to English than Polish, the observed differences do not seem substantial enough to treat this assumption as particularly significant. However, it can be summed up that in general, the similarities between the linguistic features of SL pragmatemes and their TLs equivalents are frequent enough to support several typical characteristics of pragmatemes that became evident in the analysis discussed in Chapter 4 (see p. 151).

The context-based approach to translation techniques proposed in this subsection has proved to be applicable to all analyzed pragmatemes. Furthermore, unlike in the previous typologies, no larger categorization challenges related to the insufficient description of techniques were encountered. All the suggested techniques were identified in translations of pragmatemes under study (although not all were found in French and Polish separately). The frequency of these techniques is illustrated in Figure 69.

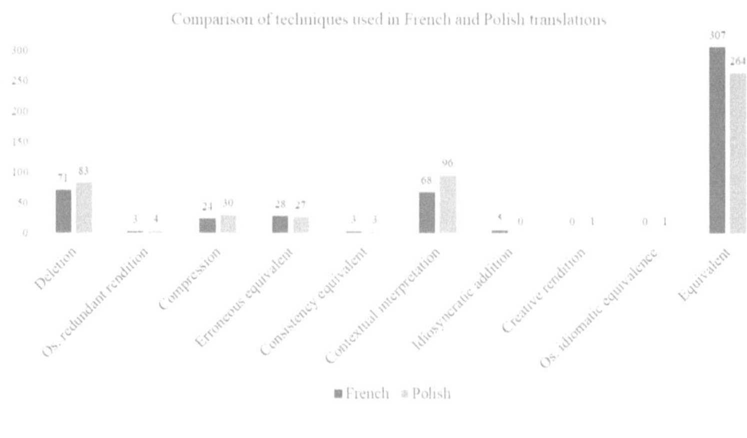

Figure 69. Comparison of the number of pragmatemes translated to French and Polish with the use of the main techniques according to Mężyk's (2024) technique typology

The most common technique in both TLs was the use of an equivalent, and the two other frequently used techniques were deletion (the second most common in French translations and the third in Polish) and contextual interpretation (the second most common in Polish and the third in French). The prevalence of deletion in both TLs not only underscores the unique nature of subtitling within the landscape of various types of translation but also highlights the unique nature of the pragmatemes that could be deleted based on the specificity of the context surrounding them. The unique nature of subtitling is further attested to by the presence of compression technique (the fourth most common in French and third in Polish), which is also particularly common for this type of translation. Another frequently used technique observed in both French and Polish translations was the erroneous equivalent, which ideally should be infrequent, as it is considered a translation mistake. However, the frequency of erroneous equivalents can be attributed to a significant number of occurrences of the pragmateme *Love you* which tended to be incorrectly translated in both TLs. Techniques such as ostensibly redundant rendition, consistency equivalent, idiosyncratic addition, creative rendition, and ostensible idiomatic equivalence were not common, which is understandable given the fact that they are typically applied in specific instances. Overall, although this study focused on pragmatemes and effectively identified the techniques used to translate these units, the typology proposed in this subsection should not be limited to pragmatemes alone, as its primary focus is on context. That is why the use of this typology in research concerning subtitling and other language units is highly encouraged.

The final significant observation concerns the frequency of how often French and Polish translators used the same technique. This was the case in 330 instances (65%), which constitutes the highest level of agreement between the translators across all four analyzed technique typologies. Therefore, it suggests a potential correlation that the more specific the technique typology, the greater the agreement between translators despite the language difference.

This chapter and the previous one provided a comprehensive analysis of pragmatemes from two different perspectives: linguistic and translational. Thanks to the analysis, it is now possible to derive conclusive insights regarding the present study on pragmatemes.

Conclusions

The primary aim of this study was to conduct an investigation into the phenomenon of pragmatemes. Such an investigation could have been approached from various perspectives, given that studies on pragmatemes are not plentiful. In the end, an approach based on contrastive and translational perspectives was chosen to explore this phenomenon from the *building blocks*, i.e., its linguistic traits across languages, to the *big picture*, i.e., its practical application in actual contexts in translation.

The first research question involved defining pragmatemes in a manner that could be universally applicable. The literature review presented in Chapter 1 revealed a multitude of definitions and defining criteria proposed by various researchers studying this phenomenon (e.g., Kauffer [2019], Blanco and Mejri [2018], and Kecskés [2000], among others). Furthermore, the literature review showed that while most theoretical frameworks on the topic might suit the language in which a particular study was conducted, they often lack accuracy when applied to a different language. Therefore, based on the existing studies discussed in Chapter 1, the following definition was proposed:

> pragmatemes are language units that are fixed, i.e., used without changes in their form, in a language and predictably used in situations of communication which are typical, repeatable, and specific. Furthermore, pragmatemes themselves trigger a mental representation of the specific communication situation.
>
> *(see p. 49)*

In addition to proposing a universal definition of pragmatemes, this study introduced a typology of these units based on Kecskés (2000). This typology includes plain pragmatemes, which are compositional units, loaded pragmatemes, which are idiomatic units, and charged pragmatemes, whose meaning is ambiguous without the context, which makes them either compositional or idiomatic expressions, depending on the context. Such a theoretical framework for understanding pragmatemes facilitates contrastive studies on the topic, as it does not impose any formal linguistic criteria, for instance, compositionality, that could restrict the identification of pragmatemes across different languages.

The next step of examining pragmatemes aimed to explore whether these units can be characterized with any linguistic properties that could potentially be considered defining across different languages. The analysis of pragmatemes in English, French, and Polish, Indo-European languages from different subgroups, ensured that the results would not be based on the similarities existing in one language subgroup. The analysis involved 290 English pragmatemes, 186 French pragmatemes, and 106 Polish pragmatemes found in corpora consisting of captions from various TV series (with the Polish corpus also including captions from four movies), typically reflecting ordinary life situations. As anticipated in the General Introduction (see p. 21), no linguistic traits were found to be consistent enough to be considered universal. Nonetheless, a number of noteworthy observations emerged from the analysis.

Firstly, certain characteristics were found to be consistent across all three languages under study, creating an image of a prototypical conversational pragmateme. Such a pragmateme would be composed of fewer than five words, would be plain (compositional), non-imperative, not in a question form, and non-elliptical. Furthermore, it would be likely to include deictic expressions, especially of the person[264] type. However, while this depiction aligns with the majority of pragmatemes gathered from the corpora in this study, the majority it represents is not overwhelming. Therefore, while the concept of a *prototypical pragmateme* is worth further investigation, it does not help in the general identification of pragmatemes. A substantial number of valid, but not fitting the prototype, pragmatemes could be omitted in a search with the application of properties of a prototypical pragmateme. Additionally, it is essential to acknowledge that the category of pragmatemes studied here involved units used in everyday conversations; pragmatemes from different domains, such as juridical contexts, may be characterized with different linguistic properties.

Secondly, although pragmatemes are fixed units, some minor variations can be noted, with pragmatemes of two to five variants being the most prevalent across all three languages. These variations mostly concern punctuation,

[264] "In the verb" deixis, which was the most common among Polish pragmatemes, also refers to a person.

which should be further examined in future research to either support or challenge claims regarding the significance of pragmatemes' prosody (e.g., Banyś 2020). Variations were also found in pragmatemes with slots, which were a result of the application of pragmatemic patterns in the corpus search. Pragmatemes with slots constitute an intriguing phenomenon, which is also worth further investigation.

Thirdly, a significant percentage of monolexical pragmatemes identified across the studied languages challenges the assumption about the nature of pragmatemes noted in the literature – that monolexical pragmatemes are scarce (e.g., Blanco and Mejri 2018). Furthermore, a tendency noted across the three languages revealed that the smaller the complexity of a pragmateme, the higher its frequency, attesting to language users' preference for simplification and minimalization of cognitive overload.

Other intriguing observations also emerged in the study of linguistic traits of pragmatemes; however, their verification in future research is needed to substantiate their significance in terms of the nature of pragmatemes in different languages. These observations include, among others: the higher expected frequency of Polish pragmatemes compared to English and French, the prominence of expressive pragmatemes in English and French and directive pragmatemes in Polish, and the differences between the general characteristics and the characteristics of loaded pragmatemes, noted especially in French and Polish (e.g., higher likelihood of lacking deixis, a tendency to be verbless, and a smaller probability of being imperative).

Following a thorough investigation of linguistic properties of pragmatemes, the translational analysis was conducted. For time and space constraints of the present dissertation, the analysis involved charged pragmatemes found in the English corpus and their French and Polish translations. To analyze the translations, three typologies of translation techniques were applied: Molina and Hurtado Albir's (2002) dynamic and functionalist approach, Hejwowski's (2015) approach to translation of idioms, and Díaz-Cintas and Remael's (2007) approach to translation of cultural elements in subtitling. The typologies had been deliberately selected to represent different approaches, ranging from the most general to the most specific, and to address different aspects of the studied units (idiomaticity, subtitles, and cultural elements). Nonetheless, although the typologies were adjusted to best apply to the concept of pragmatemes, a few methodological problems arose. These issues were mostly concerned with how the techniques had been described. Insufficient specificity in the descriptions led to questioning decisions on established equivalents (a technique proposed by Molina and Hurtado Albir [2002]) and formulaicity (a defining problem observed in the majority of techniques proposed by Hejwowski [2015]). Furthermore, in many cases, one translation could be assigned to several different techniques. This lack of clarity, not addressed by either of the authors of the applied typologies, resulted in hesitation in assigning techniques.

In the analysis with the use of the three typologies, it was noticed that in addition to the methodological issues, one crucial element was missing: context. All techniques referred to translations in isolation rather than considering them within their surrounding context. As a response, a new typology, representing a context-based approach to subtitling, was suggested. This typology involved ten main techniques: deletion, ostensibly redundant rendition, compression, erroneous equivalent, consistency equivalent, contextual interpretation, idiosyncratic addition, creative rendition, ostensible idiomatic equivalence, and equivalent. In this typology, a detailed description was provided for each technique to avoid previously mentioned methodological issues. For example, the criterion of acknowledgement by a machine translation engine, specifically DeepL, was added as a defining trait of the equivalent technique. In the analysis with the use of the new typology, all studied translations were assigned with a technique and all techniques were observed, which was not the case in the previously used techniques. The suggested typology, aside from emphasizing the role of context in translation, highlighted the importance of subtitling constraints. For instance, the omission technique (described by both Hejwowski [2015] and Díaz-Cintas and Remael [2007] in their typologies), here called "deletion", is further divided into three types: context-based deletion, constraints-based deletion, repetition-based deletion, and visual-based delation, most of them resulting from different technicalities of this AVT type.

The choice to analyze charged pragmatemes stemmed from their ambiguous nature, due to which, as it had been speculated in the General Introduction (see p. 21), this type of pragmatemes proved to pose certain problems in translation. This can be observed not only by the fact that the translators had to use a number of different techniques to translate these units but also by the number of erroneous equivalents present in the analyzed translations. Often, erroneous translation was the result of translating pragmatemes literally, leading to expressions that would not naturally occur in a similar situation in the TL.

The analysis with the use of the suggested typology showed that context influences the translation of charged pragmatemes within AV content. The use of screenshots provided a comprehensive view of the situation. As noted by Tomaszkiewicz (2006: 80), linguistic and visual codes mutually influence each other, with linguistic elements helping with the understanding of the visual elements, and visual elements illustrating linguistic elements. Screenshots demonstrated the instances where the visual context was either necessary (e.g., the examples of visual-based deletion and idiosyncratic addition, see p. 239 and p. 251) or additionally helpful (e.g., the examples of erroneous equivalent and contextual interpretation discussed on p. 244 and p. 248) to understand the full meaning of an utterance. While in other AV materials, such as David Attenborough's nature documentaries, the visual image may play a more pivotal role, in most cases of the studied conversations, linguistic context sufficed for understanding the meaning, and the visual image did not change it. Yet, including the visual context in the analysis was still beneficial, as both layers are meant to create the overall picture. Therefore, maintaining a proper balance between the analysis of linguistic and visual layers is essential, depending on the type of the AV material under examination.

The link between the contrastive and the translational analyses was found in the equivalent technique. The linguistic analysis of the translations executed with the use of the equivalent technique revealed similarities in several common traits of pragmatemes discussed in Chapter 4. These include a small percentage of question and imperative forms, a significant percentage of person deixis, and a median word count at two. These findings align with the results of the linguistic analysis of pragmatemes presented in Chapter 4, which may be perceived as challenging in regard to claims such as the one made by Baker (1993: 234) who notes that "translational behaviour is different from other types of linguistic behaviour." This statement does not seem to hold true for the majority of the formulaic units studied here, i.e., pragmatemes. However, despite these similarities, some discrepancies were observed, such as variations in the most common speech act. Therefore, it would be valuable to extend this study to include plain and loaded pragmatemes to examine whether such discrepancies are also present in other pragmateme types.

After the discussion of the primary findings of both analyses, it is now appropriate to address the study's limitations. As in all research, the main limitations of this study related to time and space. These limitations notably restricted the translational analysis to only one type of pragmatemes, i.e., charged pragmatemes. Due to the same restrictions, the method of pragmatemes identification relied on sources such as dictionaries, without the use of questionnaires that could be filled by native speakers (an approach used for the identification of formulaic sequences noted, for instance, in Wray 2002). This reliance on pre-existing sources introduced limitations, particularly regarding the contemporaneity of the units. Furthermore, given the absence of a dedicated dictionary of pragmatemes, sources containing also units of other types had to be carefully explored. After all, what Wood (2015: 160) observes regarding formulaic units in general remains applicable also for pragmatemes: "in many cases absolute certainty in identification is likely difficult to achieve."

Other limitations concerned the studied corpora. Although the method of using Language Reactor for accessing subtitles and captions from Netflix facilitates compiling corpora of different spoken registers, the scope of any research based on such corpora is limited solely to the Netflix library. In this study, this restriction notably impacted the size of French and Polish corpora, in which no choice regarding the TV series that constituted the corpora was possible: all of the TV series available with translations were used. Additionally, using captions for studying units such as oral pragmatemes may also raise questions, given that they may not always reflect the text exactly as it is uttered due to temporal and spatial subtitle constraints (although Netflix's guidelines advise to "include as much of the original content as possible", see Netflix Partner Help Center[265]). Furthermore, while captions can serve as a rich source of spoken discourse for corpus linguistic research (as discussed on p. 123), especially given various issues related to collecting

[265] Source: https://partnerhelp.netflixstudios.com/hc/en-us/articles/217350977-English-Timed-Text-Style-Guide. Accessed on July 25, 2023.

transcripts of real-life conversations, it can be argued that captions only mimic real-life conversations because, in most cases, everything that the actors say is scripted. Lastly, it is important to note that this thesis focused on pragmatemes used in everyday conversations. Therefore, its results cannot be applied universally to all categories of pragmatemes, but they may rather serve as a good starting point for comparative analyses with pragmatemes from other registers.

Despite the acknowledged limitations, the findings of the present study cannot be undermined. This study investigated the phenomenon of pragmatemes, the proficiency of which is an important factor in language fluency (Fillmore 1979) and avoidance of communicational problems. Although no universal defining traits that would help with the identification of pragmatemes in corpora were found, the applied research method was not only novel but also promising. Firstly, the use of Language Reactor to access Netflix's subtitles and captions represents a new avenue for corpus linguistic and audiovisual translation research, a cooperation that has been so far limited, mainly due to copyright reasons. Secondly, the use of Unitex facilitates studying units such as pragmatemes, which are not regular expressions, by allowing the examination of multiple different units at once. Thirdly, the compiled list of pragmatemes may serve not only as a starting point for future research but also as a valuable resource for language learners. Lastly, from a translational perspective, the study not only introduced a practical methodology for the examination of pragmatemes in translation but also offered a new typology of translation techniques in subtitling, a one that prioritizes the context. This typology holds promise, for example, for integration into translation training, particularly within audiovisual translation. This research might serve to direct students' attention to the translation process, highlighting the importance of context and technical constraints, as well as the challenges related to both in AVT.

Given the spectrum of the study, it is hoped that it will inspire future research from various standpoints. Pragmatemic patters are an example of a phenomenon worthy of a separate study. Similarly, monolexical pragmatemes as units more widespread than initially portrayed in the existing literature (e.g., Blanco and Mejri 2018) can be subject to a separate analysis, for instance, by means of MCA. Furthermore, more advanced stastical analyses, such as multifactorial statistics (see, e.g., Gries 2021, Winter 2019) can also prove useful to further explain the multi-faceted phenomenon of pragmatemes. The findings of the linguistic analysis could serve as a foundation for comparing the linguistic characteristics of pragmatemes across various registers, while the translational analysis could be replicated for other types of pragmatemes (i.e., plain and loaded) and other language pairs[266], in order to compare the results of the analysis of English charged pragmatemes and their French and Polish translations. Additionally, the proposed context-based approach to translation techniques in subtitling holds promise beyond pragmatemes, offering potential applicability in research involving various language units. Finally, it would be interesting to see this study replicated in other languages, which could constitute a significant contribution to a more comprehensive understanding of the nature of pragmatemes.

[266] With the corpora already collected, the study can continue for French pragmatemes and their English and Polish translations, and for Polish pragmatemes and their English and French translations.

Academic references

Altman, D. G. (1991). *Practical Statistics for Medical Research.* London: Chapman and Hall.

Alves, F., & Gonçalves, J. L. V. R. (2003). A Relevance Theory approach to the investigation of inferential processes in translation. In Alves, F. (Ed.) *Triangulating Translation: Perspectives in process oriented research*, 3-24. John Benjamins.

Amosova, N. N. (1963). *Osnovy angliiskoi frazeologii.* Leningrad.

Anscombre, J.-C., & Mejri, S. (Eds.). (2011). *Le figement linguistique: la parole entravée.* Paris: Honoré Champion.

Antonini, R. (2005). The Perception of Subtitled Humour in Italy: An Empirical Study. In *Humor: International Journal of Humor Research, 18(2)*, 209–225.

Arabski, J., Łyda, A., & Warchał, K. (2009). *Słownik angielskich frazemów akademickich.* Oficyna Wydawnicza Wacław Walasek.

Aryani, D. (2009). *Ellipsis in English Printed Media Headlines.* Jakarta: Gunadarma University.

Austin, J. L. (1962). *How to do things with words.* Harvard University Press.

Awdiejew A., (1998). *Zarys gramatyki funkcjonalnej współczesnego języka rosyjskiego*, Kraków.

Bach, K., & Harnish, R. (1979). *Linguistic Communication and Speech Acts.* Cambridge: MIT Press.

Bahns, J., Burmeister, H., & Vogel, T. (1986). The pragmatics of formulas in L2 learner speech: Use and development. In *Journal of Pragmatics, 10*, 693–723.

Baker, M. (1992). *In other words: A course book on translation*. Routledge.
Baker, M. (1993). Corpus Linguistics and Translation Studies: Implications and Applications. In M. Baker, G. Francis, E. Tognini-Bonelli (Eds.) *Text and Technology: In Honour of John Sinclair*, 233-250. John Benjamins.
Baker, M., & Saldanha, G. (2009). *Routledge Encyclopedia of Translation Studies*. Routledge.
Baker, P. (2006). *Using Corpora in Discourse Analysis*. Continuum.
Ballard, M. (2010). The unit of translation. In J. Delisle & J. Woodsworth (Eds.), *Handbook of Translation Studies Volume 1*, 437–440. John Benjamins.
Bally, C. (1921). *Traité de stylistique française*. Heidelberg.
Baños, R. (2020). Fandubbing. In Ł. Bogucki & M. Deckert (Eds.), *The Palgrave Handbook of Audiovisual Translation and Media Accessibility*, 209–226. Palgrave Macmillan.
Banyś W. (2020). Pragmatèmes au pays de la prosodie. In *Neophilologica*, *32*, 89-116.
Bardovi-Harlig, K. (2009). Conventional expressions as a pragmalinguistic resource: Recognition and production of conventional expressions in L2 pragmatics. In *Language Learning, 59, 755-795.*
Bardovi-Harlig, K. (2012). Formulas, Routines, and Conventional Expressions in Pragmatics Research. In *Annual Review of Applied Linguistics*, *32*, 206-227.
Barnas, M. (2017). *Les pragmatèmes dans les dialogues dans les romans de Marc Lévy.* Retrieved from https://dumas.ccsd.cnrs.fr/dumas-01630131/document. Accessed August 12, 2020.
Barnier, M. (2004). *Des films français made in Hollywood. Les versions multiples 1929-1935*. L'Harmattan.
Bartmiński, J. (2007). Stereotyp jako przedmiot lingwistyki. In J. Bartmiński (Ed.), *Stereotypy mieszkają w języku*, 53-71. Lublin.
Belczyk, A. (2007). *Tłumaczenie filmów.* Dla szkoły.
Benenowska, I. (2001). Funkcje frazemów w języku mówionym na przykładzie dialogów filmowych. In *Frazeografia słowiańska : księga pamiątkowa poświęcona prof. dr hab. Halinie A. Lilicz*, 209-213. Opole.
Bennett, P. (1994). The translation unit in human and machine. In *Babel*, *40*(1), 12-20.
Biber, D. (2006). *University language: A corpus-based study of spoken and written registers*. John Benjamins.

Bjerre Rosa, P., & Øveraas, K. M., (2019). *Retningslinjer for undertekstning i Danmark*. Retrieved from: https://translatorforeningen.dk/wp-content/uploads/2019/03/Retningslinjer_Undertekstning_DK_v1_januar_2019.pdf. Accessed on December 27, 2023.

Blanco, X. (2013). *Les pragmatèmes : définition, typologie et traitement lexicographiqe*. In *Verbum, 4*, 17-25.

Blanco, X., & Mejri, S. (2018). *Les Pragmatèmes*. Paris: Classiques Garnier.

Bogacki, K. (2012). Phrasèmes et pragmatèmes : problèmes de délimitation et de description. In A. Kacprzak & M. Gajos (Eds.), *Pluralité des cultures: chances ou menaces?*, 57-64. Łask: Oficyna Wydawnicza Leksem.

Bogucki, Ł. (2004). The constraint of relevance in subtitling. In *The Journal of Specialised Translation, 1*, 71–88.

Bogucki, Ł., & Díaz-Cintas, J. (2020). An excursus on audiovisual translation. In Ł. Bogucki & M. Deckert (Eds.), *The Palgrave Handbook of Audiovisual Translation and Media Accessibility*, 11–32. Palgrave Macmillan.

Bogucki, Ł., Dubiec-Gajer, J., Piotrowska, M., & Tomaszkiewicz, T. (2019). *Słownik polskiej terminologii przekładoznawczej*. Kraków: Księgarnia Akademicka.

Bolander, M. (1989). Prefabs, patterns and rules in interaction? Formulaic speech in adult learners' L2 Swedish. In K. Hyltenstam & L. K. Obler (Eds.), *Bilingualism across the lifespan: Aspects of acquisition, maturity, and loss*, 73-86. Cambridge University Press.

Bolaños-García-Escribano, A. (2021). Audiovisual Localisation in the Age of Streaming (Platforms). *ColNet* seminar.

Bolaños-García-Escribano, A., & Díaz-Cintas, J. (2020). The Cloud Turn in Audiovisual Translation. In Ł. Bogucki & M. Deckert (Eds.), *The Palgrave Handbook of Audiovisual Translation and Media Accessibility*, 519–544. Palgrave Macmillan.

Bolaños-García-Escribano, A., Díaz-Cintas, J., & Massidda, S. (2021). Latest advancements in audiovisual translation education. In *The Interpreter and Translator Trainer, 15*(1), 1-12.

Bolinger, D. (1975). On the Passive in English. In *LAUCUS 1*, 51-80.

Boxer, D. (2002). *Applying Sociolinguistics*. John Benjamins.

Brezina, V. (2018). *Statistics in Corpus Linguistics: A Practical Guide*. Cambridge University Press.

Brezina, V., R. Love and K. Aijmer (eds.). (2018). *Corpus Approaches to Contemporary British Speech: Sociolinguistic studies of the Spoken BNC2014*. New York: Routledge.

Brooke, J., Hammond, A., Jacob, D., Tsang, V., Hirst, G., & Shein, F. (2015). Building a Lexicon of Formulaic Language for Language Learners. In *Proceedings of the 11th Workshop on Multi-word Expressions*, 96-104.

Bruti, S. (2020). Corpus Approaches and Audiovisual Translation. In Ł. Bogucki & M. Deckert (Eds.), *The Palgrave Handbook of Audiovisual Translation and Media Accessibility*, 381-395. Palgrave Macmillan.

Bühler, K. (1934). The Deictic Field of Language and Deictic Words. In R. J. Jarvella, & W. Klein (Eds.) *Speech, Place, and Action. Studies in Deixis and Related Topics*, 9-30. Chichester: John Wiley & Sons LTD.

Burger, H. (1973). *Idiomatik des Deutschen*. Tübingen: Max Niemeyer.

Burger, H., Buhofer, A., & Sialm, A. (1982). *Handbuch der Phraseologie.* W. de Gruyter.

Bygate, M. (1988). Units of oral expression and language learning in small group interaction. In *Applied Linguistics*, *9*(1), 59-87.

Bywood, L. (2020). Technology and Audiovisual Translation. In Ł. Bogucki & M. Deckert (Eds.), *The Palgrave Handbook of Audiovisual Translation and Media Accessibility*, 503-517. Palgrave Macmillan.

Bywood, L., Volk, M., Fishel, M., & Georgakopoulou, P. (2013). Parallel Subtitling Corpora and Their Application in Machine Translation and Translatology. In *Perspectives: Studies in Translatology, 21(4)*, Special Issue: Baños Piñero, R., Bruti, S., Zanotti, S. *Corpus Linguistics and Audiovisual Translation: In Search of an Integrated Approach*, 577-594.

Carrillo Darancet, J. M. (2020). The drama of surtitling: Ever-changing translation on stage. In Ł. Bogucki & M. Deckert (Eds.), *The Palgrave Handbook of Audiovisual Translation and Media Accessibility*, 173-188. Palgrave Macmillan.

Carter, R., & McCarthy, M. (1988). *Vocabulary and language teaching.* Longman.

Carter, R., & Schmitt, N. (2004). Formulaic sequences in action: An introduction. In N. Schmitt (Ed.), *Formulaic Sequences: Acquisition, processing and use*, 1-22. John Benjamins Publishing Company.

Cattrysse, P., & Gambier, Y. (2008). Screenwriting and translating screenplays. In J. Díaz-Cintas (Ed.), *The Didactics of Audiovisual Translation*, 39-55. Benjamins Publishing.

Chaume, F. (2004). Synchronization in dubbing: a translational approach. In P. Orero (Ed.), *Topics for Audiovisual Translation*, 35-52. John Benjamins.

Chaume, F. (2012). *Audiovisual Translation: Dubbing.* Routledge.

Chaume, F. (2020). Dubbing. In Ł. Bogucki & M. Deckert (Eds.), *The Palgrave Handbook of Audiovisual Translation and Media Accessibility*, 103-132. Palgrave Macmillan.

Chaves-Fernández, L., & Sevilla-Morales, H. (2021). Análisis semántico-traductológico de un texto: una perspectiva de lingüística de corpus. In *Memoria del V Congreso Internacional de Lingüística Aplicada*, 209-219.

Cheng, W., C. Greaves, and M. Warren. (2006). From n-gram to skipgram to concgram. In *International Journal of Corpus Linguistics* 11/4: 411-33.

Cheng, W., Greaves, C., Sinclair, J. M., & Warren, M. (2009). Uncovering the extent of the phraseological tendency: Towards a systematic analysis of concgrams. In *Applied Linguistics, 30*, 236-252.

Chesterman, A. (1997). *Memes of Translation: The Spread of Ideas in Translation Theory.* John Benjamins.

Chlebda, W. (1993). Frazematyka. In *Współczesny język polski*, 327-334. Wrocław.

Chlebda, W. (2003). *Elementy frazematyki: wprowadzenie do frazeologii nadawcy.* Pruszków: Oficyna Wydawnicza LEKSEM.

Chunbai, Z. (2009). The translation of film dialogues for dubbing. In *Dubbing and Subtitling in a World Context*, 149-160. The Chinese University of Hong Kong.

Chuquet, H., & Paillard, M. (1987). *Approche linguistique des problèmes de traduction anglais--français.* Editions OPHRYS.

Coulmas, F. (1979). On the sociolinguistic relevance of routine formulae. In *Journal of Pragmatics, 3*, 239-266.

Coulmas, F. (1981). *Routine im Gespräch. Zur pragmatischen Fundierung der Idiomatik.* Wiesbaden.

Cowie, A. P. (1988). Stable and creative aspects of vocabulary use. In R. Carter & M. McCarthy (Eds.), *Vocabulary and language teaching*, 126-139. New York: Longman.

Cruse, D. A. (1992). Antonymy revisited: Some thoughts on the relationship between words and concepts. In A. Lehrer & E. Kittay (Eds.), *Frames, fields and contrasts*, 289-309.

Crystal, D. (1997). *English as a global language*. Cambridge: Cambridge University Press.

Culpeper, J. (2010). Conventionalized impoliteness formulae. In *Journal of Pragmatics, 42*, 3232-3245.

Cunningham, S., & Silver, J. (2012). On-Line Film Distribution: Its History and Global Complexion. In S. Cunningham & D. Iordanova (Eds.), *Disruption: Cinema Moves On-Line*, 934-1013. St Andrews.

Dąbrowska, M. (2013). Functions of code-switching in Polish and Hindi Facebook users' posts. In *Studia Linguistica 130(1)*, 63-84.

Dallı, H. (2023). *Pivot subtitling: Reasons and results in the Korean-Turkish context*. Boğaziçi University. Retrieved from: https://www.researchgate.net/profile/Harun-Dalli/publication/372661333_Pivot_subtitling_Reasons_and_results_in_the_Korean-Turkish_context/links/64c2601a04d6c44bc35ec13f/Pivot-subtitling-Reasons-and-results-in-the-Korean-Turkish-context.pdf. Accessed on July 23, 2023.

De Linde, Z. (1996). Le sous-titrage intralinguistique pour les sourds et les malentendants. In Y. Gambier (Ed.), *Les transferts linguistiques dans les médias audiovisuels*, 173–184. Presses Universitaires du Septentrion.

Deckert, M., & Bogucki, Ł. (2018). Polish audience preferences regarding audiovisual translation: A reception study. In M. Deckert (Ed.), *Audiovisual Translation: Research and Use*, 67–79. Peter Lang.

Díaz Cintas, J. (2001). Striving for quality in subtitling: The role of a good dialogue list. In Y. Gambier, and H. Gottlieb (Eds.), *(Multi) Media translation*, 199–211. John Benjamins.

Díaz Cintas, J. (2022). *Teaching Subtitling on the Cloud.* Tutorial at New Trends in Technology and Translation Conference, Rhodes, Greece.

Díaz-Cintas, J. (2003). Audiovisual translation in the third millennium. In G. Anderman & M. Rogers (Eds.), *Translation Today. Trends and Perspectives*, 192-204.

Díaz-Cintas, J. (2018). 'Subtitling's a carnival': New practices in cyberspace. In *Journal of Specialised Translation (30)*, 127-149.

Díaz-Cintas, J. (2020). The name and nature of subtitling. In Ł. Bogucki & M. Deckert (Eds.), *The Palgrave Handbook of Audiovisual Translation and Media Accessibility*, 149-172. Palgrave Macmillan.

Díaz-Cintas, J. (Ed.) (2009). *New trends in audiovisual translation*. Multilingual Matters.

Díaz-Cintas, J., & Massidda, S. (2019). Technological advances in audiovisual translation. In O'Hagan, M. (Ed.), *The Routledge Handbook of Translation and Technology*, 255-270. Routledge.

Díaz-Cintas, J., & Remael, A. (2007). *Audiovisual Translation: Subtitling.* Routledge.

Diessel, H. (2019). Deixis and demonstratives. In C. Maienborn, K. Heusinger, & P. Portner (Eds.), *Semantics – Interfaces*, 463-493. De Gruyter Mouton.

Diessel, H. (2019). *The Grammar Network: How Linguistic Structure Is Shaped by Language Use*. Cambridge University Press.

Durrant, P., & Mathews-Aydınlı, J. (2011). A function-first approach to identifying formulaic language in academic language. In *English for Specific Purposes, 30*, 58-72.

Dziadkiewicz, A. (2007). La traduction automatique de phraséologismes pragmatiques : quelles représentations à travers la diversité formelle et culturelle? In *Corela [Online]*, 5-2. Retrieved from http://journals.openedition.org/corela/383. Accessed on August 12, 2020.

Ellis, N. (1996). Sequencing in SLA: phonological memory, chunking and points of order. In *Studies in Second Language Acquisition, 18*, 91-126.

Ellis, N. (2012). Formulaic Language and Second Language Acquisition: Zipf and the Phrasal Teddy Bear. In *Annual Review of Applied Linguistics, 32*, 17-44.

Encyclopedia Britannica Online. *Netflix.* Retrieved from: https://www.britannica.com/topic/Netflix-Inc. Accessed on July 25, 2022.

Fillmore, C. (1979). On fluency. In C. Fillmore, D. Kempler, & W. S-Y. Wang (Eds.), *Individual differences in language ability and language behavior*, 85-101.

Fillmore, C. (1992). "Corpus linguistics" or "Computer-aided armchair linguistics". In J. Svartvik (Ed.) *Directions in Corpus Linguistics: Proceedings of Nobel Symposium 82 Stockholm, 4-8 August 1991*, 35-60. De Gruyter Mouton.

Firth, J. R. (1951). Modes of meaning. In J. R. Firth (Ed.), *Essays and studies*, 118-149. Oxford University Press.

Fléchon, G., Frassi, P., & Polguère, A. (2012). Les pragmatèmes ont-ils un charme indéfinissable? In P. Ligas & P. Frassi (Eds.), *Lexiques. Identités. Cultures*, 81-104. QuiEdit.

Forsyth, R., & Grabowski, Ł. (2015). Is there a formula for formulaic language? In *Poznan Studies in Contemporary Linguistics, 51*(4), 511-549.

Fox, W. (2016). Integrated Titles: An Improved Viewing Experience? In S. Hansen-Schirra, & S. Grucza (Eds.) *Eyetracking and Applied Linguistics*, 5-30. Language Science Press.

Francis, G. (1993). A corpus-driven approach to grammar. In M. Baker, G. Francis, E. Tognini-Bonelli (Eds.), *Text and technology: in honour of John Sinclair*, 137–156. John Benjamins.

Franco, J., & Orero, P. (2005). The research in audiovisual translation: Some objective conclusions, or the birth of an academic field. In J. D. Sanderson (Ed.), *Research on Translation for Subtitling in Spain and Italy*, 79–9. Universidad de Alicante.

Gambier Y. (2014). The position of audiovisual translation studies. In Y. Gambier & L. van Doorslaer (Eds.), *The Routledge Handbook of Translation Studies*, 45-59. Routledge.

Gambier, Y. (2022). Revisiting certain concepts of translation studies through the study of media practices. In E. Bielsa (Ed.), *The Routledge Handbook of Translation and Media*, 91–107. Routledge.

Garcarz, M. (2007). *Przekład slangu w filmie*. Tertium.

Gębka-Wolak, M., & Moroz, A. (2014). O nieswobodnej grupie syntaktycznej. In *Prace Językoznawcze XVI/1*, 45-61.

Genzel, R. B. (1991). *Getting the hang of idioms and expressions*. New York: MacMillan.

Georgakopoulou, P. (2006). Subtitling and globalisation. In *The Journal of Specialised Translation*, *6*, 115–120.

Georgakopoulou, P. (2019). Template files: The Holy Grail of subtitling. In *Journal of Audiovisual Translation*, *2*(2), 137–160.

Gil-Bardají, A. (2009). Procedures, techniques, strategies: translation process operators. In *Perspectives, Studies in Translation Theory and Practice, 17(3)*, 161-173.

Gottlieb, H. (1998). Subtitling. In M. Baker (Ed.) *Routledge Encyclopedia of Translation Studies*, 244-248. Routledge.

Gottlieb, H. (2004). Subtitles and International Anglification. In *Nordic Journal of English Studies, 3(1)*, 219–230.

Gottlieb, H. (2009). Subtitling against the current: Danish Concepts, English Minds. In J. Díaz-Cintas (Ed.) *New Trends in Audiovisual Translation*, 21-43. Multilingual Matters.

Gournay, L. (2009). La traduction comme travail de (r)écriture. In M. Ballard (Ed.) *Traductologie et enseignement de traduction à l'Université*, 127-144. Artois Presse Université.

Grabowski, Ł. (2018). Kilka słów o formuliczności z różnych perspektyw językoznawczych. In A. Pstyga, T. Kananowicz, M. Buchowska (Eds), *Słowo z perspektywy językoznawcy i tłumacza. Tom VII. Frazeologia z perspektywy językoznawcy i tłumacza*, 67-76. Gdańsk: Wydawnictwo Uniwersytetu Gdańskiego.

Greco, G. M., & Jankowska, A. (2020). Media accessibility within and beyond audiovisual translation. In Ł. Bogucki & M. Deckert (Eds.), *The Palgrave Handbook of Audiovisual Translation and Media Accessibility*, 57–82. Palgrave Macmillan.

Greenacre, M. J. (2007) *Correspondence Analysis in Practice*. 2nd Edition, Chapman & Hall/CRC.

Greenacre, M. J. (2010). Correspondence analysis. In *Wiley Interdisciplinary Reviews: Computational Statistics, 2(5)*, 613-619.

Greenacre, M., & Blasius, J. (Eds.). (2006). *Multiple Correspondence Analysis and Related Methods* (1st ed.). Chapman and Hall/CRC.

Gries, S. (2021). (Generalized Linear) Mixed-Effects Modeling: A Learner Corpus Example. *Language Learning*, 71(3), 757-798.

Griffiths, P. (2006). *An Introduction to English Semantics and Pragmatics*. Edinburgh University Press Ltd.

Guillot, C. (2006). Démonstratif et déixis discursive : analyse comparée d'un corpus écrit de français médiéval et d'un corpus oral de français contemporain. In *Langue française*, 4, 56-69.

Gut, U. (2020). Spoken corpora. In: Paquot, M., Gries S. Th. (Eds.) *A Practical Handbook of Corpus Linguistics*, 235-256.

Hatim, B., & Munday, J. (2004). *Translation - An Advanced Resource Book*. Routledge.

Hejwowski, K. (2004). *Kognitywno-komunikacyjna teoria przekładu*. Wydawnictwo Naukowe PWN.

Hejwowski, K. (2015). *Iluzja przekładu*. Wydawnictwo Naukowe Śląsk.

Hermans, T. (1999). *Translation in Systems: Descriptive and System-oriented Approaches Explained* (1st ed.). Routledge.

Hickey, T. (1993). Identifying formulas in first language acquisition. In *Journal of Child Language, 20*, 27–41.

Huang, H. J., & Wu, C. (2009). The unit of translation: Statistics speak. In *Meta, 54*(1), 110–130.

Hyland, K. (2008). As Can Be Seen: Lexical Bundles and Disciplinary Variation. In *English for Specific Purposes, 27*(1), 4–21.

Ivarsson, J. (2009). The history of subtitles in Europe. In G. C. F. Fong, & K. K. L. Au (Eds.) *Dubbing and subtitling in a world context*, 3-12. Hong Kong: The Chinese University Press.

Ivarsson, J., & Carroll, M. (1998). *Subtitling.* Simrishamn: TransEdit.

Jakobson, R. (1959). On linguistic aspects of translation. In R. Brower (Ed.), *On Translation*, 232-239. Harvard University Press.

Jalali, Z. S., Moini, M. R., & Arani, M. A. (2015). Structural and Functional Analysis of Lexical Bundles in Medical Research Articles: A Corpus-Based Study. In *International Journal of Information Science and Management, 13*(1), 51-69.

Jalilifar, A., Ghoreishi, S. M., & Roodband, S. A. E. (2016). Developing an inventory of core lexical bundles in English research articles: a cross-disciplinary corpus-based study. In *Journal of World Languages, 3*(3), 184-203.

Jenner, M. (2014). Is this TVIV? On Netflix, TVIII and binge-watching. In *New Media and Society. 18(2)*, 257-273.

Jenner, M. (2018). *Netflix and the Re-invention of Television*. Palgrave Macmillan.

Jespersen, O. (1924/1976). Living grammar. In *The philosophy of grammar*. London: George Allen & Unwin, 17–29. Reprinted in D.D. Bornstein (ed.) 1976. Readings in the theory of grammar. Cambridge, MA: Winthrop Publishers, 82-93.

Jesperson, O. (1924). *The philosophy of language*. London: Allen and Unwin.

Jibreen, M. K. (2010). The speech act of greeting: A theoretical reading. In *Journal of Kerbala University, 8(1)*, 1-25.

Johns, T. (1988). Whence and whither classroom concordancing. In T. Bongaerts, P. De Haan,, S. Lobbe, H. Wekker (Eds.), *Computer applications in language learning*, 9-27. Dordrecht: Foris.

Kabara, T. (2015). What is Gained in Subtitling: How Film Subtitles Can Expand the Source Text. In *TranscUlturAl, 7(1),* 166-179.

Käding, J. (1897). *Häufigkeitswörterbuch der deutschen Sprache*. Selbstverlag.

Karamitroglou, F. (1998). A proposed set of subtitling standards in Europe. In *Translation Journal 2(2)*. Retrieved from: https://translationjournal.net /journal/04stndrd.htm. Accessed on December 27, 2023.

Kauffer, M. (2011). Lexicographie bilingue des phraséologismes: le cas des actes de langage stéréotypés. In M. Lipinska (Ed.), *L'état des recherches et les tendances du développement de la parémiologie et de la phraséologie romanes*, 155-167. Oficyna Wydawnicza Leksem.

Kauffer, M. (2018). Le sens contextuel des « actes de langage stéréotypés ». *Lublin Studies in Modern Languages and Literature*, *42*(4), 39-59. UMCS Wydawnictwo.

Kauffer, M. (2019). Les « actes de langage stéréotypés » : essai de synthèse critique. In P. Frassi & P. Ligas (Eds.), *Cahiers de lexicologie. Les phrases préfabriqués : Sens, fonctions, usages*, 149-172. Classique Garnier.

Kecskés, I. (2000). A cognitive-pragmatic approach to situation-bound utterances. In *Journal of Pragmatics*, *32*, 605-625.

Kecskés, I. (2003). *Situation-Bound Utterances in L1 and L2*. Mouton de Gruyter.

Kecskés, I. (2010). Situation-bound utterances as pragmatic acts. In *Journal of Pragmatics, 42 (11),* 2889-2897.

Kecskés, I. (2014). The evaluative function of situation-bound utterances in intercultural interaction. In G. Thompson & L. Alba-Juez (Eds.), *Evaluation in Context*, 137-152.

Kecskés, I. (2017). Implicitness in the use of situation-bound utterances. In P. Cap & M. Dynel (Eds.), *Implicitness: From lexis to discourse*, 201-215.

Kenny, D. (2001a) Equivalence. In: M. Baker (ed.), *Routledge Encyclopedia of Translation Studies*. London & New York: Routledge, 77-80.

Kenny, D. (2001b). *Lexis and Creativity in Translation. A Corpus-Based Study.* Manchester: St. Jerome.

Kenny, D. (2006). Corpus-based Translation Studies: a Quantitative or Qualitative Development? In *Journal of Translation Studies 9(1),* 43-58.

Kenny, D. (2009). Unit of translation. In M. Baker & G. Saldanha (Eds.), *Routledge Encyclopedia of Translation Studies*, 2nd ed., 304–306. Routledge.

Kiefer, F. (1995). *Situational utterances.* Keynote presented at the semantics and pragmatics conference at Brighton.

Kitao, S. K. (2012). Using a spoken corpus compiled from subtitles to study apologies. In *Asphodel, 47,* 50-77.

Kryk, B. (1990). Deixis – a pragmatic universal? In J. Bechert (Ed.), *Toward a Typology of European Languages,* 49-61. Mouton de Gruyter.

Krzyżanowska, A., Grossmann, F., & Kwapisz-Osadnik K. (Eds.) (2021). *Les formules expressives de la conversation. Analyse contrastive : français-polonais-italien*. Wydawnictwo Episteme.

Kuhn, A., & Westwell, G. (2012). *A Dictionary of Film Studies.* Oxford University Press.

Kunin, A. V. (1970). *Angliiskaia frazeologiia*. Moscow: Higher School.

Laks, S. (1957). *Le sous-titrage de films: Sa technique, son esthétique.* Paris: Propriété de l'auteur.

Latos, A. (2020). Feminatywy w stanowiskach Rady Języka Polskiego. Język a ewolucja normy społecznej. In *Postscriptum Polonistyczne, 26(2)*, 227-242.

Le Blanc, S. (2020). Le public préfère le doublage au sous-titrage. In *L'Orient-Le Jour.* Retrieved from: https://www.lorientlejour.com/article/1210910/le-public-prefere-le-doublage-au-sous-titrage.html. Accessed on July 25, 2022.

Leech, G. (1983). *Principles of Pragmatics.* Longman.

Lefer, M.-A. (2020). Parallel corpora. In: Paquot, M., Gries S. Th. (Eds.) *A Practical Handbook of Corpus Linguistics*, 257-283.

Leppihalme, R. (1997). *Culture Bumps: An Empirical Approach to the Translation of Allusions.* Multilingual matters.

Levinson, S. C. (2004). Deixis and pragmatic. In L. Horn & G. Ward (Eds.). *The Handbook of Pragmatics*, 97-121. Oxford: Blackwell.

Lieven, E., Salomo, D., & Tomasello, M. (2009). The acquisition of lexical phrases in academic writing: A longitudinal case study. In *Journal of Second Language Writing, 18*(2), 85-105.

Lipińska, M. (2009). Les fonctions du langage et la déixis dans les slogans publicitaires français. In *Studia Romanica Posnaniensia, 36*, 97-109.

Longhi, J., & Sarfati, G.-E. (2012). *Dictionnaire de pragmatique.* Paris: Armand Colin.

Longrée, D., & Mellet, S. (2013). Le motif: une unité phraséologique englobante? Étendre le champ de la phraséologie de la langue au discours. In *Langages, 1 (189)*, 65-79.

Lorenzo, L., Pereira A., & Xoubanova, M. (2003). The Simpsons / Los Simpson. Analysis of an Audiovisual Translation. In *The Translator 9*(2), 269-291.

Loska, K. (2007). Benshi jako współautor filmu. In *Kwartalnik Filmowy, 57*, 59-65.

Louw, B. (1997). *The Role of Corpora in Critical Literary Appreciation*. Routledge.

Luczaj, K., & Hoły-Luczaj, M. (2014). The Polish Subtitles Scene in Context of Postmodern Civil Society. In: A. Jarosz (Ed.) *Good Governance and Civil Society*, 151-170, Cambridge Scholars Publishing.

Lüger, H. H. (1999). *Satzwertige Phraseologismen. Eine pragmalinguistische Untersuchung*. Wien.

Lyons, J. (1977). *Semantics*. Cambridge University Press.

Lyons. J. (1977). *Semantics. Vols 1 & 2*. Cambridge University Press.

Mailhac, J.-P. (1998). Optimising the linguistic transfer in the case of commercial videos. In Y. Gambier (Ed.), *Translating for the Media*, 207-223. University of Turku.

Malinowski, B. (1923). The Problem of Meaning in Primitive Languages. In C. K. Ogden and I. A. Richards (Eds.) *The Meaning of Meaning*, 296-336. London: Trubner.

Malinowski, B. (1935). *Coral gardens and their magic: A study of the methods of tilling the soil and of agricultural rites in the Trobriand Islands*. Routledge.

Mandelstamm, V. (1932). *Le dubbing*. Cinés.

Manes, J., & Wolfson, N. (1981). The compliment formula. In F. Coulmas (Ed.), *Conversational routine: Explorations in standardized communication situations and prepatterned speech*, 115-132. The Hague, the Netherlands: Mouton.

Marks, J. (2005). The Truth Revealed: Phrasal Verbs in Writing and Speech. In *MED Magazine 34*.

Marque-Pucheu, C. (2007). Les énoncés liés à une situation : mode de fonctionnement et mode d'accès en langue 2. In *Hieronymus, I*, 25-48.

Martín, C. G. (2018). Traduction des énoncés liés à une situation d'énonciation: les pragmatèmes. In *Lublin Studies in Modern Languages and Literature, 42(4)*, 171-183.

Martínez Sirés, P. (2016). Making the Inaccessible Accessible: A Panorama of Audiovisual Translation, Accessibility and Audio Description in Japan. In *Asiadémica: revista universitaria de estudios sobre Asia Oriental*, *7*, 24-50.

Massida, S. (2020). Fansubbing: Latest trends and future prospects. In Ł. Bogucki & M. Deckert (Eds.), *The Palgrave Handbook of Audiovisual Translation and Media Accessibility*, 189-208. Palgrave Macmillan.

Matamala, A. (2019). Voice-over: Practice, research and future prospects. In L. Pérez-González (Ed.), *The Routledge Handbook of Audiovisual Translation*, 64-81. Routledge.

Matamala, A., Perego, E., & Bottiroli, S. (2017). Dubbing versus subtitling yet again? An empirical study on user comprehension and preferences in Spain. In *Babel*, *63(3)*, 423-441.

Matthiessen, C. M. I. M. (2001). The Environments of Translation. In E. Steiner and C. Yallop (Eds.), *Exploring Translation and Multilingual Production: Beyond Context*, 127-160. Mouton de Gruyter.

Mazur, I. (2020). Audio description: Concepts, theories and research approaches. In Ł. Bogucki & M. Deckert (Eds.), *The Palgrave Handbook of Audiovisual Translation and Media Accessibility*, 227–248. Palgrave Macmillan.

Mazur, J. (1990). Styl i tekst w aspekcie pragmatycznym. In *Socjolingwistyka IX*, 72-73.

McCarthy, M. (1991). *Discourse Analysis for Language Teachers*. Cambridge University Press.

McEnery, T., & Wilson, A. (2001). *Corpus Linguistics*. Edinburgh University Press.

Mejri, S. (2018). Les pragmatèmes et la troisième articulation du langage. In *Verbum XL*, 7-19.

Mel'čuk, I. (1995). Phrasemes in Language and Phraseology in Linguistics. In M. Everaert et al. (Eds.), *Idioms. Structural and Psychological Perspectives*, 167-232. Hillsdale, NJ: Lawrence Erlbaum Associates.

Mel'čuk, I. (1998). Collocations and lexical functions. In A. P. Cowie (Ed.), *Phraseology: Theory, analysis and applications*, 23-54. Oxford: Clarendon Press.

Mel'čuk, I. A. (2012). Phraseology in the Language, in the Dictionary, and in the Computer. In *Język i metoda*, *1*, 217-239.

Mey, J. (2001). *Pragmatics*, Blackwell, Oxford.

Mężyk, J. (2021). Nauka języków obcych przy użyciu dwujęzycznych napisów do filmu. Presentation at the *Języki obce – klucz do dialogu* conference organized by the Silesian University of Technology.

Mikhailov, M., Tommola, H., & Isolahti, N. (2010). Spoken to Spoken vs. Spoken to Written: Corpus Approach to Exploring Interpreting and Subtitling. In *Polibits, 41*, 5-9.

Minzheong, S. (2021). A comparative study on over-the-tops, Netflix & Amazon Prime Video: Based on the success factors of innovation. In *International Journal of Advanced Smart Convergence, 10(1)*, 62-74.

Molina, L., & Hurtado, A. (2002). Translation Techniques Revisited: A Dynamic and Functionalist Approach. In *Meta, 47(4)*, 498-512.

Mollin, S. (2014). *The (Ir)reversibility of English Binomials: Corpus, constraints, developments*. John Benjamins.

Myles, F., & Cordier, C. (2016). Formulaic Sequences (FS) Cannot be an Umbrella Term in SLA: Focusing on Psycholinguistic FSs and Their Identification. In *Studies in Second Language Acquisition, 39(1)*, 1-26.

Myles, F., Hooper, J., & Mitchell, R. (1998). Rote or rule? Exploring the role of formulaic language in classroom foreign language learning. In *Language Learning, 48*(3), 323–363.

Myskja, K. (2013). Foreignisation and resistance: Lawrence Venuti and his critics. In *Nordic Journal of English Studies, 12(2)*, 1-23.

Nation, P., & Read, J. (2004). Measurement of formulaic sequences. In N. Schmitt (Ed.), *Formulaic Sequences: Acquisition, processing and use*, 23-35. John Benjamins Publishing Company.

Natsuko, T (1997). *Jimaku no naka no jinsei*. Hakusuisha.

Nattinger, J. R., & DeCarrico, J. S. (1992). *Lexical phrases and language teaching*. Oxford University Press.

Nedergaard-Larsen, B. (1993). Culture-bound problems in subtitling. In *Perspectives. Studies in Translation Theory and Practice, 1(2)*, 207-240.

Nelli, F. (2014). Bar Charts with jqPlot. In: *Create Web Charts With jqPlot*. Apress, Berkeley, CA.

Newmark, P. (1988). *Textbook of Translation*. Prentice Hall International.

O'Sullivan, C., Cornu, J. F. (2018). History of Audiovisual Translation. In L. Pérez-Gonzáles (Ed.) *The Routledge Handbook of Audiovisual Translation*, New York, Routledge, 15-30.

Ogiermann, E. (2009). Politeness and in-directness across cultures: A comparison of English, German, Polish and Russian requests. In *Journal of Politeness Research 5(2)*, 189-216.

Orero, P. (2009). Voice-over in Audiovisual Translation. In J. Díaz-Cintas, G. Anderman (Eds.), *Audiovisual Translation: Language Transfer on Screen*, 130-139. Palgrave Macmillan.

Osur, L., (2016). *Netflix and the Development of the Internet Television Network*. Retrieved from: https://surface.syr.edu/etd/448. Accessed on July 23, 2022.

Oziemblewska, M., & Szarkowska, A. (2020). The quality of templates in subtitling. A survey on current market practices and changing subtitler competences. In *Perspectives. Studies in Translation Theory and Practice, 30*, 432-453.

Palion-Musioł, A. (2012). Przekład audiowizualny jako wyzwanie dla współczesnego tłumacza. Narzędzia oraz metody wykorzystywane w procesie translatorycznym. In *Rocznik Przekładoznawczy*, 7, 95-106.

Palmer, H. (1933). *Second Interim Report on English Collocations*. Tokyo: Kaitakusha.

Park, D. (2007). Identifying and using formal and informal vocabulary. In *IDP Education*. The University of Cambridge and the British Council, the Post Publishing Public Co. Ltd.

Parry, M. (1928). *L'Epithète traditionelle dans Homère*. Paris: Société Editrice Les Belles Lettres.

Parry, M. (1930). Studies in the epic technique of oral verse-making. I: Homer and Homeric Style. In *Harvard Studies in Classical Philology, 41*, 73-147.

Parry, M. (1932). Studies in the epic technique of oral verse-making. II: The Homeric language as the language of oral poetry. In *Harvard Studies in Classical Philology, 43*, 1-50.

Pawley, A. (1986). On Speech Formulas and Linguistic Competence. In *Kansas Working Papers in Linguistics, 11*, 57-87.

Pedersen, J. (2003). *Scandinavian Subtitles: A Pilot Study Based on the ESIST Project*. Örebro University, unpublished pilot study.

Pedersen, J. (2018). From old tricks to Netflix: How local are interlingual subtitling norms for streamed television? In *Journal of Audiovisual Translation, 1(1)*, 81-100.

Pedersen, J. (2020). Audiovisual Translation Norms and Guidelines. In Ł. Bogucki & M. Deckert (Eds.), *The Palgrave Handbook of Audiovisual Translation and Media Accessibility*, 417-436. Palgrave Macmillan.

Pedersen, J. (2022). *Birth of a New Era? Investigating the Nature and Quality of Machine-translated Subtitles*. Presentation at the *Languages and the Media* conference in Berlin.

Perego, E., & Pacinotti, R. (2020). Audiovisual translation through the ages. In Ł. Bogucki & M. Deckert (Eds.), *The Palgrave Handbook of Audiovisual Translation and Media Accessibility*, 33-56. Palgrave Macmillan.

Peters, A. M. (1983). *Units of language acquisition*. Cambridge: Cambridge University Press.

Pęzik, P. (2014). *Spokes search engine for Polish conversational data*, CLARIN-PL digital repository, http://hdl.handle.net/11321/47.

Rabadán, R. (1991). *Equivalencia y traducción. Problemática de la equivalencia translémica inglés-español*. Universidad de León, Secretariado de Publicaciones.

Ramos Pinto, S. (2022). *Translating the Verbal and Beyond: from Reception Data to Directors' and Translators' Views*. Presentation at the Languages & The Media Conference in Berlin.

Raupach, M. (1984). Formulae in second language speech production. In H.W. Dechert, D. Möhle & M. Raupach (Eds.), In *Second language production*, 114-137. Tübingen: Gunter Narr.

Reiss, K. (1971/2000). *Translation criticism: The potentials and limitations. Categories and criteria for translation quality assessment*. St. Jerome Publishing.

Remael, A., Orero, P., & Carroll, M. (2012). Audiovisual translation and media accessibility at the crossroads. In A. Remael, P. Orero, & M. Carroll (Eds.), *Audiovisual Translation and Media Accessibility at the Crossroads. Media for All 3, Approaches to Translation Studies*, Vol. 36, 13-21.

Richards, J. C., & Schmidt, R., (2011). *Longman Dictionary of Language Teaching and Applied Linguistics*. Longman.

Romero-Fresco, P. (2015). Final thoughts: Viewing speed in subtitling. In P. Romero-Fresco (Ed.), *The Reception of Subtitles for the Deaf and Hard of Hearing in Europe*, 335–341. Peter Lang.

Rosales Sequeiros, X. (2004). Formulaic Expressions in Translation. In *Trans. Revista de Traductología*, 105-114.

Rushton, A. (2022). Motivating Japanese university EFL learners to produce longer speaking turns with web based machine translation: A pilot study. In *Kobe Kaisei Jogakuin University Research Bulletin*, *66*, 73-81.

Santamaria Guinot, L. (2001). Función y traducción de los referentes culturales en traducción. In L. Lorenzo, & A. M. Pereira (Eds.) *Traducción subordinada (II): El subtitulado (inglés-español/galego)*, 237-248. Servicio de Publicacións, Universidade de Vigo.

Sarfati, G.-E. (1997). *Éléments d'analyse du discours*. Paris: Nathan.

Schegloff, E., & Sacks, H. (1973). Opening up closings. In *Semiotica*, *7*(4), 289-327.

Schmidt, R. (1992). Psycholinguistic mechanisms underlying second language fluency. In *Studies in Second Language Acquisition*, *14*, 357-385.

Schmidt, R. W. (1983). Interaction, acculturation, and the acquisition of communicative competence: A case study of an adult. In N. Wolfson & E. Judd (Eds.), *Sociolinguistics and language acquisition*, 137-174. Rowley, MA: Newbury House.

Schmitt, N., & Underwood, G. (2004). Exploring the processing of formulaic sequences through a self-paced reading task. In N. Schmitt (Ed.), *Formulaic Sequences: Acquisition, processing and use*, 173-189. John Benjamins.

Searle, J. R. (1969). *Speech Acts*. Cambridge University Press.

Searle, J. R. (1979). *Expression and Meaning*. Cambridge University Press.

Sepielak, K. (2016). Synchronization Techniques in Multilingual Fiction Voice-over Films in Poland. In *International Journal of Communication*, *10*. 1054-1073.

Sharifian, F. (2008). Cultural schemas in L1 and L2 compliment responses: A study of Persian-speaking learners of English. In *Journal of Politeness Research: Language, Behavior, Culture*, *4*, 55-80.

Sinclair, J. & Renouf, A. (1988). A lexical syllabus for language learning. In R. Carter & M. McCarthy, *Vocabulary and Language Teaching*, 140-158. Longman.

Sinclair, J. (1991). *Corpus, concordance, collocation: Describing English language*. Oxford University Press.

Skandera, P. (2004). What are idioms? In D. J. Allerton, N. Nesselhauf, & P. Skandera (Eds.) *Phraseological units : basic concepts and their application*. Basel: Schwabe.

Snell-Hornby, M. (2006). *The Turns of Translation Studies*. John Benjamins Publishing Company.

Sperber, D., & Wilson, D. (1995). *Relevance: Communication and Cognition*. Blackwell, Oxford.

Stede, M., & Schmitz, B. (1997). *Discourse particles and routine formulas in spoken language translation*, Berlin Technical University.

Sułkowska, M. (2023). O frazeologii i pragmatemach z perspektywy dydaktyki i translacji. In *Neofilolog, 60/1*, 88-100.

Sung-Eun, C. (2014). *Basic concepts in the theory of audiovisual translation*. Retrieved from https://builder.hufs.ac.kr/user/ibas/No31/15.pdf. Accessed on July 12, 2022.

Szarkowska A, & Gerber-Morón O. (2018). Viewers can keep up with fast subtitles: Evidence from eye movements. In *PLoS ONE 13(6)*: e0199331.

Szarkowska, A. (2009). Przekład audiowizualny w Polsce – perspektywy i wyzwania. In *Przekładaniec, 20*, 8-25.

Szarkowska, A. (2016). Report on the results of an online survey on subtitle presentation times and line breaks in interlingual subtitling. Part 1: Subtitlers. London. Retrieved from: https://dev-avt.ckc.uw.edu.pl/wp-content/uploads/sites/170/2016/10/SURE_Report_Survey1.pdf. Accessed on July 23, 2022.

Szarkowska, A., & Laskowska, M. (2015). Poland – a voice-over country no more? A report on an online survey on subtitling preferences among Polish hearing and hearing-impaired viewers. In Ł. Bogucki and M. Deckert (Eds.), *Accessing audiovisual translation*, 179-197. Peter Lang.

Szpyra-Kozłowska J. (2019). Premiera, premierka czy pani premier? Nowe feminatywy w badaniu ankietowym. In *Język Polski*, 2, 22-40.

Tardzenyuy, N. (2016). Revisiting Translation Strategies and Techniques. In *International Journal of Comparative Literature and Translation Studies*, *4*(4), 48-56.

Taylor, J. R. (2002). *Cognitive grammar*. Oxford, UK: Oxford University Press.

Teubert, W. (2002). The role of parallel corpora in translation and multilingual lexicography. In B. Altenberg & S. Granger (Eds.), *Lexis in Contrast*, 189–214. John Benjamins.

Tognini-Bonelli, E. (2001). *Corpus Linguistics at Work*. John Benjamins.

Tomala, K. (2021). Kształtowanie się w polszczyźnie formacji feminatywnych o nacechowaniu pejoratywnym (na przykładzie derywatów formowanych od męskich podstaw na -nik i -arz). In *Acta Universitatis Lodziensis. Folia Linguistica 55*, 89-104.

Tomaszkiewicz, T. (2006). *Przekład audiowizualny*. Wydawnictwo Naukowe PWN.

Toury, G. (1995). *Descriptive Translation Studies and Beyond*. John Benjamins.

Trosborg, A. (1997). *Text Typology and Translation*. John Benjamins Publishing Company.

Tryuk, M. (2009). Co to jest tłumaczenie audiowizualne. In *Przekładaniec, 20*, 26-39.

Van Lancker, D. R., & Kempler, D. (1987). Comprehension of familiar phrases by left- but not by right-hemisphere damaged patients. In *Brain and Language, 32(2)*, 265-277.

Venuti, L. (1995). *The Translator's Invisibility: A History of Translation*. Routledge.

Vergaro, C. (2008). On the pragmatics of concessive constructions in Italian and English business letter discourse. In *Multilingua, 27*, 255-283.

Vinay, J.-P. & Darbelnet, J. (1995). *Comparative Stylistics of French and English. A methodology for translation*. John Benjamins.

Vinogradov, V. V. (1947). Ob osnovnuikh tipakh frazeologicheskikh edinits v russom yazike. In A. A. Shakhmatov (Ed.), *Sbornik statei i materialov*. Moscow: Nauka, 339-364.

Vinogradov, Viktor V. (1947). *Russkij jazyk: Grammaticheskoe uchenie o slove*. Moscow: Gosudarstveoye uchebno-pedagogicheskoye izdatel'stvo Ministerstva prosveshcheniya RSFSR.

Wedel, M. (2012). Universal, Germany, and ALL QUIET ON THE WESTERN FRONT: A case study in crisis historiography. In *NECSUS. European Journal of Media Studies, 1(1)*, 126–147.

White, J. (2013). Ellipsis as a Marker of Interaction in Spoken Discourse. In *Research in Language*, 11(3), 251-276.

Widdowson, H. G. (1989). Knowledge of Language and Ability for Use. In *Applied Linguistics, 10(2)*, 128-137.

Wierzbicka, A. (1985). Different cultures, different languages, different speech acts: Polish vs. English. In *Journal of Pragmatics*, *9(2-3)*, 145-178.

Winkler, S. (2005). *Ellipsis and Focus in Generative Grammar.* Mouton De Gruyter.

Winter B. (2019). *Statistics for Linguists: An Introduction Using R*. London: Routledge.

Wong, M. L.-Y. (2010). Expressions of gratitude by Hong Kong speakers of English: Research from the International Corpus of English in Hong Kong (ICE-HK). In *Journal of Pragmatics, 42*, 1243-1257.

Wood, D. (2010). *Formulaic language and second language speech fluency: Background, evidence, and classroom applications*. London/New York: Continuum.

Wood, D. (2012). Formulaic Language in Acquisition and Production: Implications for Teaching. In *TESL Canada Journal, 20*, 1-15.

Wood, D. (2015). *Fundamentals of Formulaic Language*. Bloomsbury Academic.

Wood, M. M. (1986). *A definition of idiom*. Indiana University Linguistics Club.

Wray, A. (2008). *Formulaic language. Pushing the boundaries*. Oxford.

Wray, A. (2012). What Do We (Think We) Know About Formulaic Language? An Evaluation of the Current State of Play. In *Annual Review of Applied Linguistics, 32*, 231-254.

Wray, A., & Namba, K. (2003). Use of formulaic language by a Japanese-English bilingual child: A practical approach to data analysis. *Japanese Journal for Multilingualism and Multiculturalism, 9*(1), 24-51.

Wray, A., & Perkins, M. R. (2000). The functions of formulaic language: An integrated model. In *Language & Communication, 20*(1), 1-28.

Wray, A., (2002). *Formulaic language and the lexicon*. Cambridge.

Yang, Y. (2011). A cognitive interpretation of discourse deixis. Theory and Practice. In *Language Studies, 1(2),* 128-135.

Yorio, C. (1980). Conventionalized language forms and the development of communicative competence. In *TESOL Quarterly, 14*, 433-442.

Zanotti, S. (2018). Historical approaches to AVT reception: Methods, issues and perspectives. In E. Di Giovanni & Y. Gambier (Eds.), *Reception Studies and Audiovisual Translation*, 133-156. John Benjamins.

Zinken, J., & Ogiermann, E. (2013). Responsibility and action: Invariants and diversity in requests for objects in British English and Polish interaction. In *Research on Language and Social Interaction*, 46(3), 256-76.

References for the list of pragmatemes

Sources used to prepare the lists of pragmatemes (see p. 134):

1) For English pragmatemes:

Baltrušaitytė, J. (2008). *Lithuanian-English, English-Lithuanian dictionary & phrasebook*. Hippocrene Books.

Bartnicki, K. et al. (2003). *Duży słownik polsko-angielski*. LektorKlett.

Bernacka, A., Motyliński, R. (2005). *Rozmówki angielskie*. Buchmann.

Boudjedid-Meyer, M. (1998). *Dictionary of American English Colloquial Phrases and Expressions: French-English/English-French*. Hippocrene Books.

Braginski, A. (1984). *English-Polish Phrasebook with useful wordlist: Samouczek języka angielskiego dla Polaków w USA*. Versus.

Czarnowska-Fenrych, E. (2003). *Rozmówki biznesowe : język angielski: najważniejsze sytuacje, praktyczne dialogi, profesjonalne zwroty*. Langenscheidt.

Gerber, J. (2014). *650+ English phrases for everyday speaking*. Self-published.

Government of New Brunswick (2011). *Langues officielles : Expressions et vocabulaire courants*. Retrieved from: https://www2.gnb.ca/content/dam/gnb/Departments/ohr-brh/pdf/tk/TK-Expressions-FR.pdf. Accessed on July 22, 2021.

Harvey-Smith, N., Ratajczak, P. (1998). *Słownik konwersacyjny języka angielskiego*. Wydawnictwo Kanion.

Häublein, G., Jenkins, R., Staniszewska-Kowalak, D. (1997). *Angielsko-polski słownik tematyczny*. Wydawnictwo Naukowe PWN.

Hoszowska, B. (1997). *Porozmawiajmy o interesach - po angielsku: business English dla przedsiębiorców i menedżerów oraz ich sekretarek*. Wydawnictwo Profesjonalnej Szkoły Biznesu.

Howatt, A., Szkutnik, L. (1972). *Make your choice: conversation exercises and problems for class-use or self-instruction to practise semantic relationships in context*. Państwowe Wydawnictwo Naukowe.

Jacek, S. (1992). *Konwersacje handlowe angielsko-polsko-niemieckie*. RZG.

Jackowska, T. (1991). Rozmówki angielskie. Wiedza Powszechna.

Jankowski, M., Nadstoga, Z., Sawala, K. (1990). *Wielka Brytania: informacja turystyczna, rozmówki polsko-angielskie, mini-słownik*. Atena.

Kaczmarski, S., Wójcik, A. (1990). *Z angielskim w podróży*. Wiedza Powszechna.

Keane, L. (1997). *International restaurant English: [communicating with the international traveller]*. Prentice Hall International.

Keller, E., Warner, S. T. (1998). *Conversation gambits: real English conversation practices*. Language Teaching Publications.

Kowalczyk, M., Widawski, M. (2017). *Czarny slang: słownik slangu afroamerykańskiego*. Stara Szuflada.

Kurek-Evans, M. (2010). Na podbój Wielkiej Brytanii: dwujęzyczny poradnik dla wyjeżdżających. Videograf II.

Maclean-Hańćkowiak, U., & Ratajczak, P. (1993). *Słownik tematyczny języka angielskiego*. Wydawnictwo Kanion.

Multiple authors. (2015). Rozmówki amerykańskie ze słownikiem i gramatyką. Lingea.

Office of English Language Programs. (2013). Everyday Conversations: Learning American English. Retrieved from: https://americanenglish.state.gov/resources/everyday-conversations-learning-american-english. Accessed on July 22, 2021.

Olejnik, D. (2012). *Angielski w firmie: rozmowy telefoniczne*. Pons.

Pawlikowska, B. (2010). *Blondynka na językach: angielski brytyjski*. National Geographic.

Pawlikowska, B. (2010). *Blondynka na językach: angielski USA*. National Geographic.
Retman, B., Retman, R. (1959). *How to say it in Polish? : a conversation guide with the phonetic transcription*. Wiedza Powszechna.
Spears, R. A., Niezgoda, E. (1997). *Słownik idiomów amerykańskich dla Polaków = Essential Americ an idioms for Polish speakers*. NTC Publishing Group.
Teslar, J. A. (1941). *Angielsko-polska książka dla żołnierza = An English phrase and reading book for Polish soldiers*. Robert Gibson & Son.
Widawski, M. (1997). *Nowy słownik slangu i potocznej angielszczyzny*. Wydawnictwo L&L.
Wolfram-Romanowska, D., Kaszubski, & P., Parker, M. (2007). *Idiomy polsko-angielskie = Polish-English idioms*. Wydawnictwo Naukowe PWN.
Yates, C. (1992). *May I help you? [a course for restaurant and bar staff]*. Prentice Hall.

2) For French pragmatemes:

Amette, C., Ferrer, P. R., Stanisławska, A. (2016). *Księga idiomów, czyli vous avez la parole !* PONS.
Beacco, J., Care, J. M. (1988). *Parlez-lui d'amour : le français des relations amoureuses.* CLE International.
Blanco, X., Mejri, S. (2018). Index des pragmatèmes. In: Blanco, X., & Mejri, S. (Eds.) *Les Pragmatèmes*. Classiques Garnier, 193-204.
Boudjedid-Meyer, M. (1998). *Dictionary of American English Colloquial Phrases and Expressions: French-English/English-French.* Hippocrene Books.
Drzymała, P. (1991). *Francja: informacja turystyczna, rozmówki polsko-francuskie , mini-słownik.* Atena.
Government of New Brunswick (2011). *Langues officielles : Expressions et vocabulaire courants.* Retrieved from: https://www2.gnb.ca/content/dam/gnb/Departments /ohr-brh/pdf/tk/TK-Expressions-FR.pdf. Accessed on July 22, 2021.
Jedlińska, A., Szwykowski, L., & Tomalak, J. (1979). *Słownik turystyczny francusko-polski, polsko-francuski*. Wiedza Powszechna.
Kochan, B. Zaręba, L. (2004). *Idiomy polsko-francuskie*. Wydawnictwo Naukowe PWN.
Pawlikowska, B. (2011). *Blondynka na językach: francuski.* National Geographic.

Platkow, A. (1974). *Rozmówki francuskie.* Wiedza Powszechna.
Platkow, A. (1979). *Comment le dire en polonais? : guide pratique de conversation avec la transcription phonétique française.* Wiedza Powszechna.
Słobodska, M. (1998). *Słownik francusko-polski, polsko-francuski z rozmówkami.* Harald G.
Therond, M. (1978). *Du tac au tac : formules, reflexes et images de la conversation française actuelle.* Marcel Didier.

3) For Polish pragmatemes:

Bartnicki, K. et al. (2003). *Duży słownik polsko-angielski.* LektorKlett.
Bernacka, A., Motyliński, R. (2005). *Rozmówki angielskie.* Buchmann.
Braginski, A. (1984). *English-Polish Phrasebook with useful wordlist: Samouczek języka angielskiego dla Polaków w USA.* Versus.
Chlebda, W. (Ed.) (2006-2019). *Podręczny idiomatykon polsko-rosyjski.* Zeszyty 1-10. Wydawnictwo Uniwersytetu Opolskiego.
Czarnowska-Fenrych, E. (2003). *Rozmówki biznesowe : język angielski: najważniejsze sytuacje, praktyczne dialogi, profesjonalne zwroty.* Langenscheidt.
Drzymała, P. (1991). *Francja: informacja turystyczna, rozmówki polsko-francuskie , mini-słownik.* Atena.
Harvey-Smith, N., Ratajczak, P. (1998). *Słownik konwersacyjny języka angielskiego.* Wydawnictwo Kanion.
Häublein, G., Jenkins, R., Staniszewska-Kowalak, D. (1997). *Angielsko-polski słownik tematyczny.* Wydawnictwo Naukowe PWN.
Hoszowska, B. (1997). *Porozmawiajmy o interesach - po angielsku: business English dla przedsiębiorców i menedżerów oraz ich sekretarek.* Wydawnictwo Profesjonalnej Szkoły Biznesu.
Jacek, S. (1992). *Konwersacje handlowe angielsko-polsko-niemieckie.* RZG.
Jankowski, M., Nadstoga, Z., Sawala, K. (1990). *Wielka Brytania: informacja turystyczna, rozmówki polsko-angielskie, mini-słownik.* Atena.
Jedlińska, A., Szwykowski, L., Tomalak, J. (1979). *Słownik turystyczny francusko-polski, polsko-francuski.* Wiedza Powszechna.
Kaczmarski, S., Wójcik, A. (1990). *Z angielskim w podróży.* Wiedza Powszechna.
Keane, L. (1997). *International restaurant English: [communicating with the international traveller].* Prentice Hall International.

Kochan, B. Zaręba, L. (2004). *Idiomy polsko-francuskie.* Wydawnictwo Naukowe PWN.

Kowalczyk, M., & Widawski, M. (2017). *Czarny slang: słownik slangu afroamerykańskiego.* Stara Szuflada.

Kurek-Evans, M. (2010). *Na podbój Wielkiej Brytanii: dwujęzyczny poradnik dla wyjeżdżających.* Videograf II.

Lawendowski, B., Wójcik, A. (1979). *Minirozmówki angielskie.* Wiedza Powszechna.

Maclean-Hańćkowiak, U., Ratajczak, P. (1993). *Słownik tematyczny języka angielskiego.* Wydawnictwo Kanion.

Multiple authors (2015). *Rozmówki amerykańskie ze słownikiem i gramatyką.* Lingea.

Olejnik, D. (2012). *Angielski w firmie: rozmowy telefoniczne.* Pons.

Pawlikowska, B. (2010, 2011). *Blondynka na językach (angielski brytyjski, angielski USA, francuski).* National Geographic.

Platkow, A. (1974). *Rozmówki francuskie.* Wiedza Powszechna.

Platkow, A. (1979). *Comment le dire en polonais? : guide pratique de conversation avec la transcription phonétique française.* Wiedza Powszechna.

Retman, B., Retman, R. (1959). *How to say it in Polish? : a conversation guide with the phonetic transcription.* Wiedza Powszechna.

Słobodska, M. (1998). *Słownik francusko-polski, polsko-francuski z rozmówkami.* Harald G.

Spears, R. A., Niezgoda, E. (1997). *Słownik idiomów amerykańskich dla Polaków = Essential Americ an idioms for Polish speakers.* NTC Publishing Group.

Teslar, J. A. (1941). *Angielsko-polska książka dla żołnierza = An English phrase a nd reading book for Polish soldiers.* Robert Gibson & Son.

Therond, M. (1978). *Du tac au tac : formules, reflexes et images de la conversation française actuelle.* Marcel Didier.

Widawski, M. (1997). *Nowy słownik slangu i potocznej angielszczyzny.* Wydawnictwo L&L.

Wolfram-Romanowska, D., Kaszubski, & P., Parker, M. (2007). *Idiomy polsko-angielskie = Polish-English idioms.* Wydawnictwo Naukowe PWN.

Yates, C. (1992). *May I help you? [a course for restaurant and bar staff].* Prentice Hall.

Other references

Bond, E. (2018). Why Netflix Shut Down Its Translation Portal Hermes. In *Slator.* Retrieved from: https: //slator.com/why-netflix-shut-down-its-translation-portal-hermes/. Accessed on July 23, 2022.

Brown, A., & Patterson, J. (2017). *Designing Subtitles for 360° Content.* BBC Research & Development. Retrieved from http://www.bbc.co.uk/rd/blog/2017-03-subtitles-360-video-virtual-reality. Accessed on July 25, 2022.

Chrome web store. *Language Reactor reviews.* Retrieved from: https://chrome.google.com/webstore/detail/language-reactor/hoombieeljmmljlkjmnheibnpciblicm. Accessed on March 2, 2022.

Chrome web store. *Language Reactor.* Retrieved from: https://chrome.google.com/webstore/detail/language-reactor/hoombieeljmmljlkjmnheibnpciblicm. Accessed on March 2, 2022.

Coelho, L. J. (2007). *Subtitling and Dubbing: Restrictions and Priorities.* Retrieved from https://www.translationdirectory.com/article326.htm. Accessed on July 23, 2022.

Cook, S. (2022). Netflix statistics & facts. In *Comparitech.* Retrieved from: https://www.comparitech.com/blog/vpn-privacy/netflix-statistics-facts-figures/. Accessed on July 25, 2022.

Długosz. D. (2020). Co piąty Polak planuje zrezygnować z kablówki na rzecz streamingu. Chcemy płacić mniej. In *Komputer Świat.* Retrieved from: https://www.komputerswiat.pl/aktualnosci/internet/co-piaty-polak-planuje-zrezygnowac-z-kablowki-na-rzecz-streamingu-chcemy-placic-mniej/vk67079. Accessed on July 25, 2022.

Dondzik, A. (n.d.). *Polish Proverbs Word-Play project [Illustrated Proverbs Word-Play]*. Retrieved from https://www.behance.net/gallery/6712111/Illustrated-Proverbs-Word-Play. Accessed on June 27, 2022.

Estopace, E. (2017). Talent Crunch Hits Media Localization as Amazon, Netflix Accelerate Market Growth. In *Slator*. Retrieved from: https://slator.com/talent-crunch-hits-media-localization-as-amazon-netflix-accelerate-market-growth/. Accessed on July 25, 2022.

Fletcher, W. (2002-2007). *KfNgram. Annapolis, MD: USNA*. Retrieved from http://www.kwicfinder.com/kfNgram/kfNgramHelp.html. Accessed on March 16, 2021.

GALA. Globalization and Localization Association. *Knowledge Center*. Retrieved from: https://www.gala-global.org/knowledge-center/about-the-industry/language-services. Accessed on July 25, 2022.

Goren, O. (2018). UK Milestone: Streaming TV Becomes More Popular Than Traditional Pay TV. In *Cord Busters*. Retrieved from: https://www.cordbusters.co.uk/streaming-tv-uk-more-popular-than-cable/#:~:%20text=According%20to%20a%20new%20Ofcom,such%20as%20Sky%20and%20BT. Accessed on July 25, 2022.

Iqbal, M. (2020). Netflix Revenue and Usage Statistics. In *Business of Apps*. Retrieved from: www.businessofapps.com/data/netflix-statistics/. Accessed on July 23, 2022.

Khan Academy. Retrieved from: https://www.khanacademy.org/. Accessed on July 25, 2022.

Kowalczyk, K. (2021). Discussion on Audiovisual Translation in Poland [Interview]. J. Mężyk (Interviewer).

Language Reactor Forum. Retrieved from: https://forum.languagelearningwithnetflix.com/. Accessed on December 27, 2022.

Language Reactor. Retrieved from: https://www.languagereactor.com/. Accessed on July 25, 2022.

Learning Languages with Netflix. Retrieved from: https://languagelearningwithnetflix.com/. Accessed on December 27, 2022.

Morning Consult Pro. *The International Content Boom Has Made Subtitles and Dubbers the Lifeblood of Streaming*. Retrieved from: https://morningconsult.com/2022/04/25/subtitles-dubbing-streaming/. Accessed on July 25, 2022.

Netflix Partner Help Center. *English Timed Text Style Guide.* Retrieved from: https://partnerhelp.netflixstudios.com/hc/en-us/articles/217350977-English-Timed-Text-Style-Guide. Accessed on July 25, 2023.

Netflix Partner Help Center. *French Timed Text Style Guide.* Retrieved from: https://partnerhelp.netflixstudios.com/hc/en-us/articles/217351577-French-Timed-Text-Style-Guide. Accessed on July 25, 2022.

Netflix Partner Help Center. *Legacy Workflow. Pivot Language Dialogue List.* Retrieved from: https://partnerhelp.netflixstudios.com/hc/en-us/articles/360001610707-Legacy-Workflow-Pivot-Language-Dialogue-List-SOW. Accessed on July 25, 2022.

Netflix Partner Help Center. *Polish Timed Text Style Guide.* Retrieved from: https://partnerhelp.netflixstudios.com/hc/en-us/articles/216787928-Polish-Timed-Text-Style-Guide. Accessed on July 25, 2022.

Netflix Partner Help Center. Retrieved from: https://partnerhelp.netflixstudios.com/. Accessed on July 25, 2022.

Netflix Partner Help Center. *Timed Text Style Guide: General Requirements.* Retrieved from: https://partnerhelp.netflixstudios.com/hc/en-us/articles/215758617-Timed-Text-Style-Guide-General-Requirements. Accessed on July 25, 2022.

Netflix Partner Help Center. *Timed Text Style Guide: Subtitle Templates.* Retrieved from: https://partnerhelp.netflixstudios.com/hc/en-us/articles/216787928-Polish-Timed-Text-Style-Guide. Accessed on July 25, 2022.

Netflix Partner Help Center. *What is the maximum number of characters per line allowed in Timed Text assets?* Retrieved from: https://partnerhelp.netflixstudios.com/hc/en-us/articles/215274938-What-is-the-maximum-number-of-characters-per-line-allowed-in-Timed-Text-assets-. Accessed on March 2, 2022.

Netflix Technology Blog. (2017). The Netflix HERMES Test: Quality Subtitling at Scale. In *Medium.* Retrieved from: https://netflixtechblog.com/the-netflix-hermes-test-quality-subtitling-at-scale-dccea2682aef. Accessed on July 25, 2022.

Netflix. Centre d'aide. *Pays où l'application Netflix est disponible.* Retrieved from: https://help.netflix.com/fr/node/14164#:~:%20text=Netflix%20is%20available%20for%20streaming,Korea%2C%20Russia%2C%20and%20Syria. Accessed on July 25, 2022.

OpenSubtitles. Retrieved from: https://www.opensubtitles.org/. Accessed on December 27, 2022.

Quartz. *Netflix finds dubbing doesn't work in Poland and other local TV nuances.* Retrieved from: https://qz.com/1231253/netflix-finds-dubbing-doesnt-work-in-poland-and-other-local-tv-nuances/. Accessed on July 25, 2022.

Rodriguez, A. (2017). What's "demogorgon" in French? How Netflix translated "Stranger Things". In *Quartz.* Retrieved from: https://qz.com/1107696/how-netflix-translated-stranger-things-so-it-worked-globally. Accessed on July 25, 2022.

Romanowski, P. (2021). Netflix od kablówki – czy takie rozwiązanie się opłaca? In *Pan Wybierak.* Retrieved from: https://panwybierak.pl/blog/netflix-od-kablowki-czy-warto/. Accessed on July 25, 2022.

Solsman, S. (2022). Netflix's Most Popular Shows and Movies Ever, Ranked (According to Netflix). In *Cnet.* Retrieved from: https: //www.cnet.com/tech/services-and-software/netflixs-most-popular-shows-and-movies-ever-ranked-according-to-netflix/. Accessed on July 25, 2022.

Statista. *Quaterly number of Netflix subscribers.* Retrieved from: https://www.statista.com/statistics/250934/quarterly-number-of-netflix-streaming-subscribers-worldwide/. Accessed on July 25, 2022.

Subbotko, D. (2008). Kapitulacja BBC Prime. In *Gazeta Wyborcza* dated January 11, 2008. Retrieved from: http://wyborcza.pl/1,76842,4827095.html. Accessed on July 23, 2022.

TED. Retrieved from: https://www.ted.com/. Accessed on July 25, 2022.

The BBC Subtitle Guidelines. Retrieved from: https://bbc.github.io/subtitle-guidelines/index_r1.html. Accessed on March 2, 2022.

Unitex/GramLab. Retrieved from: https://unitexgramlab.org/fr. Accessed on December 27, 2022.

Zurich, M. (2021). New Survey Shows 27 Percent of U.S. Households Plan to Cut Cable TV Subscriptions in 2021. In *Businesswire.* Retrieved from: https://www.businesswire.com/news/home/20210112005291/en/New-Survey-Shows-27-Percent-of-U.S.-Households-Plan-to-Cut-Cable-TV-Subscriptions-in-2021. Accessed on July 25, 2022.

Appendix

Pragmatemes found in the English, French, and Polish corpora

Pragmateme	Page number[267]
English	
After you	141
Afternoon	
All cash	
All done	
All set	158
Another round	
Anyone here	
Anything else	213, 231
Can I get you anything else	
Is that all	213, 229
Are you all right	136, 145
You all right	145
Are you OK	136, 236
You ok	
Are you there	224, 248
Arms up	
Careful, it's hot	
Be quiet	
Quiet	
Bingo	209, 212, 224
Bottoms up	
Break a leg	
Bye	
All right, bye	
Okay, bye	
So long	

(Continued)

267 If specifically mentioned in this thesis.

Pragmateme	Page number
Peace out	
Peace	
Call 911	
Call an ambulance	
Call me [PERSON]	
Call me	
Call me back	
Call the cops	
I'll call you later	
I gotta call you back	
I'll call you back	177
Can I come in	
Can I get you something to eat/drink	
Can I get you anything	
Can I have [NOUN]	
Can I have another	
Can/May I/we help you	
What can I help you with [TIME]	
What do you need	
What can I do for you	158
Can you hear me	165, 209, 248
Pass me [NOUN]	
Check	50, 158, 210, 215, 225, 243
Cheers	158, 217, 222, 232
Cheers to that/us	
Clear	51, 84, 216, 224
Cut	213
Deal	
We have a deal	
We got a deal	
Dig in	
Don't cry	
Don't move	219
Don't touch me	
Enjoy yourself	
Enjoy	215, 224, 226, 250

(*Continued*)

Pragmateme	Page number
Everything all right	
Is everything all right	
Everything's fine	219
Excuse me	
Fancy seeing you here	
I'm/We're fine	50, 210, 214, 219, 225, 231, 236, 244, 249, 256, 257
I'm fine, thanks	
I'm fine, thank you	145, 181
Fingers crossed	
Follow me	138
Freeze	
Get in here	
Get in the car	
Get in there	
Get in	
God bless you	
Going once, going twice, sold for [PRICE]	
Good afternoon	43, 63, 64, 79
Goodbye	
Good evening	79
Good morning	41, 42, 43, 49, 59, 63, 180, 215
Good night	
Happy anniversary	
Happy birthday	23, 28, 49
Happy Hanukkah	
Happy New Year	
Have a [POSITIVE ADJECTIVE] day	54,158, 161, 165, 178
Have a [POSITIVE ADJECTIVE] evening	159, 224
Have a [POSITIVE ADJECTIVE] night	158, 178
Have a good one	178
Have a [POSITIVE ADJECTIVE] time	178
Have fun	
Hello	49, 62, 63, 139, 163
Hello again	
Hello there	
Hello?	29, 180, 215, 216, 230, 238, 239, 240

(Continued)

Pragmateme	Page number
Help yourself	223, 237, 253, 256
Help	
Here it is	
Here we are	210
Here you go	209, 210, 216, 225, 232
Here	210, 211, 214, 218, 240, 241
Here's your [NOUN]	
Hey there	
Hey	210, 220
I'm talking to you	237
I'm/We're here to see [PERSON]	
Hi again	
Hi there	
Hi	173, 220, 229
Hey, hey	236
Hey, hey, hey	
Hi, hi	
Hi, hi, hi	
Hey, it's [PERSON]	
Hi, it's [PERSON]	
Sorry, this is [PERSON]	
Hi, I'm [PERSON]	
Hello, I'm [PERSON]	
Hold it right there	
Hold on a [TIME]	
Hold on	
Hang on a [TIME]	
Hang on	
Wait a [TIME]	
Just a [TIME]	
Please wait	
One moment	210
Please hold	138
How are you doing	
How are you feeling	
How are you holding up	

(Continued)

Pragmateme	Page number
How are you	22, 49, 59, 63, 135, 139, 158, 165, 181, 231
How are you today	
[GREETING], how are you	49
How's it going	
How can/may I help you	37
How much (is it)	
How much	210
I can't hear you	
I/We gotta go	
Gotta go	
I/We've gotta go	
I/We have to go	
To [SOMETHING/PERSON]	210, 229, 253
Here's to [SOMETHING/PERSON]	
Can I call you back	
I'll take it	210, 217, 226, 255
Coming	
I'm coming	
Happy to help	
[POSITIVE ADJECTIVE] to see you too	
I'm not hungry	
Not hungry	
I'm sorry too	
I'm sorry I'm late	173, 177
Sorry I'm/we're late	
Sorry to interrupt	
I'm sorry to bother you	
I'm/We're so sorry to bother you	
Sorry, I don't speak [LANGUAGE]	
Have we met	
Nice to meet you, too	
It's [POSITIVE ADJECTIVE] to meet you	168
It's [INTENSIFIER] nice to meet you	
Nice to meet you	75, 136, 168
Very nice to meet you	
Hi, nice to meet you	

(*Continued*)

Pragmateme	Page number
Pleasure to meet you	
It was [POSITIVE ADJECTIVE] to meet you	136
It's [POSITIVE ADJECTIVE] to see you	47
It('s)[268] [INTENSIFIER] [POSITIVE ADJECTIVE] to see you	
[POSITIVE ADJECTIVE] to see you	
So [POSITIVE ADJECTIVE] to see you	
[POSITIVE ADJECTIVE] to see you again	
I'm/We're so happy to see you	
It was good to see you	
It smells [POSITIVE ADJECTIVE]	
Smells [POSITIVE ADJECTIVE]	
It's a boy	161, 177
It's a date	215, 224
It's my fault	
My pleasure	
My treat	
Keep the change	177
Take your seats	181
Language	
Give it up for [PERSON]	
Please welcome	
Leave a message	
Let me get that for you	
Let me in	220, 243
Let's get this party started	
Get down	
Long live the [PERSON]	67
Long time no see	
Love ya	245
Love you	50, 210, 225, 245, 248, 261
Love you too	217, 245
Make yourself at home	

(Continued)

268 "('s)" appears in English pragmatemes in which two verb forms were found: one with "is" and the other with the contracted form.

Pragmateme	Page number
Merry Christmas	22, 45
Morning	
My turn	
It's my turn	
Next in line	162
Next	
Who's next	
No more/further questions, Your Honor	
No need to apologize	
No phone	
On the house	
Get on your knees	
On your knees	
Open the door	
Pardon me	
Police	
See ya	
I'll see ya	
See you	
See you [DAY]	23, 49, 138, 161, 165
I'll see you [TIME]	
See you around	
I'll see you at [PLACE]	
See you at [PLACE]	
See you soon	138
I'll see you soon	
I'll see you later	
See you later	73, 136, 138
Later	
Set	
Shall we go	
Shh	
Sit down	
Sit	
Sit, sit	
Have a seat	

(Continued)

Pragmateme	Page number
Slow down	210, 220
Smile	
Speaking	
This is [PERSON] speaking	
Surprise	
Stop right there	210, 219
Take care	145
Take a deep breath	
Deep breath	
Breathe	
Thank you all for being here	
Thank you for coming	50, 138, 173
Thanks for coming	
That's it	210, 253
There you are	
This way	
It's this way	
Watch your step	
Welcome back	
Welcome to [PLACE/EVENT]	161
Welcome	
What('s) going on here	
What's up	
Hey, what's up	
Sup	
What up	
Yo, what's up	
What happened to you	
What happened	
What('s) going on	
What's wrong	
What's the matter	
What('s) the problem	
What('s) your problem	
Who is it	
Who('s) that	

(*Continued*)

Pragmateme	Page number
Will you marry me	28, 165
Yo	219, 220, 229
Yo, yo	
You have the right to remain silent	
Your turn	
It's your turn	
Your move	
You're up next	
You're up	77, 210, 212
You're welcome	158
You('ve) reached [PERSON]	
Yuck	
French	
À plus tard	138
À plus	
Salut	220, 229
Salut, c'est [PERSON]	
Ciao	
Attention, c'est fragile	
C'est M. [PERSON]	
[PLACE] clair(e)	
C'est fermé	
Je t'embrasse	
Je t'embrasse aussi	
Merci de votre appel	
C'est ouvert	
Votre/Ton rendez-vous est arrivé	
Mon rendez-vous est arrivé	
J'ai rendez-vous avec [PERSON]	
Silence	
À [SOMETHING/PERSON]	230, 253
Police !	
À toute	
À tout de suite	
À la prochaine	
À [NUMBER] h	

(*Continued*)

Pragmateme	Page number
À tout à l'heure	
À vite	
À bientôt	
À demain	138, 165
À [DAY]	138
À ce soir	
Santé.	232
À votre service	
À vos armes	
À ton/votre tour	
À l'appareil	
Ça fait plaisir de te voir	
C'est pour moi	
À toi/vous (de jouer)	212
Bonne journée	165, 178
Merci et bonne journée	
Feu	
Adieu	
Bonne route	178
C'est bon, merci	
Merci de ton/l'/votre aide	
[PERSON], merci de laisser un message	
Merci pour l'invitation	
Bonne nuit	178
Bonne soirée	178
Très bonne soirée	
Bonnes vacances	
Bonsoir	
Merci, bonsoir	
Bye	
Besoin d'aide	173
Je vous accompagne	
Vous allez bien	
Ça va	49, 168
Ça va ou quoi	
Salut, ça va	

(*Continued*)

Pragmateme	Page number
Salut, [PERSON], ça va	
Ça va et toi/vous	
Ça va, toi	
Ça va ?	
Ça va bien	
Tu vas bien	
Ça va, ça va	
Comment allez/vas-vous/tu	158
Bisous	245
Au lit	
Allô ?	
Allô, bonjour	
Allô	215, 216
Allô, c'est/ici [PERSON]	
Y a quelqu'un	
Amen	
Joyeux anniversaire	23
Après vous	
Au revoir	
Bienvenu(e)	
Bienvenue à/chez [PLACE/TIME/EVENT]	
Bon appétit	215, 250
Bon voyage	138
Bonjour	49, 215
[PERSON], bonjour ?	
Vous êtes sur le répondeur de [PERSON]	157
Bonjour, c'est [PERSON]	
Enchanté(e)	
Excuse(z)-moi	
Il coûte combien	
Je te/vous doit combien	
Comment ça va	168
Comment puis-je vous aider	
Je peux vous aider	
Qu'est-ce que vous avez	
Qu'est-ce qui se passe	

(Continued)

Pragmateme	**Page number**
Qu'est-ce qui se passe ici	
Qu'est-ce qui t'/vous amène	
Qu'y a-t-il	
Que se passe-t-il	
Qui est là	216
Tu/Vous te/vous sens/sentez comment	
Coucou	
De rien	
Pardon pour le retard	
Pardon de (vous) déranger	
Psst	
En joue	
Entendu	
Tu peux/veux fermer la porte	
Il faut que j'y aille	
J'arrive	
Je t(vous)'en prie	158
Je te/vous le/la passe	
Joyeux Noël	
L'addition, s'il vous plaît	243, 246
La porte	
[NOUN], s'il vous plaît	
Je suis [ADJECTIVE EXPRESSING HAPPINESS] de te/vous voir	
J'/On appelle la police	
C'est la police	
Une minute	256
Motus.	
On/Je se/me casse	
On se rappelle	
Je te/vous rappelle [TIME]	
Je te/vous rappelle	
On se tire	
(C'est/Viens/Venez) Par ici	
Ravie de vous rencontrer	
[Bien] Reçu	

(Continued)

Pragmateme	Page number
Respire [ADVERB]	
Vous avez choisi	
Vos papiers	
Vive la Fraternité	
Un, deux, trois, soleil	
Un instant	
Très bien, merci	
Merci, ça va très bien	
Toutes mes condoléances	
Taxi	
Signature, s'il vous plaît	
Pas de souci	
Je vais prendre [NOUN]	
Je veux bien [NOUN]	
[TIME], s'il vous/te plaît	
Bon app	
C'est moi	
C'est pas grave	
C'est pour toi/vous	
Wesh	142, 229
Wesh ?	
Polish	
Alarm	
Amen	
Baczność	
Bierz go	
Chwileczkę	
Ciało Chrystusa	180
Cisza	
Ciszej	
Co ci jest	
Co jest grane	
Co jest	
Co mogę dla ciebie/pana zrobić	158
Co się dzieje	
Co się stało	

(*Continued*)

Pragmateme	Page number
Co tam	
Co tu się dzieje	
Coś jeszcze	213, 256
Czołem	
Cześć	220
Mogę prosić o [NOUN]	138
Czym mogę pani służyć	
Czysto	51
Do nogi	139
Do widzenia	
Do zobaczenia	
Dobranoc	
Dobry wieczór	79
Dzień dobry	49, 79, 168
[NOUN], proszę	111
Dziękuję za pomoc	
Fajnie, że przyszłaś	
Halo	240
Jest tam kto	
Hej	220
Hejka	143
Hej, cześć	
Ile	
Jak się czujesz	
Jak się masz	49
Jak wyglądam	
Jestem	
Kopę lat	
Kto mówi	
Kto tam	
Miłego dnia	165, 178
Miło mi	
Bardzo mi miło	
Moje uszanowanie	
Musimy/muszę lecieć	
Musimy/muszę iść	

(*Continued*)

Pragmateme	Page number
Muszę kończyć	
Na pomoc	
Na razie	
Na wieki wieków, amen	
Na ziemię	
Nic się nie stało.	
Nie przepraszaj	
O co chodzi	
O co ci chodzi	
Odbiór	
Opuść broń	
Pa	
Policja	
Proszę bardzo	
Proszę o spokój	
Proszę poczekać	
Proszę tu podpisać	
Proszę wchodzić	
Proszę wyjść	
Proszę za mną	
Przepraszam na chwilę	
Przepraszam za spóźnienie	173
Ratunku	
Ręce do góry	
Siad	
Siema	
Sio	
Słucham	
Słucham?	
Tak, słucham	
Smacznego	215, 250
Szczęść Boże	
Szukaj	
Tędy	
To (jest) rozkaz	
To wszystko	

(*Continued*)

Pragmateme	Page number
To wszystko?	213, 229
Trzymaj się	
Twoje/Wasze zdrowie	
Uważaj na siebie	
W czym mogę pomóc	
W imię Ojca i Syna, i Ducha Świętego, amen.	156
Wesołych Świąt	
Witaj(cie)	
Witam(y)	
Witam(y) w/na [PLACE]	
Witam w klubie.	
Wszystkiego dobrego	
Wszystkiego najlepszego	
Wszystko (jest) w porządku	257
Wszystko w porządku?	
Zdrowie [PERSON]	135
Zdrowie	217
Złodziej	
Zostaw!	
Żegnam	

ŁÓDŹ STUDIES IN LANGUAGE

Edited by

Barbara Lewandowska- Tomaszczyk and Łukasz Bogucki

Vol. 1 Barbara Lewandowska- Tomaszczyk / Patrick James Melia (eds.): PALC'99: Practical Applications in Language Corpora. Papers from the International Conference at the University of Łódź, 15- 18 April 1999. 2000.

Vol. 2 Lou Burnard / Tony McEnery (eds.): Rethinking Language Pedagogy from a Corpus Perspective. Papers from the Third International Conference on Teaching and Language Corpora. 2000.

Vol. 3 Barbara Lewandowska- Tomaszczyk / John Osborne / Frits Schulte: Foreign Language Teaching and Information and Communication Technology. 2001.

Vol. 4 Piotr Cap: Explorations in Political Discourse. Methodological and Critical Perspectives. 2002.

Vol. 5 Ewa Waniek- Klimczak / Patrick James Melia (eds.): Accents and Speech in Teaching English Phonetics and Phonology. EFL perspective. 2002.

Vol. 6 Barbara Lewandowska- Tomaszczyk / Kamila Turewicz (eds.): Cognitive Linguistics Today. 2002.

Vol. 7 Barbara Lewandowska- Tomaszczyk (ed.): PALC 2001: Practical Applications in Language Corpora. 2003.

Vol. 8 Corpus Linguistics by the Lune. A Festschrift for Geoffrey Leech. Edited by Andrew Wilson, Paul Rayson and Tony McEnery. 2003.

Vol. 9 Barbara Lewandowska- Tomaszczyk (ed.): Practical Applications in Language and Computers. PALC 2003. 2004.

Vol. 10 Imagery in Language. Festschrift in Honour of Professor Ronald W. Langacker. Edited by Barbara Lewandowska- Tomaszczyk and Alina Kwiatkowska. 2004.

Vol. 11 Seana Coulson / Barbara Lewandowska- Tomaszczyk (eds.): The Literal and Nonliteral in Language and Thought. 2005.

Vol. 12 Piotr Cap (ed.): Pragmatics Today. 2005.

Vol. 13 Jacek Waliński / Krzysztof Kredens / Stanisław Goźdź-Roszkowski (eds.): Corpora and ICT in Language Studies. PALC 2005. 2007.

Vol. 14 Krzysztof Kosecki (ed.): Perspectives on Metonymy. Proceedings of the International Conference "Perspectives on Metonymy", held in Łódź, Poland, May 6- 7, 2005. 2007.

Vol. 15 Barbara Lewandowska- Tomaszczyk / Tomasz Płudowski / Dolores Valencia Tanno (eds.): The Media and International Communication. 2007.

Vol. 16 Krzysztof Kredens / Stanisław Goźdź-Roszkowski (eds.): Language and the Law: International Outlooks. 2007.

Vol. 17 Barbara Lewandowska- Tomaszczyk (ed.): Corpus Linguistics, Computer Tools, and Applications – State of the Art. PALC 2007. 2008.

Vol. 18 Barbara Lewandowska- Tomaszczyk / Katarzyna Dziwirek (eds.): Studies in Cognitive Corpus Linguistics. 2009.

Vol. 19 Barbara Lewandowska- Tomaszczyk / Marcel Thelen (eds.): Meaning in Translation. 2010.

Vol. 20 Łukasz Bogucki / Krzysztof Kredens (eds.): Perspectives on Audiovisual Translation. 2010.

Vol. 21 Piotr Stalmaszczyk (ed.): Turning Points in the Philosophy of Language and Linguistics. 2011.

Vol. 22 Stanisław Goźdź-Roszkowski: Patterns of Linguistic Variation in American Legal English. A Corpus- Based Study. 2011.

Vol. 23 Kamila Ciepiela (ed.): Identity through a Language Lens. 2011.

Vol. 24 Stanisław Goźdź-Roszkowski (ed.): Explorations across Languages and Corpora. PALC 2009. 2011.

Vol. 25 Krzysztof Kosecki / Janusz Badio (eds.): Cognitive Processes in Language. 2012.

Vol. 26 Alina Kwiatkowska (ed.): Texts and Minds. Papers in Cognitive Poetics and Rhetoric. 2012.

Vol. 27 Paul A. Wilson (ed.): Dynamicity in Emotion Concepts. 2012.

Vol. 28 Piotr Pęzik (ed.): Corpus Data across Languages and Disciplines. 2012.

Vol. 29 Mikołaj Deckert: Meaning in Subtitling. Toward a Contrastive Cognitive Semantic Model. 2013.

Vol. 30 Łukasz Bogucki: Areas and Methods of Audiovisual Translation Research. 3rd Revised Edition. 2019.

Vol. 31 Janusz Badio / Kamila Ciepiela (eds.): Language, Action, Interaction. 2013.

Vol. 32 Barbara Lewandowska- Tomaszczyk / Krzysztof Kosecki (eds.): Time and Temporality in Language and Human Experience. 2014.

Vol. 33 Iwona Witczak- Plisiecka (ed.): Cognitive and Pragmatic Aspects of Speech Actions. 2014.

Vol. 34 Małgorzata Anna Kamińska: A History of the Concise Oxford Dictionary. 2014.

Vol. 35 Łukasz Bogucki / Mikołaj Deckert (eds.): Accessing Audiovisual Translation. 2015.

Vol. 36 Joanna Jabłońska- Hood: A Conceptual Blending Theory of Humour. Selected British Comedy Productions in Focus. 2015.

Vol. 37 Krzysztof Kosecki / Janusz Badio (eds.): Empirical Methods in Language Studies. 2015.

Vol. 38 Katarzyna Stadnik: Chaucer's Choices. Through the looking- glass of medieval imagery. 2015.

Vol. 39 Paulina Pietrzak / Mikołaj Deckert (eds.): Constructing Translation Competence. 2015.

Vol. 40 Małgorzata Fabiszak / Karolina Krawczak / Katarzyna Rokoszewska (eds.): Categorization in Discourse and Grammar. 2016.

Vol. 41 Marcel Thelen / Gys- Walt van Egdom / Dirk Verbeeck / Łukasz Bogucki / Barbara Lewandowska- Tomaszczyk (eds.): Translation and Meaning. New Series, Vol. 1. 2016.

Vol. 42 Łukasz Bogucki / Barbara Lewandowska- Tomaszczyk / Marcel Thelen (eds.): Translation and Meaning. New Series, Vol. 2, Pt. 1. 2016.

Vol. 43 Łukasz Bogucki / Barbara Lewandowska- Tomaszczyk / Marcel Thelen (eds.): Translation and Meaning. New Series, Vol. 2, Pt. 2. 2016.

Vol. 44 Przemysław Łozowski / Katarzyna Stadnik (eds.): Visions and Revisions. Studies in Theoretical and Applied Linguistics. 2016.

Vol. 45 Marek Kuźniak / Bożena Rozwadowska / Michał Szawerna (eds.): From Motion to Emotion. Aspects of Physical and Cultural Embodiment in Language. 2016.

Vol. 46 Anna Rędzioch- Korkuz: Opera Surtitling as a Special Case of Audiovisual Translation. Towards a Semiotic and Translation Based Framework for Opera Surtitling. 2016.

Vol. 47 Mateusz Sajna: Video Game Translation and Cognitive Semantics. 2016.

Vol. 48 Kamila Ciepiela (ed.): Identity in Communicative Contexts. 2016.

Vol. 49 Mikołaj Nkollo: The Entrenchment of the 'unus alterum' Pattern. Four Essays on Latin and Old Romance Reciprocal Constructions. 2016.

Vol. 50 Paweł Rydzewski: Backness Distinction in Phonology. A Polish Perspective on the Phonemic Status of y. 2016.

Vol. 51 Piotr Pęzik / Jacek Tadeusz Waliński (eds.): Language, Corpora and Cognition. 2017.

Vol. 52 Janusz Badio (ed.): Events and Narratives in Language. 2016.

Vol. 53 Mikołaj Deckert (ed.): Audiovisual Translation – Research and Use. 2017. 2nd Expanded Edition 2019.

Vol. 54 Michał Szawerna: Metaphoricity of Conventionalized Diegetic Images in Comics. A Study in Multimodal Cognitive Linguistics. 2017.

Vol. 55 Artur Gałkowski / Monika Kopytowska (eds.): Current Perspectives in Semiotics. Signs, Signification, and Communication. 2018.

Vol. 56 Artur Gałkowski / Monika Kopytowska (eds.): Current Perspectives in Semiotics. Text, Genres, and Representations. 2018.

Vol. 57 Łukasz Bogucki / Piotr Cap (eds.): Exploration in Language and Linguistics. For Professor Piotr Stalmaszczyk on the Occasion of His 60th Birthday. 2018.

Vol. 58 Michał Kornacki: Computer- assisted Translation (CAT) Tools in the Translator Training Process. 2018.

Vol. 59 Marcin Walczyński / Piotr Czajka / Michał Szawerna (eds.): On the Verge between Language and Translation. 2018.

Vol. 60	Łukasz Bogucki / Paulina Pietrzak / Michał Kornacki (eds.): Understanding Translator Education. 2018.
Vol. 61	Marcin Walczyński: Psycho- Affective Factors in Consecutive Interpreting. 2019.
Vol. 62	Kamila Ciepiela (ed.): Language, Identity and Community. 2019.
Vol. 63	Olga Łabendowicz: Audiovisual Translation in Poland. Changing Audiences. 2019.
Vol. 64	Enrique Bernárdez / Joanna Jabłońska- Hood / Katarzyna Stadnik (eds.): Cognition in context. New insights into language, culture and the mind. 2019.
Vol. 65	Montse Corrius / Eva Espasa / Patrick Zabalbeascoa (eds.): Translating Audiovisuals in a Kaleidoscope of Languages. 2019.
Vol. 66	Barbara Lewandowska- Tomaszczyk / Valeria Monello / Marco Venuti (eds.): Language, Heart, and Mind. Studies at the intersection of emotion and cognition. 2020.
Vol. 67	Marta Chodkiewicz: Understanding the Development of Translation Competence. 2020.
Vol. 68	Urszula Paradowska: Developing Information Competence in Translator Training. 2021.
Vol. 69	Luca Valleriani: Upper- class English in Natural and Audiovisual Dialogue. 2021.
Vol. 70	Michał Kornacki and Gary Massey (eds.): Contextuality in Translation and Interpreting. Selected Papers from the Łódź-ZHAW Duo Colloquium on Translation and Meaning 2020–2021. 2022.
Vol. 71	Monika Kopytowska / Artur Gałkowski / Massimo Leone (eds.): Thought- Sign- Symbol. Cross- Cultural Representations of Religion. 2022.
Vol. 72	Bartosz Pietrzak: The Concept of Honor in the Language of Early Arabic Poetry. A Cultural Linguistic Study. 2022.
Vol. 73	Aleksandra Beata Makowska: Terminology and phraseology in research papers in the domains of new technologies. A cognitive corpus- based perspective. 2024.
Vol. 74	Marco Venuti / Emanuela Campisi / Ester Di Silvestro (eds.): Strategies of Inclusion and Exclusion in online and offline Interaction. 2024.
Vol. 75	Łukasz Dutka: The Quality of Live Subtitling. Technology, User Expectations and Quality Metrics. 2024.
Vol. 76	Klaudia Gajewska: Voice Assistants in Action-oriented Mediation Practice. 2025.
Vol. 77	Julie Lefort: Overview of the Sociolinguistic Context of the Dongxiang Language. 2025.
Vol. 78	Judyta Mężyk: Pragmatemes in Audiovisual Translation in English, French, and Polish. 2025.

www.peterlang.com

www.ingramcontent.com/pod-product-compliance
Ingram Content Group UK Ltd.
Pitfield, Milton Keynes, MK11 3LW, UK
UKHW041825100926
8556IPUK00002B/30

9 783631 931806